A few determined men, even one

* * *

Like a giant sledge, the explosion of the shell shakes and rattles the deepest core. Some men lie in their beds for a lifetime after, stunned, winded, jarred mute by that hammer blow.

Except for the helmet and olive drab wool uniform, Kerley was the movie image of a Texas Ranger, tanned, tall and spare, tough and mature.

Sergeant Corn fiddled with the eyepieces, rotated the scope and carefully scrutinized the sloping hillside and hedgerows in front of us. He crouched down in the tall grass beside the tripod, and after a time he turned to me and in a calm voice asked, "Want to shoot some Jerries, Lieutenant?" From the casual, even tone of his voice he might have been asking if I wanted an apple or if I liked the way the French cultivated their fields. I wondered if he was testing me.

In a sweeping series of orders, Hitler replaced Field Marshal Karl von Rundstedt and others in the west who held to the same view, although Field Marshal Erwin Rommel stayed on. Von Rundstedt's replacement, Field Marshal Gunther von Kluge, the epitome of German military leadership, arrived fresh and vigorous from Hitler's headquarters, determined to carry out Hitler's demand to stand fast at any price.

In the early daylight that followed the initial hours of von Kluge's midnight counterattack, a leaden mist covered the landscape. Gradually the day's lightening found us sightless and drifting in a moist, low-hanging cloud, like a ship on a flat, windless sea. Only a fool would have stepped out of the fog.

With this technique well honed, my binoculars soon became a gun sight. When I shouted "Fire Mission" to Sasser, it was as if I were tensing my trigger finger, beginning the squeeze to detonation that would send a deadly missile to the target.

Conservation of radio batteries now became of the utmost importance.

Corn wouldn't be needing his web belt. I pulled it through the loops of his trousers, took it off and wrapped it around his right leg above the knee and buckled it. It was all there was for a tourniquet.

**Portions of this book
have previously appeared in:**

Prologue: Quarterly of the National Archives
FA Journal
MHQ: The Quarterly Journal of Military History

Other Publications

Throughout his law career, the author has published numerous articles on tax and law issues. He actively writes short stories, poetry, and plays. His poetry has been included in Volumes 1, 2, and 3 of *Twelve Oregon Poets*, and was included as a theme piece in *Fishing Beyond the Buoys: Salmon Trolling.*

Fire Mission!

The Siege at Mortain, Normandy, August 1944

By

Robert Weiss

BURD STREET PRESS
SHIPPENSBURG, PENNSYLVANIA

Second, Revised, Updated Edition Copyright © 2002 by Robert Weiss
First Edition Copyright © 1998 by Robert Weiss, originally published as
Enemy North, South, East, West: A Recollection of the "Lost Battalion" at Mortain, France

Unless otherwise listed, all photographs are courtesy of the author.
Maps by Tom Bennett.

The acid-free paper used in this book meets the guidelines for permanence and durability of the Committee on Production Guidelines for Book Longevity of the Council on Library Resources.

First Printing by
Strawberry Hill Press
3848 S.E. Division Street
Portland, OR 97202-1641

ISBN 1-57249-313-5 (formerly ISBN 0-89407-123-8 pbk.)

For a complete list of available publications
please write
Burd Street Press
Division of White Mane Publishing Company, Inc.
P.O. Box 708
Shippensburg, PA 17257-0708 USA

Library of Congress Cataloging-in-Publication Data

Weiss, Robert (Robert L.), 1923-
    Fire mission! : the siege at Mortain, Normandy, August 1944 / by Robert Weiss.--2nd, rev., updated ed.
        p. cm.
    Rev., updated ed. of: Enemy north, south, east, west. c 1998.
    Includes bibliographical references.
    ISBN-13: 978-1-57249-313-1   ISBN-10: 1-57249-313-5 (alk. paper)
    1. Mortain, Battle of, Mortain, France, 1944. 2. Mortain (France)--History, Military. 3. World War, 1939-1945--Campaigns--France--Mortain. I. Weiss, Robert (Robert L.), 1923- Enemy north, south, east, west. II. Title.

D756.5.M67 W45 2002
940.54'21421--dc21

                                                                2002027938

PRINTED IN THE UNITED STATES OF AMERICA

To the men of the "Lost Battalion"
who fought at Mortain

Contents

There are many...

who have joined with me in writing this book.

The original stimulus came from my dear friend Stephen Ellis, who after reading an account of the Battle of Mortain said to me that I should tell my own story. In the early stages of developing the tone and direction of the book, Sherron Norlen, who is a poet and writer, and Bruce Hamilton, a creative editor, author and book designer, gave me much guidance.

Dan Garrott, a comrade during the battle, spent many hours with me both in person and by telephone, and provided a unique perspective of that event so long ago. Armon Sasser, also with me at the battle, was able to confirm and add to the story. My regret is that he did not live to see the book.

Mary C. Ryan, managing editor of *Prologue: Quarterly of the National Archives*, provided needed encouragement early on by inviting me to write an article drawn from the book. She helped me locate many of the fine photographs from the National Archives that are reproduced in the book. She has been a good friend and supporter. I have been similarly heartened by Patrecia Slayden Hollis, editor of *FA Journal*, who published another article based on the book; and then by Robert Cowley, editor, *MHQ: The Quarterly Journal of Military History*, who gave me confidence with publication of a third article from the book and John Tarkov of *MHQ* who pushed and tugged to give the article its final shape.

I thank Kristi Burke for her continuing support and for giving the book its final polish. Tom Bennett prepared the excellent maps that illustrate terrain features and show the disposition of armed forces.

There are others: National Archives personnel, friends who have read drafts, my college roommate Herman Bement, himself a naval hero of World War II, who helped me thumb through files at the National Archives in the tedious search for whatever might be there, and many more. I thank them all.

only summer grass
still stands, bent before the winds—
the old soldiers sleep

Prologue

If the SS troops that surrounded us had overrun our position, they would have executed me summarily. Their failure to do so created a magnificent irony of the war. I did not reflect on it at the time, but as the years envelop me the magnitude grows. In some sense it is like an irony of well-plotted fiction, preposterous to imagine but engaging to contemplate.

That the SS troops failed to overrun our position, to capture and destroy us, verifies that individuals can affect outcomes, that in the sweep of large events a few can touch the lives of many.

The script of a battle bears many stories. The author who describes a battle must consider which to tell. The greater the scale of that battle the more difficult for the writer to make space for individual stories.

Descriptions of modern battles tend to reflect the grand scope of modern warfare which employs armed forces of huge size supported by intense mechanization, instant communication and weapons of terrifying destructive capability. On the one hand, if the story is to be fully understood, the reader must learn in overwhelming detail which small units, all numbered and named, supported by how many guns and tanks, and what kinds, were at what places between what hours on what days.

On the other hand, the writer may record only the broad-sweeping, strategic movements of large units, along with the thinking of the masterminds who directed these maneuvers. For example, the totality of the warfare in the Cotentin peninsula of France, beginning on D-Day, has been subsumed under "The Battle of Normandy" or "The Battle of France." Take your pick. Lesser engagements that make up this great "Battle," often significant battles themselves by the standards of any age, may be fitted in if the generals and other military historians find room. Eventually, some stories are reduced to a paragraph or a line, or may even disappear.

In either case, however, statistics and information overwhelm, and body heat, dirt, noise, taste and smell fade. As a result, modern military history has produced little literature of general or lasting interest. By contrast, battle tales from bygone eras, often of the cut and thrust variety, continue to survive. Agincourt still stirs the blood. The tale of George Washington and 120 men stuck in the woods of Pennsylvania for a winter lives on. The extraordinary feat of Sergeant York in World War I looms large among war stories while the battle in which he worked his magic molders in the history books.

Such smaller engagements are easier to grasp. The reader, at least in imagination, can relate to the bravery—or the fear—of a single soldier in a foxhole. The Alamo is not a statistic or a diagram on a map. It is about blood and death and the resoluteness of a few men.

In the postmodern world where the individual most often feels overwhelmed and powerless, such tales provide a toehold for a continuing belief that each person can have an influence, that a few determined men, that even one man, can make a difference. Tales of smaller engagements revive and give life to individual human endeavor and spirit.

The "Lost Battalion" in August 1944 fits the image. It was a fragment of a larger battle action. General Omar Bradley called it "one of the epochal struggles of the war."[1] This account describes only part of the story, what I saw as a field artillery forward observer. But it is the story that I alone can tell.

The name "Lost Battalion" was a concoction of World War II journalists who copied the name from an event of World War I, no doubt in order to impart a bit of eye-catching hype to their columns. Lieutenant Ralph A. Kerley, who was one of the heroes of the engagement, wrote that the battalion was isolated but never "lost." Nonetheless, the phrase caught on and occasionally pops up in descriptions of this battle action.

Kerley also wrote that had it not been for the artillery, the battalion "would have been destroyed or captured." In achieving that result, a field artillery forward observer group of three men and myself played a significant role. In the context of statistics that now measure by millions whatever is deemed worth counting, where land strategies focus on armies and where the use of overwhelming force is key, it is not inappropriate to note that four men made a difference in the lives of many others.

Before time brings men and their memories to an end, it seemed that an affectionate regard for family, friends and colleagues required the telling of my story. Many of these people are vaguely aware that I shared with other soldiers a battle experience that was a singular event. A few know that some high point of ground, a hill, had something to do with it. Even fewer know about Mortain, let alone where it is or what its significance was to the Battle of France. This story shares a part of the past that, for one reason or another, has been secluded from casual conversation. Friends, family, colleagues may draw conclusions as to what the impact was on me. I still reflect on that myself. Those readers who are strangers may find value in turning this vicarious experience inward and reflecting how their lives might have been different had they been there, too.

*For the convenience of many readers,
this edition designates time in
standard rather than in military format.*

Music

January 1995. To the left of our table, a new wall climbs high to an old ceiling, the remains of a small neighborhood movie house in Portland, Oregon, now carved up into a tavern. The wall splits the old theater into two parts, separating the performers and listeners, where we sit, from the serious drinkers in the bar on the other side. What had once been the right half of the theater has become a long, narrow room with a too-high ceiling, a world turned on its side.

At the end of the room is a stage lit by spotlights. The rest is dark. A monstrous mural on the dividing wall reflects light from the stage, and half-lit, pasty faces and vacuous, bagel-like eyes, look out from the wall at me and across the room into nowhere. Except for this painting, the setting is stark and devoid of any decoration or color. A small crowd in jeans, sweats, T-shirts and jackets fills the few simple tables and cheap metal chairs scattered across the hard, black landscape of the floor. Overhead, plastic netting, spray-painted a dirty, mud-brown or maybe GI olive drab—it is hard to tell against the black ceiling in that light—hovers ominously as if waiting, like a huge trap, to flop down and swallow us all up.

On the stage at the end of this barren, sideways room, a slender, wild man of a drummer, bespectacled, wearing an earring and a striped shirt, madly flays the drums, cymbals and gongs in front of him, stomps the foot pedal of a bass drum and drives the rest of the rock and roll band with a pounding, incessant beat. How does he know when to strike which instrument? As if preprogrammed, he never hesitates, never goes through a moment of indecision, but flails his arms wildly, beating the instruments in such rapid succession that sometimes it seems as if he is striking them all at once.

In front of him, two young women, one in shirt and jeans and the other in a plain sweater, skirt and boots, violently strum flat, electric guitars. One guitar is a brilliant, shining red. Occasionally its motion catches a spotlight, and then for an instant it blazes like gunfire or a lacquered Valentine's Day heart. From time to time the women slow the pace for a moment or two while the drummer solos or a young man standing shyly to the side hits deep notes on an electric bass guitar. Then the young women speed up, strum until their bodies shake and bounce with the rhythm and motion of their hands against the strings. At intervals they sing at the tops of their lungs into microphones, the words adding to and becoming lost in the drone and whine of the guitars and the pulverizing blows of the drums.

The audience can't understand the words over the amplified noise of the music-making. The singers surely know that. But the players don't mute their instruments, and the singers sing on, louder and louder, almost to the point of screeching, as if the only thing that matters is to shout out the lyrics. It is the voice of a generation that accepts that its message may not be heard but nonetheless cries out the lyrics full blast, pounds its drums, turns up the amplifiers. The louder they sing, the louder the band plays and the more the young women bounce, shake and pulsate. There are no gyrations to their movements, nothing sexual, only intensity, a strident, unified vibration that joins the energy coming from the amplifiers and which makes my eardrums ring uncomfortably.

I shove my fingers into my ears, already stuffed with cotton, and rest my elbows on the table so as not to be conspicuous even in the dark. I shut my eyes and try to hide, but I can't escape the beat of their music. Unconsciously, I tap my foot. I move my leg away from my wife's, embarrassed that she might discover me tapping. It isn't my kind of music. But what is? To what sounds do I listen—and march?

I sit with closed eyes. The music becomes violent, explosive, and it rattles my head. Other explosions ring through it, too, almost the same sound as this music. At the end of the upside-down, black room of my mind there is a stage, and I am on it, a young soldier, a field artillery forward observer, in a foxhole, dirty and tired, dust, sweat and a week's growth of beard covering my cheeks. To my front, clouds of smoke and dust blur the morning sunlight, and the explosions of hundreds of shells shatter the air in time with the drumbeat on the other stage. I shout commands into the microphone of a radio and then listen for an answer, but there is none. If there were, the shellfire would drown it out just as the drums and amplified guitars stifle the singing. But I continue to shout into the microphone at the top of my lungs. Unlike the words of the young singers, my words *have* to be heard. They have to make a *difference*. The explosions rip the air and muffle my voice, like bursts of sound from the band.

And then the noise stops. The musicians put down their instruments, the audience applauds. Some cross to the other side of the wall for beer.

The pounding in my head gradually crumbles.

2

Three Fourteen

August 6, 1944. In the isolating darkness that fell across Hill 314, (the Hill), E Company riflemen and we artillery observers rooted around in foxholes, trying to wriggle into positions of comfort, grinding against the shallow, rocky sides as if we could wear them into a body shape. We stirred restlessly. Comfort became a dream to be dreamed at another time in another place. Earlier, when we had first settled into our foxholes, we had felt secure and at ease, but with the passing of only a few hours, the night no longer offered time for rest, let alone for stretching out.

Overhead, the exhaust trails of German aircraft soiled the sky, and their engines hummed a warning to our ears. During daylight hours in the days to come, intense surveillance by overwhelming Allied airpower would keep enemy planes bottled up at Paris and other airfields. But for now, they found a way through the defensive net and droned in the darkness above us.

To the immediate front, tanks were also active. We had been told that we faced an army in retreat. But the grinding and meshing of gears, the muffled growl of heavy engines, the rhythm of steel chains and treads pounding on roads voiced a desperate purpose, and we listened tensely to the ominous refrain.

The guttural droning of this enemy traffic disturbed the night, an unsettling dissonance that turned and twisted us in our rocky beds. The tale of a retreating enemy grew less convincing as the noise level increased. The night seemed to be turning treacherously against us.

Well below the southeastern promontory of the Hill, our right flank was guarded by H Company, a heavy weapons unit. Men were dug in along a minor road that ran generally easterly below the southern cliffs of the Hill and connected an outlying, quasi-rural, residential area with the town of Mortain, 1,000 yards to the rear. The company's lone 57mm antitank gun was sighted down the road toward the enemy. Tucked away in the bushes along the side, its slender barrel reflected no stray gleam of light that would give the roadblock away. The gun crew hunkered down next to it. Only a short distance farther east on the same road, panzer troops were making last-minute checks of radios, ammunition, and firing mechanisms of the superior and dreaded 88mm guns. Mechanics examined treads, engines and operating systems of powerful German tanks. Helmeted tank commanders, goggles pushed up, pored over maps one last time.

After midnight, messengers from E Company's listening posts and patrols brought reports of enemy activity below us. The Germans were not retreating.

To the right, tanks rumbled toward Mortain. Shouts echoed weakly in the moist night air and the high-pitched crackle of gunfire stood out from the steady undertone of the tanks. Like those infantrymen at the outposts, I felt danger move closer, waited anxiously as beads of sweat flecked my forehead and dribbled slowly into my eyebrows, blotted moisture with my shirt sleeve, touched the wetness with my other hand. The sweat kept on dribbling despite the cool night air. It wasn't the GI long johns that brought it up.

The noises of the panzers increased, seemed close by as each infantryman squeezed the stock of his rifle nervously with clammy hands. It would be useless against a panzer. If only Lieutenant Kerley, the company commander, were nearer.

The field artillery forward observer group that I commanded from the 230th Field Artillery Battalion—four of us—went to work to get artillery support from our guns which were miles away to the rear. Telephone lines to Fire Direction Center, the artillery nerve hub at our battalion headquarters, were still intact. Our field telephone rested in a beautiful leather case, saddle-soaped and polished to a parade-ground shine that gleamed softly, even at night. Again and again Sergeant Sasser cranked it and relayed to our Fire Direction Center the artillery fire missions I fed to him. In that first darkness, on unfamiliar ground, and with no well-coordinated infantry runner system in place, I used the artillery defensive fire plan that Lieutenant Lee, the artillery liaison officer, had given when he had called earlier.

"Crow," the code name for the 230th Field Artillery Battalion, splattered the landscape and dropped a curtain of hot, exploding steel in the face of the enemy. Each shell carried death in its 33-pound steel casing and through the long night barred the Germans from advancing across the Hill.

That curtain of jagged steel fragments also fell in the faces of the men on the perimeter of our position, but there was no retreat from it. I wasn't on the very edge as the shells blasted close by and roared furiously across the hillsides, but I was close enough. Many other times I was on the very edge—even beyond—and endured what those men did, crouched low in foxholes that were barely scratches on the Hill's rocky slope, hardly deep enough to give comfort, hanging on as the hillside shuddered under the force of erupting shells.

All thought ceases when overhead, without warning, the half-whisper, half-whistle of a shell suddenly cracks the night air and breaks into a scream as it closes in. That night it was our own "friendly artillery" shrieking at us: same sound, enemy, friendly, equally deadly. Push hard, that's what you do, try to drive deep into earth's unyielding rocks. "Lower! Get down!" Time shortens to zero. Like a giant sledge, the explosion of the shell shakes and rattles the deepest core. Some men lie in their beds for a lifetime after, stunned, winded, jarred mute by that hammer blow. For most, the recovery time is short, and for a few it is only an instant or two. Even for the latter, it becomes a black interval, not to be remembered, but unable to be forgotten. The explosion blasts away all sense of time. A thumping heart beats hard against the chest as will struggles against the heart's deep, essential palpitation. "Was I hit?" The search for damage follows. None. "Jesus, that was close. Look around, now, see if anything's over the edge of the foxhole. Careful. Grip your rifle—dammit—your insides are shaking like jelly." After a moment, a quiet settles in like an eternity come to rest, followed by one breathless second after another. The time has come to flatten out again, and lie against the earth in tense, suspended animation, waiting for the whistle of the next shell.

Movies always show dirt and fragments of rock blowing sky-high. Sometimes there is a roar or a blasting sound. The screen may go totally white or black for an instant to convey the impression of an explosion. The actors often look stunned, shake their heads and wipe dirt and sweat away. Sometimes they duck or run for cover. It is the best the cinema can offer.

Even in a reinforced, concrete bunker or in the catacombs and underground chambers of a church, below stone floors that have stood the test of centuries, the experience of being shelled is jarring. As if there is a way to escape, some crouch as low as possible, shrink for cover against the farthest, darkest wall. Eyes dart in all directions, unable to focus, searching vainly for a better place to hide. Then they close their eyes, cease to breathe, held in a stupor by expectation. Necks telescope and retract. Helmets flow down over hunched-up shoulders.

In a real show, the geysers of earth seen in movies are usually replaced by shells that explode in the air or on impact. Flying clods of dirt inflict little punishment, but jagged pieces of a steel shell, torn apart in its explosion, cut a man to pieces. When the explosion comes, eyes close, arms instinctively cover the face and head, hearts pound. Minds turn blank or desperate while chunks and splinters of the fractured shell whir in all directions, raking the air and ground impartially for a thigh, an arm, a chest.

Meanwhile, down below us to the right on the southern side of the Hill, the German panzers had already rolled straight over H Company. The 57mm antitank gun cracked a military joke against the powerful German tanks, heavily sheathed with steel plate. The enemy captured 19 of H Company's 20 jeeps and, of course, the antitank gun, for whatever that was worth to them. H Company troops who were not captured, scattered and sought refuge as best they could in the night. Some worked their way up the Hill and blended into E Company.

The German battle plan may have called for a swift dash north and south around Hill 314 with first priority to cut through Mortain to our rear, then drive on to the west, and deliver a lightning blow to the ocean, barely 20 miles to our rear. In that case, the enemy's battle plan would have called for mopping up on the Hill later. But maybe attacking the Hill had equal priority with the strike to the ocean but was not susceptible to swift execution because of the uncertainties inherent in a night attack over hilly, rocky terrain. The unexpected, heavy artillery fire we brought to bear in close proximity to our own position threw any attack off balance. A night assault may have suddenly become too chancy because our artillery fire made the rocky outcroppings of Hill 314 appear to be a heavily defended position. Maybe, maybe.

But the enemy had mounted a strong attack that caught the American forces around Mortain off-guard. The strength of the attack was not immediately apparent.[1] On the eastern ridge of the Hill, sniper fire harassed us through the night. Across the Hill to the west, small enemy groups infiltrated G Company's position on the western ridge of the Hill, screaming, *"Heil Hitler."*[2] Overhead, German night fighters unsettled the skies. We stood fast in the dark and shot back as best we could against the unseen enemy. Artillery fire became the only significant shield against the German threat.

Where the Germans had cut through H Company and exposed our right flank to attack, I adjusted artillery fire by sound, a last resort method. The shelling erupted, hot, volcanic, violent. The shells which exploded close to the fringe of E Company's position added to a rapidly developing sense of uncertainty. We did not then fully comprehend the spreading menace on that flank, which the shelling, like a closed, iron gate, momentarily diverted away from E Company.

I had no choice except to bring down artillery fire close to E Company and hold off the attempt by the Germans to overrun our position on the brow of the Hill. The shelling stopped them little more than a bayonet's length away from the farthest outpost, but none of the E Company men were injured by the shelling from our artillery.

On all sides, the muffled growl of tanks rose and echoed in the night.

3

A Pleasant Little Town

Fewer than 24 hours before, we had driven a jeep rather casually up to Hill 314 in the bloom of a warm, sunny, lazy Sunday. That morning of August 6 had the prospect of being the kind of summer day when back home, after it really warmed up, you might go swimming or dig worms to fish for bluegills or pick up a softball game with some of the guys. Before the war started, there were few cars, no television, little money, no fast lane to roar off into. Our front that Sunday morning seemed somewhat similar: calm, uneventful, predictable.

The largest invasion by sea in history had brought millions of men into battle against each other in Normandy. If the Allies won, the war would be over. If the Germans could fight the Allies to a standstill or drive them into the sea, as they had in 1940, there would be time to build additional defenses and to develop and perfect the secret weapons which Hitler's scientists were working on night and day, the means to secure an armistice and, perhaps, peace for Germany. Hitler might even win. "What happened in Normandy would decide this: history has nothing to offer more dramatic."[1]

The fighting had torn through picturesque tourist resorts and across ancient farm country, the so-called *bocage*, or hedgerow country. French farmers for hundreds of years had mounded up earth and rock around the boundaries of their fields and along the edges of the roads, and these hedgerows, overgrown and bound together with trees and shrubs, had become almost impenetrable, each one a separate

Not long after the Battle of Mortain, the author *(left)* and Private Luigi Ianucci during a lunch break. Private Ianucci was later killed in action.

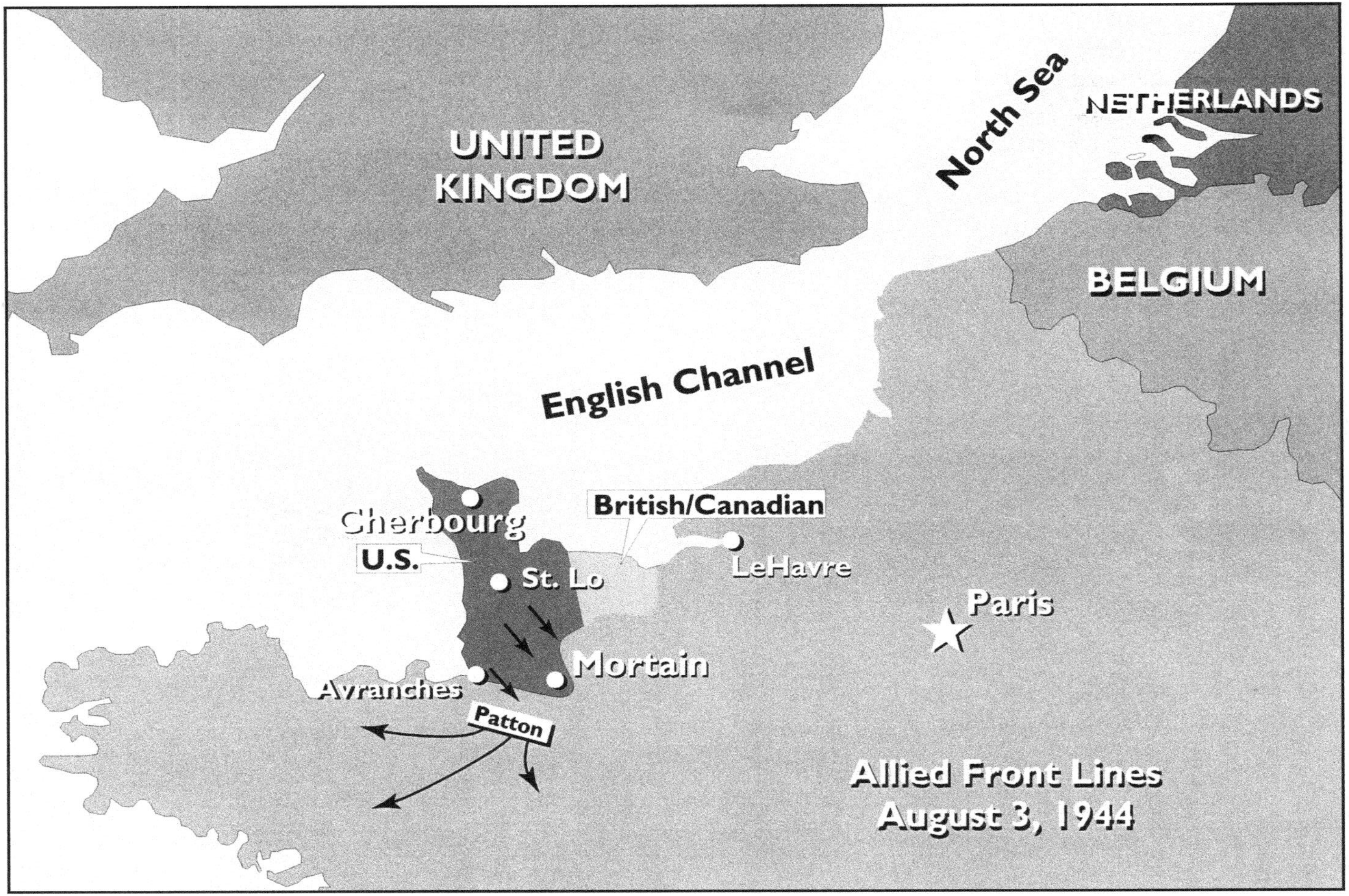

Allied Front Lines
August 3, 1944

NETHERLANDS

BELGIUM

North Sea

Paris

English Channel

LeHavre

British/Canadian

UNITED
KINGDOM

Mortain

St. Lo

Cherbourg
U.S.

Patton

Avranches

bastion to be assaulted and overcome. In seven weeks of bitter fighting since the D-Day landings on June 6, American troops had clawed their way almost yard by yard from the beaches through the endless hedgerows to St. Lô. In the narrow confines of the Cherbourg peninsula there had been barely room for one American army to fight, and a second had waited, bottled up until the American ground forces broke out into the open past St. Lô on July 25. Infantry divisions of the U.S. First Army now were mopping up to the south and east. Tanks and mobile forces of General George Patton's Third Army, in a somewhat parallel move, were sweeping south from Normandy and then turning west into Brittany and also east, driving the German forces before them. To the north, along the coast east of Normandy, the British and Canadians moved against collapsing German resistance. We thought the war was going well.

But in the ranks we didn't have much information. Just three days before, I had written to my mother:

> Well, how is everything back in old Indiana? In fact, we'd like to know how things are over here. Whenever you're in the fight you never know how it is going; that's the way it always is.

Our guns, the twelve 105mm howitzers that made up the firepower of the 230th Field Artillery Battalion, had been moving most of the night of August 5 under a full moon, and when dawn came had gone into position about forty miles south of St. Lô, ready to shoot. As the sun stretched over the fields and hills of southern Normandy that Sunday morning, I gathered my forward observer party together to load the jeep. We pushed in food, extra batteries for the radio, and observation equipment. In the cracks and spaces we jammed in personal gear—not much, because we expected to be just a short telephone or radio call away from B Battery, one of three 4-gun batteries in the 230th. B Battery was our home base. If we needed anything, a call to B Battery would fetch it to us. We did not intend to send our jeep back for supplies because that would have imprudently left the rest of our forward observer party without transportation.

Four of us made a jeepful. Corporal Dan C. Garrott was at the wheel. From Kentucky and appropriately soft-spoken, he was ever willing, dependable, but also determined not to be anybody's fool in a killing war. He was a survivor. A Kentucky license plate hung from the front bumper of the jeep, not in accord with military regulations but making its own statement about the GI. I sat next to Dan, my right foot up on the low edge of the frame of the jeep, ready for a quick exit, if need be. The canvas top was down.

Behind us, perched high on top of the jeep's load were Sergeant Armon A. Sasser, the radio operator, and Staff Sergeant John L. Corn, the survey section chief. Sasser was from North Carolina; Corn, a big hunk of a man, was from Iowa. I had grown up in Indiana. Starting with Sasser near the Atlantic Seaboard, and reaching across to Corn's home in the Midwest, we had all come from small towns, as most communities then were.

We left the B Battery gun position and set off toward the town of Mortain, which was four to five miles by road, to find Lieutenant Webster R. Lee. As the artillery liaison officer, he was the link with the infantry and would send us on to join up with units of an infantry battalion, which the 230th Field Artillery Battalion would directly support with its twelve 105mm howitzers if artillery fire was needed. We believed that we were to occupy an observation post (OP) somewhere in the vicinity of the town. Lieutenant Lee would give us final instructions.

After the breakout at St. Lô, the front had developed rapidly. Patton and his armored divisions were raising havoc with the enemy. Other divisions were on the move. Beyond that, as we drove on to Mortain, we knew very little. Most soldiers didn't care what they knew or didn't know, other than what was immediately to their front, rear or flanks. Knowledge of the big picture gave the troops in the front lines no power or edge. An infantryman couldn't throw the big picture at the enemy, hide behind it or shoot it. If pinned down by mortar or machine gun fire, his concerns were more immediate than the situation map at Allied Supreme Headquarters.

Besides, the last couple of days had been time out for our outfit, the 30th Infantry Division, more popularly known as "Old Hickory" in recognition of its Southern roots. It was the first relief from the

Corporal Dan C. Garrott
(lower right) and
Private Ianucci with a
local woman

Sergeant Armon A. Sasser,
radio operator

The author taking a helmet bath near
Ste. Mere-Eglise after landing in France

fighting since the division landed in Normandy. Many were still dazed and battered by the tons of bombs which the U.S. Army Air Corps had mistakenly dropped short of designated enemy targets in the "carpet" bombing at St. Lô. Men had been given a needed rest, time to wash up and to clean guns and equipment. Knowing that he would not be roused in the night to shoot or attack the enemy, a soldier could sleep it through—if he could separate from the penetrating consciousness of where he was.

A USO (United Service Organization) show of entertainers, for moments, masked the separate world that was the soldier's reality. Edward G. Robinson, "Little Caesar" of movie fame, paid a call. I was given the honor of driving him in a jeep when he came to our bit of turf. He was a short man with a sturdy build. In his olive-green trench coat, which he kept tightly buttoned and belted, and military cap, he looked reliable. He wore the most serious, thoughtful expression imaginable and easily could have passed for a senior commander on inspection. Never once, offstage while he was with us, did he break into the commanding smirk that was a hallmark of his screen performances, the one that said: "Let me tell you something, sweetheart." He asked many questions and appeared deeply concerned with the answers of the soldiers who clustered about him and who clearly impressed him. Perhaps he contrasted our youth, and the fragile future that the war offered to many, with his own, longer years.

This brief rest period and relief from the war also aroused suspicion. Not that everyone wasn't grateful, but no one could stand easy. For one thing, during this vacation from battle, we had still been in a battle zone, not more than 10 to 15 miles at the most from the front lines and under extreme blackout restrictions.

The American public isn't gullible, and you couldn't fool the average GI. No one had to tell him that the time off from the hedgerows of death was to ready the division for more of the same. The prospect showed in the care with which some men moved from place to place, and in simple events like standing in line for meals. Small, nervous groups would line up for chow, always on guard against gathering in large numbers, fearful of making a good target for enemy aircraft or a stray artillery shell.

Sometimes the sense of the war's nearness would flare up for the briefest instant. Underneath his helmet a soldier's head would nervously flick to one side. A boyish face would start wide-eyed at a sudden, unexpected noise, and then relax at the recognition that it was a piece of equipment banging against the metal bed of a truck, not gunfire. Lips would move secretly, silently, perhaps in prayer, or just as likely in condemnation of it all.

A few became loud and boisterous, feigning nonchalance with their trumpeting. And one sergeant who commanded a gun crew in B Battery drank so much one night during the rest period that he thought he could end the war by killing the battery commander. While he screamed with an insane, foaming rage, several men stuffed him into a foxhole and sat on him until he passed out. When morning came, he awoke with no recollection of the night before except for his aching head and bones. The war was still on, but, of course, he was no longer a sergeant.

So, beyond the simple understanding that our forces were on the move and that our division was going back on the line, we had little information as we came close to Mortain. It was just as well. Even if we had known what the generals at the highest headquarters thought they knew, it would have been of no use to us that day or in any of the days that followed.

Summer sunshine faded into a dusty halo hanging over the road, and movement was slow. Our route was crowded with army trucks, jeeps and guns and some French refugees. It was never easy to know whether the French were returning after a battle or fleeing before the next one. The farmers of Normandy and the residents of the small towns, by some underground or native intelligence or consciousness, always knew when it was safe to stay or return and when it was time to move out, like a person whose nose smells an impending storm in the wind and instinctively senses the need to take shelter.

Despite the congestion, it was not 30 minutes until we drove into the outskirts of Mortain, a pleasant little town of 1,650 inhabitants,[2] crowded between rocky hills and escarpments to the east and

French refugees from Mortain

National Archives

a swift-flowing stream to the west, the River Cance, marked with sharply falling rapids. The previous evening Colonel Hammond D. Birks, the commanding officer of the 120th Infantry Regiment of the 30th Division, had looked the town over and perceived that it was wide open with business being transacted and the hotels full.[3] Some of the advance elements that were with him thought that Mortain would make an excellent place for more rest and relaxation. Those who had preceded the 30th Division troops sized it up differently. The commander of the 18th Infantry Regiment, which was being replaced by Birks' troops, pointed out to him that Hill 314 was the key to the entire area. He noted that in case of emergency the Hill "...would have to be held at all costs."[4]

Since the previous evening when Colonel Birks rated the town as a tourist attraction, our forces had taken over and converted it to a military scene ready for battle. The 2d Battalion, 120th Infantry, had taken over the Grande Hotel de la Poste and set up its headquarters there. Army installations and roadblocks were in place on the outskirts. A tank destroyer platoon was in the town, held there in reserve for whatever action might develop in any direction. Army linemen were stringing a tangle of telephone lines, each subordinate unit being essentially responsible for its own communication network.

A café and small shops along the main street were now deserted. Although there had been warm greetings from the French along the way to Mortain, cheering, bouquets of flowers and drinks offered at every halt,[5] no frenzy of townspeople lined the streets to greet the liberating American troops. The activity in the streets looked more serious than a victory parade. The Germans had recently rolled through the town with tanks, trucks, horse-drawn vehicles and artillery. The local residents had no assurance that they would not be back. Many of the townspeople took refuge in an abandoned mineshaft not far away. Our own troops were all that we saw.

Lieutenant Lee's jeep was parked half up on a sidewalk, and he stood nearby, staring at the passing troops, looking for the forward observers that he would send ahead to the infantry. A large map case covered with fraying canvas rested on the back of the jeep. The canvas was a makeshift cover to prevent reflections that an alert enemy might spot. The radio antenna curved across the rear of the jeep from one side to the other. The driver lounged in his seat while the radio operator leaned intently against the big radio mounted in back, listening for calls. Everything seemed well organized. It was all happening the way it should, like a practice exercise or a stateside maneuver. We pulled up behind.

I hopped out of the jeep, quickly took three or four steps to where Lieutenant Lee stood and identified myself. We spoke briefly. Then he uncovered the map. Units of the 1st Infantry Division, "Big Red One," were in position along the edges of a hill in the countryside, about 1,000 yards east of the center of town where we stood. Together we leaned over the back of the jeep and studied the map.

The top of the Hill was about a mile long from north to south, and the contour lines on a map gave it a shape like a mitten or, perhaps, a T-bone steak. On the western edge, the town side, and on the south, steep cliffs dropped off sharply. Along the rim of the western edge, beginning approximately where the road from town came out on top, the ground rose in a southerly direction forming a ridge. The road itself ran almost due east across the Hill's top and continued in that direction for some distance, eventually passing a little farm settlement called Bel-Air. For simplicity, that name designates this east-west road.

Parallel to this road and to the north about 1,500 yards—less than a mile—was a main highway, what had been the principal avenue of escape for German units believed to be trapped somewhere to the east. This highway ran east to the town of Ger. At the northern outskirts of Mortain, it connected with a road that ran north from Mortain to L'Abbaye-Blanche and St. Barthélemy.

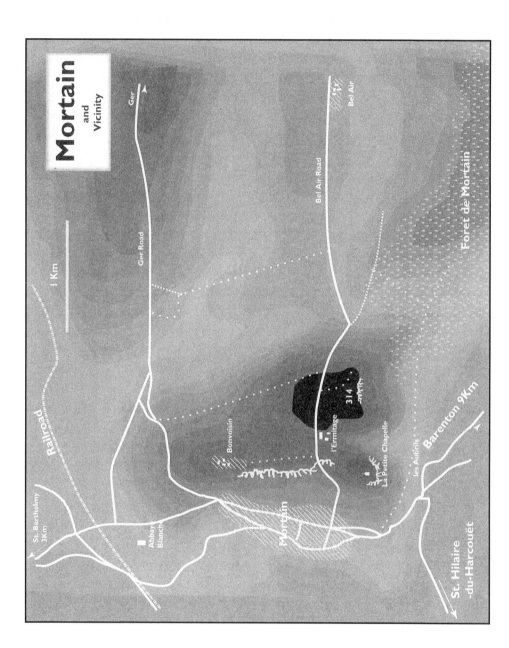

Mortain
and
Vicinity

1 Km

Ger

Ger Road

Railroad

St. Barthelmy
3Km

Abbaye
Blanche

Mortain

Bonvoisin

l'Ermitage

314

La Petite Chapelle

les Aubrits

Bel Air Road

Bel Air

Forêt de Mortain

Barenton 9Km

St. Hilaire
-du-Harcouët

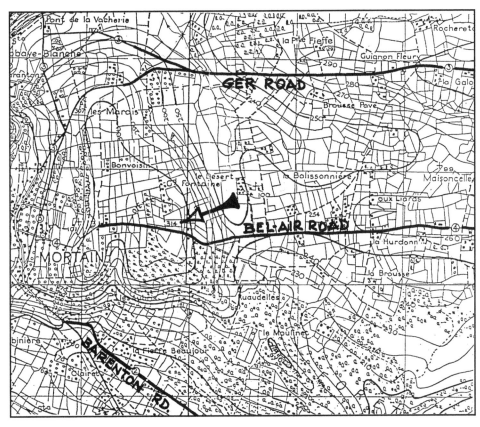

Portions of Maps—Mortain and Barenton. From RG 77, AMS, M-865, Mortain, 34/10NE and Barenton 34/10SE, Feb. 1944, National Archives at College Park, Maryland. Ger, Bel-Air and Barenton Roads are highlighted. The originals have a 10-meter contour interval. The grid is approximately 1,000 meters.

All along the eastern edge of the mitten, or T-bone, there was another, higher ridge that also ran generally from north to south, being higher at the southern end. To the east, the countryside sloped away from this ridge more gradually than on the west and the south. Between the two ridges, more or less at the center of the Hill, there was a small plain or basin, consisting mostly of farm and pasture land, which for a considerable distance sloped gently to the south. At the southern end of this plain a little draw began and quickly ran off into a sharp valley that sundered the southern end of the Hill, between the eastern and western ridges, into twin, rocky promontories. They were the highest points on the Hill.

It took only a moment to decide that my party should move forward to the eastern ridge.

Lieutenant Lee pointed with his index finger and placed it on the map. Contour lines curved around and encircled it. When he took it away, in the center of those enveloping contour lines was the number 314. It was at the highest point on the eastern ridge, and the highest place on the Hill. It was now late morning. Garrott started the jeep. We headed up to Hill 314.

4

The Forward Observer

Usually, a forward observer worked with a single infantry company. The 30th Infantry Division was broken into three regimental combat teams, each of which consisted of one infantry regiment supported by one light artillery battalion with twelve 105mm howitzers. Under this structure, the 230th Field Artillery always supported the 120th Infantry Regiment if it was "on the line." As we moved onto Hill 314 we did not know which infantry companies of the 120th would join us there.

That was not unusual. My job as forward observer generally was to observe the enemy, advise artillery battalion headquarters of what I saw—whether it was two enemy infantrymen or a battalion of tanks—note the position of what I saw and request artillery fire if I thought it was an appropriate target. Usually, although not always, the forward observer was attached to an infantry unit. In supporting the infantry, the primary objectives would be to defend the infantry unit against enemy attack and to aid it in accomplishing any special mission assigned to it, such as capturing an enemy strongpoint. Other targets were fair game if the opportunity developed. If, as forward observer, I had to move in front of the infantry in order to provide the necessary artillery support—to shoot up the enemy—within the bounds of reasonable common sense, I was expected to do it.

Often it was a lonely job, but also one which gave me a great deal of discretion. There was a freedom of enterprise associated with it, a feeling of being in business for myself, that was somehow less restrictive, less regimented than normal army routine. I liked that.

23

Any forward observer's activities were to a considerable extent dictated by energy, skill, dedication, how intrepid he was, and, of course, what the situation demanded, whether it meant being in front of the infantry or hunkering down safely behind a stout wall or fortification.

I have been asked what kind of artillery I, as a forward observer, had with me. The answer is none. Yet, in a practical sense, in addition to my Colt .45 I packed a battalion of 105mm howitzers and was capable of blasting an attacking force of infantry and tanks to bits. Often I might "shoot" many battalions of artillery at the same target at the same time. It depended upon communication and availability.

The forward observer in World War II for the most part soldiered with the infantry, marched and fought with them, using artillery instead of a rifle. The portable radio, of course, made this possible and, in this respect, *made World War II different from all previous wars.* It brought the artillery into the front lines and made it into a front-line weapon *as it never had been before.*

Organizational techniques, of course, were very important in coordinating front-line commands from the forward observer to the guns located miles to the rear. Except in the most unusual of circumstances, the actual instructions that aimed artillery came from a Fire Direction Center, a part of artillery battalion headquarters. Essential data, information and commands were relayed back and forth between the forward observer, Fire Direction Center and the guns, all of which depended upon reliable communication between them.

In a static situation, the forward observer could communicate with Fire Direction Center by telephone. In the more common mobile situation, whether fast-moving or not, fire commands went by radio. When the radio was mounted in a jeep, the jeep's electrical system provided the power to operate it. It would have been rare, however, to direct fire in the front lines from a jeep. If dismounted from the jeep, a batterypack made the radio portable. When the batteries in the batterypack ran down, they could be removed from the batterypack casing and replaced.

Although portable, the field artillery's 35-pound Model 610 radio and the almost equally heavy batterypack were sturdy, cumbersome pieces of equipment designed for reliability and durability. They were not pocket-sized like many of today's radios, but dinosaur-like and very heavy. Carrying them any distance provided a strenuous workout and required two men for the job. It was possible for one man to carry both the radio and batterypack together, but only for very short distances.

Using a cross-shoulder carrying strap, the radio operator could manage to carry the radio, his gas mask, a carbine or sidearm, binoculars and a canteen, but only if he accepted a slight deformation of the spine and a sloping of the shoulders. The same was true of the batterypack which the other man carried. Bulky though it was, this bit of technology gave the artillery front-line mobility, virtually as much as traditional infantry weapons such as the rifle, the machine gun and the mortar.

In most situations, then, a supply of replacement batteries was essential to maintain artillery as a front-line weapon.

Each gun in a field artillery battery—normally four guns in a battery—was "surveyed in" so that the direction it was pointing and its location and altitude, or elevation, were known with considerable accuracy. At the Fire Direction Center, specially trained personnel would plot this data on a map, or firing chart. When the location of a target was designated, they could then measure fairly accurately the distance from the guns and also the direction to and altitude of the target. Using printed tables, these Fire Direction Center personnel would compute data which they would send as commands to the guns. Theoretically, the shells should hit the target.

The forward observer's job in all of this was to designate the target and its location as accurately as possible to the Fire Direction Center, and, once firing had commenced, to determine where the shells hit in relation to the target. The observer did this by observing or "sensing" the shell bursts and the smoke, dust, and debris churned up from the explosion of the shells. Were the shells landing beyond the target, "over," or were they falling "short"? Were they "right" or "left"? And how far? The observer would translate his observations into data that would enable the Fire Direction Center to give further commands to the guns. If the commands were properly executed by the gun crews, again the shells should theoretically hit the target. The entire process was called "adjusting fire."

The information as to target location and accuracy, or point of impact, of the rounds that had been fired, depended on the forward observer's perception and ability to estimate the distance and direction between the target and the point of impact, often at distances of many thousands of yards from the target. If the forward observer was not directly in line between the guns and the target, estimating the location of shell bursts in relation to a target became even more complex. There were textbook procedures for doing all of this. In the end, however, the forward observer's part of the process of "adjusting fire," or "shooting," was something of an art form or personal skill.

Needless to say, some forward observers located and described targets more accurately than others. When it came to sensing where the rounds were hitting and bursting in relation to a target, there was a significant difference in skill levels between observers. Some could "shoot" better than others. I don't believe that I have ever heard a forward observer referred to as a "crack shot," but the comparison with small arms and rifle shooting is useful as a reference point. Obviously, the higher the degree of skill of the forward observer in adjusting artillery fire, the quicker and more effective the artillery fire would be. Delays of almost any sort would give the enemy warning and time to take cover.

This sounds primitive by comparison with modern techniques of laser and infrared guided missiles. It was nonetheless effective. When executed by a forward observer who knew how to "shoot," artillery fire was extremely accurate.

Once, in the States, when on major maneuvers where there were field judges who evaluated and graded performance, I was selected as the forward observer. This put my battalion commander, a lieutenant colonel, under extreme pressure because his future to some extent depended upon what a 20-year-old second lieutenant would do.

The field judges pointed out the target to me, an isolated, stout-trunked, almost leafless tree at some distance. My task was to give commands based on data which I was required to estimate in relation to a known geographic feature. I was told where the guns were in relation to that geographic feature. Only one gun would fire until the adjustment onto the target had been completed. Adjusting fire with only one gun was normal procedure, both in the States and in combat, in order to conserve ammunition. Using only the data that I had estimated, the first shell exploded in the tree, momentarily blanketing it with smoke and debris. A lucky hit. The 105mm howitzer was not designed for such accuracy. I called for two more quick rounds to verify the sensing, and, at my third command, all of the battalion's twelve guns were "firing for effect," devastating the target area completely. Crude, perhaps, but accurate, quick and effective. My battalion commander must have danced.

In France, it was no longer make-believe. Face-to-face with the enemy, life and death came down to my judgment, my ability to read a map and to estimate distances visually, both laterally and in depth. If the target was moving, it was more difficult. Shooting a tank slamming down a road with guns blazing was tougher than pecking away at an old tree.

5

We Dig In

After leaving Lieutenant Lee at the roadside in Mortain, we pushed through the confusion in the center of the town and headed east, ascending steeply past stone and stucco-covered brick structures, mostly residences. Five years of war and occupation had left their mark, and most buildings were colorfully dilapidated. The climb was steadily upwards, past rocky outcroppings and finally out into the countryside where the road topped out on the high ground that is Hill 314.

In front of us, 800 yards to the east, we saw the long line that is the top of the ridge running along the eastern edge of the Hill. As we drove east along the Bel-Air Road, at the far right we could make out the southeastern promontory of the Hill, a fierce outcropping of big rocks and jagged cliffs plunging down to the south and to the west. This was the spot to which Lieutenant Lee had pointed on the map when he gave us our instructions in Mortain. It is the highest point on the Hill.

Just short of the eastern ridge, we turned right off the Bel-Air Road. A trail made by 1st Division vehicles that had preceded us ran down through some trees to the south. The first job was to unload and get the jeep out of the way. We dismantled the radio from its jeep mounting so that it became portable, and carefully set it and a batterypack on the ground along with other equipment and gear.

While we reconnoitered the crest of the ridge, Corporal Garrott drove the jeep down toward the head of the draw running to the south. There had been a good deal of troop activity before us, and other vehicles had already beaten the beginnings of a road through the grass and brush. Garrott followed this path for some yards, and then pulled off into a grove of trees. There, with branches and brush, he carefully camouflaged the windshield, which was already in a horizontal position on top of the hood, and also the rest of the vehicle, subduing its outline and enhancing the protection from air observation already provided naturally by the grove.

Because we were occupying high ground with no apparent maneuvering or movement in prospect, we had brought along a BC scope, periscope-like binoculars of relatively high magnification, so heavy and unwieldy that a heavy-duty tripod was required to hold it steady for observation. We lugged all of this equipment, the radio and the batterypack plus personal gear up onto the east ridge of the Hill, sweating uncomfortably in the warm sunshine of that quiet, summer afternoon.

At the top, we met a field artillery forward observer attached to the 1st Division infantry regiment which was holding the Hill. He had been there for several days, with almost no action unfolding before him and with plenty of time to study the terrain in front, that is to the east. He showed us several possible observation posts, or OPs, on the ridge. In particular, one offered a view straight down the Bel-Air Road.

The Ger Highway connected with the Bel-Air Road by numerous trails, hidden from observation where they tunneled through foliage past the hedgerows. The observer on the ridge told us that shooting the retreating Germans on these roads had been a regular "picnic." All we had to do, he said, was to knock them out when clouds of dust rising up from the roads revealed their movements. He told us that the 1st Division infantry had also been supported by anti-tank units and tank destroyers which had fired from the top of the Hill not 50 yards from his artillery OP. Discarded shell casings lay around on top of the ridge.

The situation, then, as he explained it to us, would be simply a matter of the infantry continuing to hold the high ground which American forces occupied, and, for me, the artillery observer, to spot the Germans as our enveloping troops flushed them out of the hedgerows and then "shoot" them with the 105mm howitzers of our field artillery. We expected to make good use of the excellent observation which the OP afforded.

The Hill dominated the terrain to our front and to the north and northeast as well as to the south. To the southeast we had observation for perhaps 15 miles. At first we did not bother with this latter sector, supposedly a friendly flank.

The best information given to us when taking over this position was to watch to our front, that is, to the east. The observation to the north, although considerable, did not give us the same open view of the roads that we had to the east and to the southeast. In consequence of the briefing that we got, we anticipated that our most important missions would lie to our direct front. In fact, they did.

The summer grasses were tall, and small pine trees grew randomly in the rocky soil on the east ridge of the Hill. Large outcroppings of rock lent character to the scene. Down below us, fields and trees stretched away to the east, occasionally interrupted by a crossing hedgerow. A few farm buildings and groves of surrounding trees filled in the scene, a French impressionist painting come to life.

We began to set up our OP, digging in the radio, finding appropriate cover for ourselves. We contacted battalion headquarters by radio to report our location, using a very crude and simple coding procedure so that any listening enemy would not immediately know where or who we were. Because we normally were involved in fast-moving situations in which the enemy would not have the time or the equipment to break our coding system, this simple code was more than adequate.

Several hours after we set up our OP on Hill 314, E Company, 2d Battalion, 120th Infantry, relieved the last remnants of the 1st Division and they marched off. By then it was nearly 2:00 p.m. Lieutenant Ralph Kerley, a Texan, commanded E Company. Except for the helmet and olive drab wool uniform, he was the movie image of a Texas Ranger, tanned, tall and spare, tough and mature. Here was a man who looked as if he had been born to fight the Germans to the

Field artillery observation post, European Theater, WWII, with BC scope

Courtesy of the *FA Journal*

death. Kerley immediately deployed troops on both sides of the Bel-Air Road, with the bulk of them spread out to the end of the eastern ridge south of the road. He also set up a roadblock to the east, down the Bel-Air Road, and positioned outposts on trails that ran through the area.

The 2d Battalion was given essentially the same "holding" mission as the 1st Division infantry which it relieved. E Company was joined on the Hill by other infantry companies: G Company of the 2d Battalion occupied the high ground along the western ridge, across the pasture to our rear; K Company of the 3d Battalion of the 120th went into position to the north of the Bel-Air Road along the eastern high ground of the Hill; and H Company, the heavy weapons unit, protected the right flank on the southern slope of the Hill below E Company. Although loosely speaking, the infantry now covered the top of the Hill, the companies were not shoulder to shoulder, and significant distances separated each one from the others.

The positions that the departing infantry left had not been developed in depth, were sufficient only for a hasty defense and were never intended to hold off a strong counterattack. The 2d Battalion command and the individual company commanders were fully aware of this and planned to strengthen the positions which they had taken over as soon as they could by emplacing fortifications and mines.[1]

Nonetheless, a sense of security filled the air. The last few days had been an easy time for the 1st Division sitting quietly on the Hill. Moreover, "There was no concrete information regarding the enemy."[2] In fact, the first entry in the 230th Message Log for August 6 is from the liaison officer, the man who was supposed to know the situation so that he could direct forward observers to the locations that would most effectively support the infantry. The message says: "Have no maps or know anything of situation."

It was immediately evident, and more so later, that this high Hill which the 2d Battalion occupied was a key point, a pivot. If the Germans should attack—and we had no expectation that they would—and failed to spread out over the top of the Hill in all directions and envelope it, their divisions and panzers would have to maneuver around the Hill and attempt to turn the American forces like spokes around the hub of a wheel. If they were unsuccessful in this, and the Americans continued to occupy the Hill, the Germans risked being turned back or caught against its cliffs.

Kerley established his command post and headquarters well below the crest of the eastern ridge, up against a jumble of rocks near the beginning of the shallow draw that ran off to the south and which turned into the steep valley between the eastern and western promontories of the Hill. Tucked between the ridge to the east and the steep slopes to the south, nearly in the middle of the E Company position, it was a choice place for a headquarters and manifestly defensible for a front-line position, particularly with the town of Mortain to the rear and both flanks held by American troops.

6 "Want to Shoot Some Jerries?"

Sergeant Corn had set up the BC scope, which we had laboriously lugged onto the eastern ridge. Now we hoped it had been worth the effort. The grasses and bushes were high, and we were well concealed behind them. The eyes of the scope peeked gingerly over the full-headed tops of the golden grasses, searching. It would have taken a sharp-eyed enemy observer and some careless act on our part to betray this activity. With the sun at our backs, there was no likelihood of sunshine reflecting off the lenses of the scope. Despite the information that the enemy was retreating, we were exceedingly careful.

Sergeant Corn fiddled with the eyepieces, rotated the scope and carefully scrutinized the sloping hillside and hedgerows in front of us. He crouched down in the tall grass beside the tripod, and after a time he turned to me and in a calm voice asked, "Want to shoot some Jerries, Lieutenant?" From the casual, even tone of his voice he might have been asking if I wanted an apple or if I liked the way the French cultivated their fields. I wondered if he was testing me.

Only two weeks earlier, the boat which brought me to France, an LCI[1] designed for infantry assault troops, had shuddered up onto Utah Beach. With full pack on my back, I had eagerly pushed my way to the front of the troops huddled on deck in the broken light of dawn, determined to be the first one off the ship—and I was. The landing ramp slanting down from the front of the vessel had been plowing through the English Channel all night during our crossing. It was wet, slimy and slick. I had not taken that into account. The full pack made me top-heavy, and I skidded and slid down the ramp, but somehow maintained my balance, until I lurched onto the sand. After all of the training, the months of building expectations, the letdown of delays and endless waiting in lines, we were here, in France, at last. It was a moment that I silently honored. I turned around to the others still on deck and with a short, sharp movement of my head gave them a sign to follow.

On July 28, after that unsteady landing in France, I wrote home:

> ...I hope I get a chance to do a little shooting on my own the next few days...

Two days later, I was assigned to B Battery, 230th Field Artillery Battalion, a unit of the 30th Infantry Division, as a "reconnaissance" officer, that is, as a forward observer. Forward observers were on the cutting edge of battle, and they came and went. The casualty rate was very high. I was not the first replacement that these men had seen. And there would be others after me.

So when Sergeant Corn asked that question, with such apparent innocence, he was asking it of the new kid on the block. "Want to shoot some Jerries?"

I edged up to the scope and peered through it. There were Germans all right, gray-green uniforms, rifles. A company of infantry in close formation marched along the road, some 2,000 yards—a mile and a quarter or so—to the east. If the Germans were in full retreat, what were their troops doing at the edge of our front lines? I never thought to ask the question.

I felt confident. My training had been good. I knew what to do. Except for the live target in front of me, it seemed no different than any training mission. I turned and alerted Sergeant Sasser at the radio close by:

Fire Mission. Enemy infantry.

"Fire Mission" was a standard signal alerting Fire Direction Center to get ready for action. Sergeant Sasser switched on the radio and called the battalion Fire Direction Center:

Crow this is Crow Baker 3.

Sasser was from North Carolina. He spoke in muted Southern tones which would never betray our presence to any enemy patrol that might be within earshot. When he received a response from "Crow," that is, from our battalion headquarters, he repeated my message.

Thus, around four o'clock that afternoon, began the first of 193 fire missions that our party would send in before we came off the Hill, an average of one every 45 minutes for the next six days.[2]

Back at the Fire Direction Center the air crackled with the message wrapped in that low, North Carolina voice:

Fire Mission. Enemy infantry.

This was a priority call. Except for another fire mission, it would take precedence over any other activity at the Fire Direction Center. It was an attention-getter that rattled airwaves and demanded action. Shooting the enemy with artillery was what we were there for. The staff at the Fire Direction Center at battalion headquarters would make the final decision as to whether the target justified the expenditure of ammunition.

In command there was Lieutenant Colonel Lewis D. Vieman. He, too, was from Texas and, like Kerley, was tall. There the resemblance ended. Colonel Vieman was thin, rail-like, eternally erect. A product of Texas A & M, he was all spit and polish, humorless, a highly demanding and efficient officer. He was one who would stand in an open field and flatly drawl "No, *merci*" to a humble French woman who came to proffer the only gift of thanks she had for the liberating Americans, a plate of the most delicious-looking tomatoes ever grown. He would do this without emotion, looking away with contrived indifference, excluding her from his world as he turned deliberately to busy himself in the military task that had brought him uninvited onto her farm field. He really was trying to say, "Don't come too close. It's against army regulations to take your tomatoes." But "No, *merci*" was the best response he could make.

Unlike his avoidance of the tomatoes, Colonel Vieman acted on the target quickly. It was a good one. We had radioed approximate coordinates of the target's location. A noncom hung over a map and plotted with a ruler and protractor. Another checked the plot. They consulted printed firing tables. Then they converted the data into commands and telephoned them to a battery of our guns. Sergeant Sasser was soon able to announce:

The author aboard ship crossing the English Channel from Southampton to Utah Beach in early July 1944

On the way.

High-explosive shells that would burst apart into hundreds of pieces of uncaring, flesh-ripping, jagged pieces of steel[3] were in the air. I watched. There were explosions near the Jerries. I gave additional commands. There were more explosions, and dust and black smoke clouded the air. The echo of the bursting shells faded away across the hedgerows and fields. When the smoke and dust cleared, the Jerries were gone. The gray-green uniforms had disappeared into the grasses and trees.

It was an easy thing shooting Jerries. How many had we killed or wounded? We had no way of knowing. But now we knew they were there. We waited and watched.

Overhead, enemy aircraft unexpectedly became active. Kerley's men had been in position for little more than half an hour when six enemy FW190s swept the area. We heard bombing well to the rear.

As a rule, Allied air superiority kept the *Luftwaffe* out of the skies except at night. The infantry commanders were very concerned by the appearance of the FW190s because this was the first daylight air offensive they had encountered since going into battle almost seven weeks before.[4] We kept a low profile, restricted our movements, and stayed concealed in the billowing grasses and under the scattered pines on the hillside. It was important to avoid bunching up or creating a target that would have been obvious to low-flying aircraft. The infantry tried to improve their individual positions, those taken over from the 1st Division's 18th Infantry Regiment, but digging was difficult in the rocky ground. In some places, soldiers encountered solid rock just below the surface.[5]

At around 5:45 p.m., enemy mortar shells suddenly burst in our vicinity. Everyone took cover. Based on the sounds of the firing, we measured the direction of the mortars as carefully as we could and reported to battalion. The mortar shells appeared to come from a location a bit north of east. Mortars have a limited range, not able to shoot many thousands of yards like artillery. A light mortar, that is one that was easily portable and which could be carried by infantry, like our 60mm mortar, had an extreme range slightly in excess of one mile. If a plot had been made which combined the direction which we had observed with the normal range of a mortar, it would have placed the enemy to the east along the Bel-Air Road, just beyond our own infantry roadblock. If the mortars, or perhaps a single mortar with a patrol, were even closer, then the enemy was south of the roadblock and down the ridge just below us.

It didn't look like an enemy in retreat, but we didn't ask why the German army, which was falling back, was so aggressively close. That wasn't our job on the Hill. We took cover.

In the early evening, we again spotted gray-green uniforms, caught by the warm tones of sunlight which seemed to brighten as the end of the day approached. They were in and around a building about 2,500 yards to the east and a touch to the south. Again it was *"Fire Mission,"* and our artillery roared and brought a hail of exploding shells and jagged steel onto the target. Had we killed or wounded? Probably. How many? How badly? We could not say. Had we damaged an unknown Frenchman's farmhouse? Clearly, we had done that. Would he view it as a fair trade?

In the dying light, almost at 9:30 p.m. that Sunday, a messenger from an infantry outpost rushed up, breathless, rifle over shoulder, cheeks glistening with sweat. His anxious, wide eyes and earnest voice, the way his body slumped in relief at finding the artillery forward observer, showed that he knew what a dirty game he was playing so far from home. Enemy infantry had been observed. He gave us an approximate location and, still panting, laid down in the grass to cool off and gather himself before going back into the unknown. We fired our last fire mission of the day as darkness closed in. This time the enemy was only a few hundred yards from our previous target and not in full retreat. We wondered if the new target was the same infantry that had been the first target, or possibly other troops, who with the first target, formed part of a larger unit. If so, we faced a large force.

But intelligence and fitting together all of the many bits and pieces of information was not our task. We assumed somebody else was doing that. It had been a reasonable afternoon's work, and we were ready for our reward. The infantry was serving hot rations, brought in by jeep. It was a modern war that we were fighting, no grub roasted on a stick over an open campfire, but a real hot *meal,* cooked on a stove and brought up to us at the front in insulated containers that kept the food hot. The kitchen crew also passed out boxed K-rations, two per man. The K-ration, with its little tins and packets of food all carefully done up in a heavy, waterproof box, was scientifically designed by expert nutritionists. Each one contained the caloric equivalent of one meal, theoretically fit to eat even cold. We fumbled in the dark for our mess kits and lined up for chow, the last real meal anyone on the Hill would have for nearly a week.

By that time we had been connected into the telephone network that the 1st Division had left in place. Somebody had come up in the dark, left us a field telephone, hooked it up, cranked it, tested it and hustled off. We now could communicate directly with our battalion headquarters and Fire Direction Center. Lieutenant Lee, our liaison officer who was still back in the town, rang soon after and gave me a nighttime plan of defensive artillery fire, a precaution against the unexpected. I handed a copy of the fire plan to Lieutenant Kerley and also told him that I had talked to an artillery observer from the 980th Field Artillery Battalion, a 155mm "long tom" outfit, who had come onto the Hill.

Whatever assurance this other observer's presence may have implied was as fleeting as the twilight in which he had come. He disappeared minutes later, and we never saw him again. Nor did we ever hear from or see Lieutenant Lee after his telephone call. Nor could we, because, as we learned later, he was captured when the Germans swept through Mortain.

Meanwhile, however, and unknown to us, elsewhere in the early afternoon of that first day, a French civilian told our forces that artillery, paratroopers and 10 German infantry regiments from the Russian front were assembling on the high ground approximately two to three miles north of our position and east of St. Barthélemy, where bitter fighting would take place in the next few days.[6] Another civilian reported enemy artillery several miles south and east of Hill 314.[7] And by the time I had fired that last fire mission in the waning twilight, our division artillery headquarters also knew that there were enemy tanks on the road between Barenton and Mortain and that there was a tank and infantry assembly area about a mile southwest of Barenton.[8] Barenton is approximately six miles southeast of Mortain.

Our infantry was in a holding position, not in pursuit of a fleeing enemy, and not actively seeking contact with the Germans. Yet the Germans were marching around in front of us, you might say retreating in the wrong direction, very close to our lines under cover of approaching night.

In retrospect, you may well ask why all these enemy troops and tanks were there if the enemy was in flight. The answer seems obvious 50 years after the fact. But it is unlikely that the events of the next few hours would have been different or that the course of the battle would have changed if the question had been asked that first evening. One could ask similar questions about many battles and about many wars. What if? What if? The speculation is intriguing and endless but provides no answer to reward the questioner. Perhaps the reward is in the asking, however late that may be. What is certain is that in battle what is seen is often not all of what is there. Expectation rules perception. What military man on the battlefield, no matter how brilliant, can intuitively piece together such bits and scraps of information and reach the definitive and correct conclusion that only a fictional Sherlock Holmes could sense? By way of compensation, however, an intelligence failure on one side, in the confusion of the fighting, often is balanced by a failure on the other.

My forward observer party moved down behind the eastern ridge, close to Lieutenant Kerley's command post and headquarters, and bedded down for what in our continuing optimism looked like an uneventful summer's sleep. Night drew a soft veil over the French countryside. There were no campfires glowing in the darkness, no stacked rifles. No songs or humming of tunes filled the air. The airplane which could see and attack at night and modern artillery and other surface weaponry had scratched those romantic touches from the landscape. For safety's sake, we crawled into foxholes left by the field artillery forward observers whom we had replaced. There obviously had been plenty of time for them to dig in on this lazy front, or else they gave digging a priority. In either case we were grateful. We felt secure.

A week later at battalion headquarters, after the battle was over, I wrote:

> As we bedded down, everything was quiet; and we anticipated that any action we would see in our position would be slight indeed.

That first night I curled tightly into my rocky foxhole trying to find some position that would be comfortable. The helmet made an awkward pillow. As I wiggled around in the dirt and rocks, one hand rubbed across the sleeve of my shirt. It was heavy, wool serge, not government issue. I rubbed the sleeve again. The twill had a strength about it that I felt in the black of that night, as if it were passing on energy from another time and another war.

7   *Hitler's Counterstroke*

As darkness shut us in along the rocky ledges of Hill 314 that first night on August 6, the war was heating up to white-hot intensity in our front yard.

To understand why and how, it is necessary to go back to July 20, a little over two weeks earlier, roughly the day I lurched down a ship's ramp onto the beaches of France. A bomb attempt was made that day on the life of Hitler, who was meeting with the High Command of the Wehrmacht at the Wolf's Lair in East Prussia where he then maintained his headquarters. The explosion left his pants a tattered snarl of threads and nearly blew his eardrums out. Whether his hearing was permanently impaired or not, thereafter he ceased to listen to or heed his advisers with the same acceptance as before.

The escape from the death plot, which had killed some of his immediate staff, and the tracking down, torture and savage execution of the plotters "...induced in him a euphoria and sense of confidence, of a turning point in his fortunes...."[1] In a last meeting that day with the decayed shell of the once admired Mussolini, he prattled of good luck, destiny and a triumphant conclusion.

At the same time, his mood was vicious. He decreed arrest for kin of the conspirators and detention of families of the aristocratic plotters in the military. Threats of extermination were made against the entire clan that bore the name of the principal ringleader. Nonetheless, in the interest of the continuing conduct of the war, what had taken on the appearance of a vengeful attack on the entire officer corps had to be checked. A gesture allowed a military court to

43

flush and clean the army's ranks. Senior officers nervously affirmed their loyalty. Hitler accepted their pledges with skepticism.

Despite this display of solidarity, the uneasy balance between Hitler and his generals had altered. The death plot had originated within the army, and it had failed. The patriotism of the army no longer could be presumed. Suspicion hung in the air; and in their rush to reinstate lost honor, the generals gave ground. No longer were they able to challenge Hitler's military judgment or argue against his point of view. His decisions would henceforth become their decisions without question.

After the American breakthrough at St. Lô on July 25, General Bradley sensed that the breakthrough could be converted into a breakout, a wide-ranging, swift-moving maneuver. He had approximately 15 infantry divisions on line. In addition, there was General George Patton, with polished helmet, pearl-handled pistols and riding boots, who seethed like a tethered bull straining to burst into the arena. On July 27, Bradley opened the gate and sent Patton rushing out to take Brittany to the south and all the way to its western end.

Patton started with three armored divisions and four infantry divisions. In a series of swift and unconventional moves, Patton on July 30 captured Avranches, the exit city from Normandy to Brittany. By August 4 he had taken Rennes, in the center of Brittany, and his forces were well on the way to Brest at the extreme western point of the peninsula.

While Patton was making his dash out of Normandy and through Brittany, Bradley's infantry was pushing hard to clean the enemy out of Normandy and had driven resolutely south on Patton's eastern flank. On August 3, the 1st Infantry Division captured Mortain. John Keegan's analysis is:

> ...The capture of Mortain by the 1st Division on August 3rd anchored the Army's line *on high ground which dominated the routes the Germans must use if they were to attempt a counter-attack* against the break-out.

So little did Bradley count on that possibility, however, that on this day he issued orders to Patton to close down his drive into Brittany...and turn east with all available strength....[2] [Emphasis added]

On the Eastern Front, almost inevitably, the ghost of Napoleon had stalked the Germans that spring. Hundreds of thousands of men were encircled, swallowed up and destroyed on the endless plains and steppes of Russia, lost forever to the monstrous, insatiable ambitions of the Third Reich. The cracks and crevices of the German manpower barrel were scraped clean in an effort to replace the slaughtered troops. Less fit and older men, and even boys, were called up. Training, however, took time. It would be October 1944, at the earliest, before replacement, or ersatz, troops would be in some kind of fighting trim, ready to be plugged into the shattered line of battle.

What this meant strategically was that if Germany was to be saved from ruinous defeat, highest priority had to be given to preserving combat strength for a fight on a different line of defense, closer to German borders. The commanders in the west warned of the underlying seriousness of the situation and that the war might end in defeat. Field Marshal Erwin Rommel, the "Desert Fox," had been among the first to express pessimism. On July 1, the Supreme Commander in the west, Field Marshal Karl von Rundstedt, suggested that there was no alternative but to make peace.

In a sweeping series of orders, Hitler replaced von Rundstedt and others in the west who held to the same view, although Rommel stayed on. Von Rundstedt's replacement, Field Marshal Gunther von Kluge, the epitome of German military leadership, arrived fresh and vigorous from Hitler's headquarters, determined to carry out Hitler's demand to stand fast at any price. Von Kluge, one of the Wehrmacht's great battlefield generals, believed that the defense in the west was lagging because of poor leadership, mistakes in the field and the defeatist views of the commanders. He stepped forward smartly to energize his new command. After first dressing down Rommel, he set off to tour the fields of battle. What he found caused him to step back and join the escalating chorus. In a note to Hitler on July 22 he predicted that the front would break.

The air of paranoia over the generals thickened. Suspicion grew that even von Kluge had been involved in the July 20 coup attempt, despite his being away at his post in France in the west.

Next, on July 31, as Patton's forces rolled at high speed through Avranches with virtually no opposition into Brittany to the west, von Kluge proposed withdrawal from Normandy to a more defensible position near the German border. Hitler rejected the suggestion. He was incensed and reasoned that von Kluge did not understand what had to be done. Hitler dispatched a trusted ranking officer from the High Command to instruct von Kluge to fight and hold the line.

The directive to stand fast had hardly been delivered to von Kluge when Hitler seized on another strategy. Unexpectedly, he gave von Kluge an order to counterattack from positions east of Avranches and to close off the American forces in Normandy.

The idea was clear to Hitler. To the east of the American forces and along the northern coast of France, the British and the Germans had fought to a standstill, and the front there had stabilized. German troops could be withdrawn from that front and thrown into an attack to support existing German forces already on the line opposing American forces in the narrow corridor east of Avranches. By pressing fiercely with lightning speed all the way to Avranches at the sea, a scant 20 miles, the invading armies would be split in two. Patton's army would be cut off from the rest of the American forces, restricting Patton's advantage of mobility and cutting off resupply of his forces. Hitler even fantasized that the American beachhead could be isolated.

This was Hitler's counterstroke.

Armchair quarterbacks and generals abound, and for good reason. In many situations they have a fifty-fifty chance of being right. A good general often has a fifty-fifty chance of being wrong. An attack will succeed or it will fail. In that simple context, the odds are even and anyone can play. Clearly, the strength that is brought to bear, weaponry, timing, tactical execution, the determination of the soldiers in the field, and the leadership of their commanders play a significant role, often a decisive one. But it is the big strategy that engages the eye and captures the enthusiasm of armchair generals. Whether to attack, and where and when, are decisions that many political leaders find irresistible, almost as if war were some sort of board game.

Winston Churchill meddled regularly in the work of his generals and admirals. With his overarching ego, it is no wonder that Hitler also considered himself a gifted military strategist. Occasionally, he intervened directly in operational decisions. Often the odds were even that he would be right; and when the wrong guesses are thrown out, his batting average was not bad. And had he not held his grip on the levers of power in part because of his monster's instinct for an adversary's weakness? The game he played was that of decisive intervention when the strategic grouping and disposition of forces suggested a bold stroke.

That was what he then ordered. He called it "Operation Luttich," the same name as the hammer blow which the German commander Erich Ludendorff delivered against France in August 1914, almost 30 years before to the day. A soothsayer burning entrails for signs and omens would have found the smoke favorable.

Von Kluge did not. He had already seen the American battle line stretch and turn into a reverse "L" at Avranches as Patton sped west through Brittany. He was cognizant that a successful counterattack at the apex of the "L" would divide the American forces. When the lines were drawn on a map, it took no genius, military or other, to see that. In his experienced judgment, however, any advantage gained by a counterattack would be limited and would buy time only to turn and establish a new defensive line much farther to the east, near Germany. Having already dismissed the idea of a counterattack because of Hitler's fanatical insistence to stand fast, he was now under a baffling order to launch one.

Hitler's order to attack was not debatable. The aftermath of the July 20 bomb plot made that clear. Moreover, von Kluge himself was now distinctly suspect. He was aware that he might be implicated. Swift and unswerving obedience became his only chance for survival.

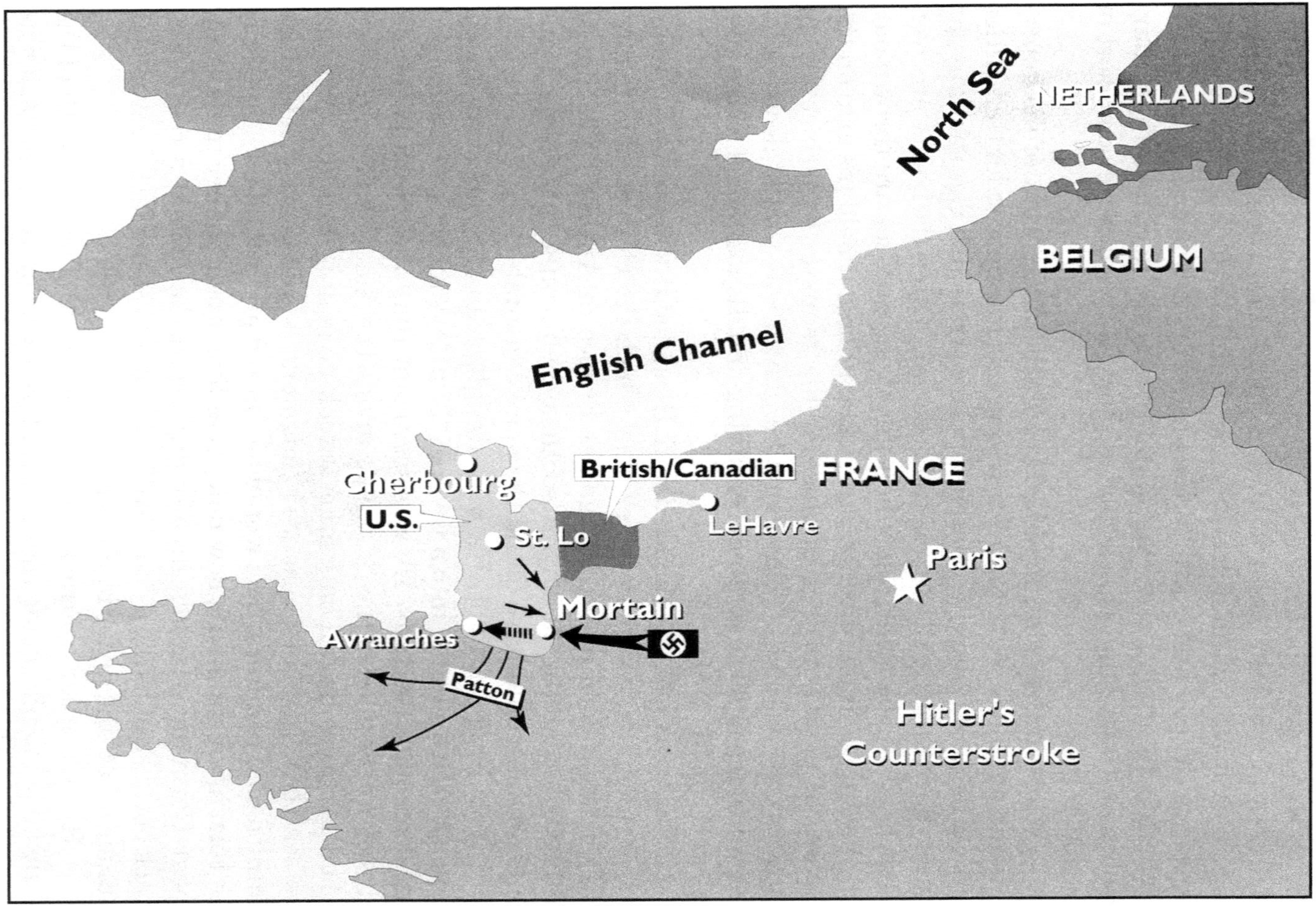
North Sea
NETHERLANDS
BELGIUM
English Channel
British/Canadian
FRANCE
Cherbourg
U.S.
St. Lo
LeHavre
Paris
Mortain
Avranches
Patton
Hitler's
Counterstroke

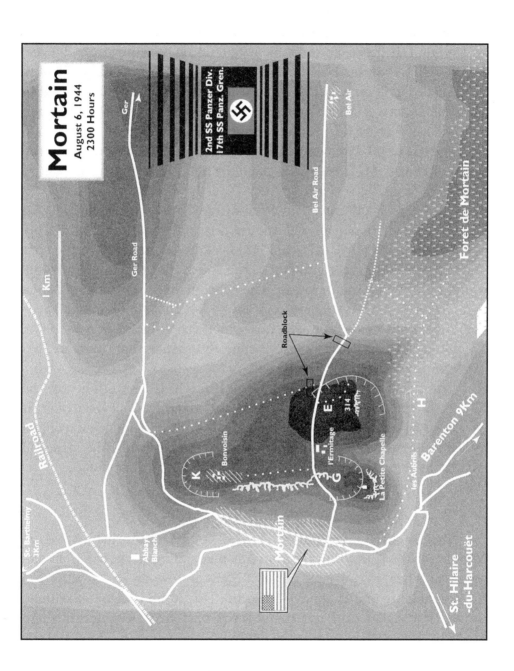

Mortain
August 6, 1944
2300 Hours

2nd SS Panzer Div.
17th SS Panz. Gren.

1 Km

Ger Road

Ger

Bel Air Road

Bel Air

Forêt de Mortain

Roadblock

E

314

Bonvoisin

l'Ermitage

La Petite Chapelle

les Aubrils

Barenton 9Km

K

G

H

Railroad

St. Barthelmy
3Km

Abbaye
Blanche

Mortain

St. Hilaire
-du-Harcouët

Von Kluge quickly developed a detailed battle plan and gathered together forces for the counterattack, some of which were widely scattered in the west. Four divisions, including the elite 2d SS Panzer, *Das Reich*, were assembled and deployed east of Avranches. The 2d SS Panzer Division was a veteran unit, one of Hitler's favorites and accustomed to winning. Von Kluge's battle plan called for the attack to begin on August 6 in the early hours after darkness. Hitler then changed his mind. He wanted to delay until other divisions, from the south of France and elsewhere, could be added to ensure a knockout blow.

This was a change that von Kluge could no longer accept. Bradley's order to Patton on August 3 to turn east out of Brittany now posed a new threat. Patton had broken out not only to the east but in a wide-sweeping end run to the south that threatened to surround all of von Kluge's forces. The concentration of German tanks and troops east of Avranches, moreover, left those forces open to attack and destruction from the air, which the Allies now controlled. To mount the counterattack immediately, rather than to delay, became an imperative for von Kluge.

But either way, his options were limited. If he waited until he had sufficient forces on hand to mount a strong counterattack, it would be too late. By then, his forces would be surrounded and trapped by superior Allied forces and devastated from the air. If he attacked earlier, he was too weak to win. But Hitler left him no choice.

Shortly after midnight on August 6, the counterattack began. No advance artillery barrage gave it away. Two divisions plus elements of other units struck north of Mortain toward Le Mesnil-Tove, St. Barthélemy and L'Abbaye-Blanche. The 2d SS Panzers streamed around Hill 314, to the north and south of it, and swarmed through Mortain. The objectives were to fan out to the north in support of the other German divisions and to charge west the 20 miles to Avranches on the Atlantic coast, just across a small bay from famed Mont St. Michel.

Earlier that night of Sunday, August 6, code breakers at Bletchley Park, England, had intercepted a message which carried strategic significance, the timing and objectives of the German counterattack. They passed the decoded dispatch to high headquarters. At the strategic level, the Allied command took note of Hill 314.[3] The number means that the hill is 314 meters—about 1,000 feet—above sea level. Not high, perhaps, but high enough when it is among the highest places in all of Normandy. An observer on that hill could see for miles. General J. Lawton "Lightning Joe" Collins at VII Corps Headquarters identified the necessity of controlling the Hill in case of attack.[4] Normally, the division was expected to take appropriate action on its own initiative to protect a key terrain feature within its sector without specific instructions.

The job of a high headquarters is to manage large units, armies and divisions, and it merely passed on the warning contained in the intercepted message and alerted our division headquarters to expect a counterattack within 12 hours.

But by then the counterattack was rolling.

8   *"...By the Dawn's Early Light..."*

In the early daylight that followed the initial hours of von Kluge's midnight counterattack, a leaden mist covered the landscape. Gradually the day's lightening found us sightless and drifting in a moist, low-hanging cloud, like a ship on a flat, windless sea. Only a fool would have stepped out of the fog. The shelling during the night had given the enemy a taste of what was waiting. But until the mist blew away, we, too, could see nothing in any direction except for a few dim shapes as our own troops, close by, moved cautiously in and out of the thick haze.

Locating targets by sound in a fog would have been impossible. Sounds seem to come from all directions under such conditions. Adjusting artillery fire would have been even more uncertain. For a brief time we were helpless. There was nothing we could have done to defend ourselves except to shoot with the arms that we carried if Germans had emerged from the blanketing mists.

Bit by bit, our understanding began to take shape in those early, hazy hours. First of all, telephone lines to the rear, ours and that of the infantry, were gone, either deliberately cut by the enemy, chewed up by their tanks or shot out in the fight back in the town. Tank and hostile infantry activity below our position on the Hill was increasing. Snipers banged away erratically at us from the rear.

My three men and I waited expectantly at Lieutenant Kerley's command post, listening to the flurry of reports brought in by one runner after another, waiting anxiously for the fog to lift. The Germans also waited. But not for long. While the mists hovered about us in the thin light, around 6:00 a.m. that Monday morning, August 7, a runner from our right flank reported 400 enemy were counterattacking on our right flank downhill, below our position. Again I called "Fire Mission," now by radio. I was shooting blind, by guesswork, but the guess was a good one, and the quick response of our guns drilled through the fog and beat back the enemy.

At Kerley's command post, in a draw down behind the eastern ridge of the Hill, frustration with the dead telephone lines heightened the growing uncertainty in those first, misty hours. This was not only because one means of communication had been destroyed, but because the infantry's portable field radios had limited range and clarity. Runners hurried breathlessly up to Kerley bringing small pieces of news from the outposts, pieces to be fitted together, but only questions and a sense of impending bankruptcy hovered in the damp air.

Then a remarkable thing occurred, perhaps a touch of the cosmos or an echo from another life. It reflected an intangible quality that made Kerley a superior field commander. I have considered this many times over the years. Intuition, or perhaps some deeper message—common only to those with special powers of recognition—is the only explanation that I have for what happened next.

Kerley sat down on the damp ground, laid his helmeted head back against a large rock, as if he were back home in Texas, and went to sleep. My God, what had happened? Was Kerley sick? Had something weird come through the fog and paralyzed him? Suddenly the fog became unnerving. The panic that ensued was greater than if he had been shot. A panting runner from one of the outposts appeared out of the mist and charged up to find Kerley dead to the world.

"Lieutenant." No answer.

Louder: "Lieutenant." Still no answer. Shaking him, desperately, but carefully, "Kerley. For Christ's sake, we're catching hell."

No response.

Then to one of the tiny group that passed for Kerley's headquarters, "What's wrong with Kerley?"

"He's been like that."

"What do we do? Can't you wake him up?"

"No. You'd better go back up on the ridge."

Lieutenant (later Lieutenant Colonel) Ralph A. Kerley, commander of E Company. Both he and Joseph C. Reaser, on the following page, were highly decorated.

Courtesy of the family of Ralph A. Kerley

The scene was repeated several times over the next hour or two while we waited in the draw near Kerley. The initial hysteria, when Kerley without forewarning had unexpectedly detached himself, gradually faded. The men grew calmer, more accepting as they stood and watched. The fog held everything in check. At length, Kerley bounced back to life. For the rest of the time on the Hill, almost six days, I never saw him again when he was not on his feet, or if sitting, he was directing and giving strength to the defense of the Hill.

It is true that most men slept very little during the days and nights ahead, but that strange injection of sleep reinforced Kerley's naturally rough and fearless way. It was as if some deep intelligence inside him, perhaps grounded in the subconscious or some other experience, had gathered together the scraps of information and analyzed them, put them in perspective, and responded: "Kerley, you're surrounded. Rest. You'll need it. It's foggy and the shooting has died down. Do it now." And he was cool enough to do it.

❖ ❖ ❖ ❖ ❖

My forward observer's job carried with it the need to think ahead independently, and a certain freedom of action from mere blind obedience to the orders of others. As I stood there in the mist watching Kerley, I, too, sensed that we might be facing a situation where we would need all the resources we could get. More than anything, we would need batteries for our radio. With telephone lines gone, the radio might be the only lifeline for both ourselves and the infantry. The sniper fire to our rear made it clear that the enemy was on the southwest part of the Hill, across the draw. The only way out would be off to our left flank to the north, and then down into the town. Sergeant Corn and Corporal Garrott volunteered to try to get through and contact Lieutenant Lee for batteries. They crept off quickly, leaving Sergeant Sasser and me to make our way up to the OP and wait for what lay hiding in the cloud of fog around us.

With radio and batterypack between us, Sasser and I scrambled up the rocky slope to the crest of the eastern ridge of the Hill. The exertion of the climb warmed us. We crouched below the tops of the bushes and grasses and I began searching the blank page that still lay to the front. When by midmorning, around 9:30 or so, the warming air lifted the mist off the Hill, I spotted enemy vehicles bringing up infantry for an attack. The sequence of messages began again:

Lieutenant (later Captain) Joseph C. Reaser, commander of K Company

Crow this is Crow Baker 3. *Fire Mission*. Enemy vehicles.

The first visual target in that suddenly bright, August daylight came clearly into view. Then more vehicles. Explosions of artillery shells reverberated across the picturesque farmland sloping away before us. The vehicles changed direction and ran off into trees and behind hedgerows. Next I saw a platoon of infantry with machine guns.

Crow this is Crow Baker 3. *Fire Mission*. Enemy infantry—twenty—with machine guns.

Shells erupted in pairs, in fours and sixes, black clouds over the countryside.

The shelling dispersed the formation. We had their range. As the landscape cleared, I warmed to my work.

But now German artillery opened up, and shells exploded close by. Although later on, both Sasser and Kerley suspected that the Germans "fixed" our positions by monitoring our radio transmissions, we had no evidence that they were doing so early on. No doubt, the shelling was part of prudent routine before attacking the crest of the Hill, to neutralize any troops that were there.

Within an hour of that first bright sunlight, machine gun fire snipped the bushes and tall grass around our OP. The sounds of the guns firing at us were lost in the fields and rocks below us. But we knew we were a target by the quick, almost imperceptible rush of air and the slightest movement back and forth of dense foliage where bullets whizzed through and air closed back around the tunnels they bored. No one had to tell us what was happening. The bullets carried a warning and sucked up my energy as they cut by, like an unseen hand that steals. We dropped to the ground and listened to the snip-snip of the bullets just above our heads.

To remain longer was not prudent. I radioed Crow:

Crow this is Crow Baker 3. Moving under machine gun fire. Over and Out.

Sasser switched off the radio. It was 10:35 a.m. Early. I swallowed hard, jerked my head at Sasser. "Come on. Let's go."

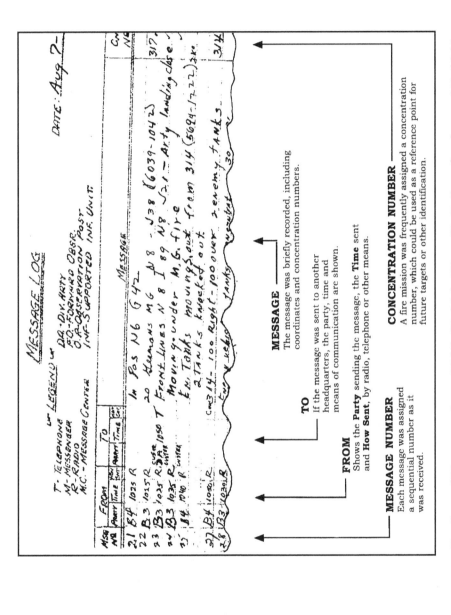

Portion of Message Log, 230th Field Artillery Battalion, for August 7, 1944

National Archives

The message log image contains the following:

MESSAGE LOG

LEGEND

T - TELEPHONE
M - MESSENGER
R - RADIO
M.C. - MESSAGE CENTER

DA - DIV. ARTY
FO - FORWARD OBSR.
O - OBSERVATION POST
INF - SUPPORTED INF. UNIT

DATE: Aug 7-

MSG No	FROM				TO				MESSAGE	Cn No
	Party	Time	How Sent		Party	Time	How Sent			
21	B4	1025	R						In Pos N6 G42	
22	B3	1015	R						20 Humans MG N8 - J38 (6039-1042)	317
23	B3	1025	R	DA 1050	T	O			Front lines N8 I89 N8 J2.1 - Arty landing close.	317
24	B3	1035	R						Moving under MG fire	
25	B4	1040	R						En Tanks moving out from 314 (5694-1222) 2xr	
									2 Tanks knocked out.	
27	B4	1040	R						Cn 314 - 100 Right -100 over 2 enemy tanks -	3/4
28	B3	1030	R						two enemy tanks knocked out 30	

MESSAGE NUMBER

Each message was assigned a sequential number as it was received.

FROM

Shows the **Party** sending the message, the **Time** sent and **How Sent**, by radio, telephone or other means.

TO

If the message was sent to another headquarters, the party, time and means of communication are shown.

MESSAGE

The message was briefly recorded, including coordinates and concentration numbers.

CONCENTRATION NUMBER

A fire mission was frequently assigned a concentration number, which could be used as a reference point for future targets or other identification.

9

"Enemy N, S, E, W"

Machine gun bullets continued to clip the tops of the bushes. Sasser and I grabbed all the gear, the BC scope, the heavy tripod, radio, batterypack and telephone. We ducked low like a couple of thieves trying to avoid detection and hustled off the ridgetop. It had taken three or four men to lug all of that equipment up the ridge. With the sudden injection of adrenalin from enemy fire, two of us now brought it down. Gravity had little to do with our swift departure.

The day before, I had climbed to the OP with total confidence, certain of my ability to "shoot" the enemy. The confidence was still there, but the experience of being shot off an OP humbled me. I had faced live ammunition during training in the States, but always with the knowledge that a safety factor protected me and that no one was trying to kill. Here, we had been lucky.

What were Sasser's feelings during those moments? As I reflect back to those minutes, still vivid in memory, I can see that I was too immature and inexperienced, too separated by the artificial barrier of rank that I had not then learned to transcend, to question him. I did not ask whether he was touched with fear or filled with anger, and whether it had been as humbling for him as for me to be shot off the ridge and to have to run for cover.

Being a forward observer meant being an outsider. To the infantry, the artillery observer personnel were always just attached personnel. We marched with them, dug in with them, fought with them. It made them feel good to have us around. But we were still only a supporting branch. This attitude even extended to recognition in the case of battle honors, such as the Presidential Unit Citation that was awarded to the 2d Battalion for its struggle on the Hill. The infantry easily acknowledged that artillery saved the battalion from being captured or destroyed,[1] but the infantry believed that my forward observer party and the other artillerymen who were also on the Hill could not be included in the citation because we were not infantry, not members of the 2d Battalion. Eventually, common sense prevailed. The commander of the 120th Infantry Regiment adopted the simple expedient of printing an order that specifically named us.

Although I eventually grew closer to some of the men who went forward with me—they were rotated regularly, rarely the same group twice in a row—between us it was always "Lieutenant" and "Sergeant" or "Corporal." This put me on the outside with them as well. So it was with Sasser and me that morning as we rushed through the brush and across rocks to safety. The military hierarchy places walls between men when they need to be closer, barriers to the heart thrown up where there should be none. Sasser was eight or nine years older than I, a significant difference then, perhaps a barrier in itself. It was as if we viewed each other through a morning mist like the one that had folded around the Hill. We moved in and out, always in contact, but never in touch.

Below the crest, a runner from Lieutenant Kerley was waiting for us, as if he knew that we couldn't stay up on that ridge for long. But we would soon be back in business. We dumped all excess equipment in the jeep which Corporal Garrott had so carefully screened from observation, everything except the essentials: radio and batterypack, personal weapons and gas mask carriers, binoculars, maps, and code templates.

By now a beautiful summer day had stretched across the countryside, rolling through farmyards and orchards, kicking up little zephyrs and rustling the needles of the pine trees around us. Kerley was on the southern end of the Hill near a harsh, rocky outcropping which was its very highest point, the place where there should have been a marker and a plaque with the legend "314." Here were the gray cliffs, *rochers*, as the French say, real "rock-ers" as the GI might. They were massive chunks, fractured and cracked along thin part lines, torn loose from the central mass, pushed up a thousand feet from an ancient sea, broken with sharp, threatening edges, piled randomly one on the other, breaking away to the south and west into sharp, gray crags that hung over the valleys and fields below. A scattering of boulders around the edges of the main promontory had tumbled away into piles of rubble, rude and unkempt, like trash from an old quarry.

To the left, to the north, a crest of golden grasses meandered toward the area from which we had just fled. An occasional small tree and clumps of bushes grew irregularly across the top. To the right of the crags, the Hill dropped away steeply through trees, the Forêt de Mortain. At the back, a broken, scraggly cliff reached down sharply into the valley below. Trees on the fringe of the Forêt de Mortain gave the cliffs cover from across the valley.

Kerley had moved his command post from the draw down below and was directing the defense of his company position from the vicinity of these crags. In the hours and days that ensued, Kerley's "management style" became intensely hands-on and personal. Kerley went wherever the situation demanded. The command post moved with him. The headquarters, however, remained where it had been during the early morning counterattack.

This highest point at the southern end of the Hill was the best all-around observation point, the point from which we could inflict, by calling in artillery fire, the most damage to the enemy. Like Kerley, we moved from time to time as the pressure of enemy movement and attack seemed to dictate, which meant that we were not always at the infantry command post. But that morning and the rest of the day we stayed close by.

Sasser and I, lugging the radio and batterypack, struggled up a little, grassy funnel that shot steeply down from the northern side of the high, gray crags into the valley below. A fringe of tumbled, broken rock lying in jumbled piles gave the funnel its shape. Below the edge of the cliff, on the backside near the top of the crags, we found an ideal spot for the radio, protected and yet close by so that Sasser could hear me shouting messages from higher up where I could see.

As we set up our OP, German infantry advanced in front of us in closed formation[2] across open fields less than a mile away. Supporting tanks moved on roads and through open areas, some coming within a thousand yards on our right flank. The troops and armor were not hard to spot as they came toward us. We took them under fire immediately using both time and ricochet fire. Deadly against infantry in the open, time fire used a fuse, which if properly set, would detonate before the shell struck the ground, focusing a hail of steel shards on the target below. Ricochet fire, especially effective against tanks and vehicles, employed a fuse set so that the shell exploded after impact, letting the shell find a target on the bounce if there was not a direct hit and penetration on impact.[3]

Fire mission followed on fire mission.

Crow this is Crow Baker 3. *Fire mission.* Enemy vehicles. Tanks. *Fire Mission.* Strong enemy force. Men milling about. Large counterattack.
Fire Mission. Tanks moving across road.
Fire Mission. Tanks in draw.

Again and again, and it was barely noon.

Concentration after concentration of shells exploded over and around the enemy. Little puffs of black smoke and swirls of dust dirtied the landscape, mingled together, and slowly drifted away. The advancing infantry took cover, and the tanks went into hiding for a time. Although we continued to shoot at other targets, principally automatic weapons installations, by two o'clock that afternoon the situation seemed well in hand. The pressure lifted from our infantry outposts. I scanned the terrain through my binoculars without spotting a target.

At such close range, spotting and locating targets and adjusting fire accurately was not difficult. Moreover, I soon knew the terrain by heart. Landscape features, buildings, road junctions, orchards and

			...100 Royal - 100 mph - 3 Enemy TANKS	314
28	B3	1030 R	Enemy vehicles - Tanks - Constructions 303 - 315 - 3K	
			(6151-1046)ᵗʰ (5784-1209) 314 (41.42.1935)	
29	C3	1105 R	Check Pt 2ᵃ Enemy vehicles (62.1 - 12.0)	304
30	B3	1110 R Gᵐᵒ	T. Strong enemy force CON 316 (6142-1055)(618-103.0) 316ᵃᵗ
		DA 1120	1st vehicle hit - Mar m. line about - large counter-attack
31	B3	1110 R	Front lines extended - N8 - J24 - from last line
33	A3	1205 R	In position RJ V07 (66.32 - 0522)
34	B3	1205 R	Tanks moving across road - 61.72 & 95
35	B3	1207 R	Tanks in draw - N8 - J43 (60.5 - 09.9)	319
36	S.6	1215 T	Tanks going W. (572 - 147)
37	Cₕ	1245 T DA 1730 T	Shell rep. 110
38	M.4	1245 R	In position (?) N6 - 621 - 11.45
39	A3	1245 R DA 1545 T	Two scout cars - Pz Pro - (6761 - 0608)
40	Radio 1245 R DA 1545 T	Tanks in vicinity 58.7 - 10.0 At 10.00
41	S-6	1300 P DA 1545 T	Wounded sent back from 3rd Bn. - Slightly wounded captured by Germans - Serious cases sent on back to our own hosp.
42	B3	1320 R DA 1545 T	Con. 308 no 200cc 400 ss - EN. AA WEAPON (6151-1046)ᵗʰ	319
43	S-6	1230 T DA 1730 T	L. Cry #111
44	6N1	1340 T	H Links, Aᶜᶜ N6 J3, J4, J12, J14, D30 - Bᶜᵒ N6 D23, Bᶜᵒ N6 D28, D46, D35, D44, D53
45	B3	1350 T DA 1545 T	EN. AUTO. WEAPP. N8K20(613-107)
46	6N1	1350 T	B3 rgts. E Co Cy Links N8 I81, J32
47	B4	1420 R DA 1545 T	Enemy infantry - tanks vicinity of houses - (57.06 - 11.90)	321
48	B.4	1420 T	In position TN.4 - D28 (56.82 - 11.58)
49	A8	1435 T	In position M6 - J28 (54.3 - 10.7)
50	B3	1440 R DA 1545 T	EN. Mortar in vicinity (62.2 - 10.8)
51	B4	1445 R DA 1545 T	CON 321 - 100 own - Tanks + inf	321
52	Hardy	1448 T DA 1545 T	Counter battery - 6 rounds Verify 105m
53	B3	1455 R DA 1545 T	EN MORTERS (6224-1073)	322
54	M.6	1510 T DA 1545 T	Tanks (568 - 098)
55	B4	1510 R DA 1545 T	1 TANK N6 J31 (564 - 119)
56	B.6	1515 T DA 1545 T	5 Rounds 42.18 cm 105m - vic. B. Btry
57	IN.4	1530 R DA 1531 T	British plane strafing our front line
58	W.1	1600 R LN 1531 R	Message from CUSTER 6 to CUFF 6
59	C4	1605 R	In position N5 612 (56.72 - 1203) - N5 612
60	I.1	1625 R DA 1730 T	Enemy tank TN.L - J51 - (52.12 - 11.91)	320
61	W.1	1630 R S-6 1630 I	Message from Cuffe & Custer 6 "Cannot say now - use your imagination"
62	S.6	1630 I 1630 T	1 tank reported 200 yds from Custer C.P. going N
63	B4	1705 R DA 1730 T	Enemy. in Infantry - Mortars vicinity house - 5 7.06 - 11.90. 322
64	S4	1730 R DA 1730 T	Receiving shelling 88 4 guns AZ 1800

Continuation of Message Log for August 7, 1944

fields became concentration numbers in my mind, targets on which I could call down artillery fire with almost no delay, or reference points from which to adjust artillery fire to other targets. This capability gave an easy rhythm to the shift from one target to another, and reduced response time. With this technique well honed, my binoculars soon became a gun sight. When I shouted "Fire Mission" to Sasser, it was as if I were tensing my trigger finger, beginning the squeeze to detonation that would send a deadly missile to the target.

It had now been many hours since Sergeant Corn and Corporal Garrott had set out to find a way north through the left flank to get batteries. We had heard nothing. I was concerned. I looked at Sasser and saw that he understood. With the German attack now at a standstill, he left to try to locate them. It could not have been an assignment that he wished for, to climb down the cliffs, through the rocks and trees into that valley, snipers a few hundred yards to the west, and then in broad daylight to make his way from rock to rock and bush to bush back up the draw below the OP that had been machine gunned out of existence just a few hours before.

Who would even know those two? "Hey, have you seen a sergeant and a corporal from the 230th?" Except for the hash marks, insignia of rank on the sleeves of their shirts, there was nothing to identify them. They did not shoulder infantry M-1 rifles, but carried pistols. But so did some infantrymen. One dirty, unshaven face under a helmet looked much like another. Corn was taller, Garrott shorter. There were hundreds of men on the Hill. Sasser was cautious, nervous; he wouldn't go too far. He wouldn't have to.

I was alone with the radio and the unseen enemy to the front and to the rear. Lieutenant Kerley and a few infantry were nearby. Kerley was constantly on the move, dealing with reports from runners coming in from the outposts and the roadblock on the Bel-Air Road along E Company's northern perimeter, seeing that his men were exactly where he wanted them, feeding raw courage into slack bellies.

While I waited alone, scrunched down near the top of the high crags, I looked down the grassy, rock-lined funnel up which Sasser and I had strained with the radio and batterypack. At the base, one of Kerley's runners trotted into view, and quickly started the scramble up the grassy slope in the hot sun, M-1 slung from his shoulder, helmet pushed back. I had seen him before, a young Native American, I believe, lithe, strong, a good choice for a runner. Before he reached the top, perhaps 15 or 20 feet from where I was, a German shell screeched over the crest and exploded down below, not dangerously close, but near enough so that it came at him with a violent concussion. He flung himself into the hillside and lay still as death. After a moment, he rolled over and looked up at me. He was physically unharmed, but he shook with fright. His helmet had fallen off, and his black hair shone in the sunlight. Dark eyes had sprung wide with terror, and the whites showed vividly against swarthy skin. He stared up at me, winded, unable to speak, breathing heavily. My eyes, shaded by my helmet, squinted back into the bright sunlight where he rested on the slope, silently trying to give him some assurance that everything was all right. Before I could say a word, he twisted to his knees, clapped on his helmet, grabbed his rifle and, still panting, ran off up the slope to find Kerley.

I turned back to the enemy whose fire had become less intense, an occasional mortar shell and sporadic spray from automatic weapons. The Germans grew more cautious now than they had been earlier that morning. Artillery fire silenced each new target that showed itself—for a time. Alone without Sasser, after spotting a target I scrambled off the top of the crags down to the radio and switched it on.

Crow this is Crow Baker 3.

This time the voice really was that of Crow Baker 3.

Fire Mission. Enemy mortars.

The Germans were using heavy mortars, dropping their deadly little bombs from a mile and a half away. I clambered back up to adjust and then observe our concentrations of high explosives erupt, destroy and do their work.

Fleeing from the OP was forgotten for the moment. I no longer felt outgunned.

The Germans hesitated. No more frontal infantry assaults in closed formations as if on parade. No more columns of tanks on open roads. The attack became piecemeal, probing, deliberate. Down below, a sniper had infiltrated the trees. An occasional burst of fire would flatten all of us at the crags. Then silence. Another shot followed. It was difficult to pinpoint the source. Where would the next bullets come from? Down among the pines below us it was easy for him to shift from place to place without being seen, ideal for picking off a careless soldier—and for harassing, for building uncertainty.

After many minutes of silence, a single shot rang out. It was close. Was he trying to pick us off one by one? Was it only a diversion to distract us from an attack from another direction? The sniper seemed to have a plan, and we were part of it. Kerley had had enough. He crawled over to one of his men and laid his carbine down.

"Give me the rifle, son."

"Yessir."

Kerley took the M-1, held out his hand for an extra clip of bullets and then crawled off to the north, disappearing behind rocks and brush. We waited. Five minutes. Ten. Twenty...and beyond counting. No one knew what to do. The men looked hesitantly to one another for some answer. In the distance we heard the muffled boom of artillery.

From down below to the front, the sharp report of two shots bounced off the rocks and echoed up the hillside. Silence. We stirred anxiously, now and then glancing quickly to the east, but staying behind cover. Nothing.

We held the air in our lungs, now grown tight with waiting. Then, as if part of a script, a tall GI sauntered up the slope of the Hill, out of the trees and scrub to our left. It was Kerley. He walked quietly over to the man—a kid like the rest of us—from whom he had borrowed the rifle. With both hands holding the rifle horizontally he pitched it back gently.

"Thanks, son."

Shortly after Kerley returned, the enemy put another sniper to work. This time it was an 88mm gun, high velocity, accurate, many would say the Germans' most deadly weapon, and terrifying at short range. The prominent outcropping of rock offered an easy target. None of my men had yet returned, and I still manned the OP by myself. The 88 blasted away. As I wrote after the battle:

> ...its fire was more annoying than anything else, although a few uncomfortably close rounds bounced off the rocks beside us....

This fire, jarring in its proximity, gave me the opportunity to measure the weapon's accuracy and consistency. It was my first exposure to it. Clearly it would be deadly against a target as large as a tank or a building. It would not, however, shoot an apple off a man's head except by chance, not with any precision or consistency. I concluded that a small target might face off an 88 with impunity—for a while—until the 88 got lucky.

One round, however, almost found a target. As I huddled behind the shelter of the crags, counting the incoming rounds—counting incoming fire, artillery or mortar, was a good distraction from what might be the inevitable—a shell grazed the crest above the tall grass and hit a boulder to the left at the head of the grassy funnel up which Sasser and I hours before had dragged ourselves and the radio, the same grassy funnel where Kerley's runner had come under fire. It happened so quickly, so unexpectedly that I had no time to react. The shell chipped a hefty fragment about the size of a baseball off the boulder and then whirred erratically into the valley behind, where it exploded an instant later.

The image of that incident of the defective round fired by the 88 remains plain: grasses the color of honey, sunburned brush and a few small pine trees, the rough cliffs pressing my shoulder and back, the gray boulder cast loose from the larger mass and nestled in tall stems a few feet away, solid, resting, waiting, as if for its turn to come. And then, the freight-train speed and scream of that shell, the almost instantaneous impact on the boulder, the chunk broken loose from the boulder and tossed at random through the air, the shell hurtling into the valley behind, its even rotation distorted into an irregular wobble, the scream now rising and falling up and down the scale in tempo with the wobble, and then the explosion on impact in the valley.

Almost simultaneously, before I could move or duck, the baseball-sized chunk of boulder flew 15 feet or so toward me and struck my forearm. No damage done. I turned back to the front. The 88 shut down.

Exploding shells scatter most of their fragments away from the long axis, to the sides and up and down. If that shell had exploded when it touched down on the boulder, I could have been dead, certainly wounded. In the larger context of the battle, the artillery forward observer would have been eliminated. At the time, the explanation of the shell's malfunction was "Polish" ammunition. But another bad Polish joke became an intuitive reference to hidden allies.

In the front lines we were unaware of the totality of the war, our outlook being limited to what we saw and the rumors that came along the grapevine. But no doubt the Germans were using ammunition that had been manufactured in countries which they had overrun and tried to absorb into the Third Reich. Not all such manufacturing facilities were as skillful or as precise as German manufacturers. The round that struck near me might have been poorly machined or assembled, made, perhaps, by enslaved Poles, who resisted their oppressors by sabotaging the production of weapons, parts and ammunition. I would like to think that the shell left me unscathed, except for the bump on the arm, because of a brave, unseen ally, who at great personal risk carefully and surreptitiously assembled that 88mm shell so that it would pass German inspection but malfunction when fired. Whatever the reason, the miraculous event lingers in my memory.

Corn, Garrott and Sasser returned empty-handed. Our little family was back together.

The 88s continued to pepper us sporadically, and the shelling took a toll among the infantry. As the afternoon ground on, snipers from the hilltop to the west made the valley between us and them untenable. All of E Company moved off the slopes to the east and south and up along the crest of the Hill near the crags. In addition, Kerley had now absorbed the remnants of H Company who had straggled cautiously up the hillsides after their bruising night. With the remains of their heavy weapons, they were deployed and mixed in with the E Company riflemen.

By that time, it was clear that we were in a pocket, enveloped on all sides. G and K Companies to the north, generally between the Bel-Air Road and the main east-west road to Ger, were also in the pocket. K Company centered on a little farm settlement, a clump of buildings known as "*Bonvoisin,*" or "good neighbor." The three infantry companies did not, however, make up a consolidated force. They were in contact with each other by runner only. E Company's radio had gone on sabbatical.

The infantry had taken a number of casualties from sniper fire and the constant bombardment of the 88s and mortars. The Germans did not appear to view our stand as more than a temporary impediment, if that. Earlier in the day a German artillery officer was captured when he came up the Bel-Air Road trying to reconnoiter positions for his guns. The information we received from him was that the tanks to our front were part of the 17th SS Panzer Grenadiers. Any fool could judge our position was critical. In the late afternoon, an uncoded message was relayed through the artillery radio network, from Kerley to his regimental commander:

Cannot say more. Use your imagination.

In retrospect Kerley's words were almost coy.

Enemy shelling continued. Behind the high, silent crags, in the gathering shadows of the afternoon sunlight, we covered our ears and tried to remain calm as one blast after another shook the dome of the Hill. At one lull in the string of explosions, Sergeant Sasser down below me stared, examining the antenna from the top surface of his radio all the way up to its end, and then shouted, "Lieutenant, Lieutenant. Look!"

He pointed in total amazement at the antenna. The antenna on a series 610 radio was a slender, telescoping, metal tube much like those on most modern automobiles. Ours had been fully extended for maximum range and effectiveness and had projected up to or perhaps slightly above the edge of the crags. Sasser continued to gesture dumbfoundedly, pointing to the ragged end where it had been shot off during the shower of 88s. Maybe he was right about radio direction finders.

It seemed time to send our own message. Besides, we had to know how effective the radio now was with its clipped-off antenna, both for sending and receiving. Unlike Kerley, I was not willing to trust anyone's imagination. This game clearly was for keeps. The message said:

Enemy N, S, E, W. Request supply and support immediately.

Conservation of radio batteries now became of the utmost importance.

We knew that our radio and the radio of the other forward observer, Lieutenant Charles A. Bartz, someplace off to the left, were the lifelines to the 2d Battalion. At the moment, we had no idea where Bartz was or if he had communication with Fire Direction Center. We did not wait for a reply to our message. Besides, within moments we had a more crucial demand and radioed for artillery fire. This next fire mission was prefaced with a more telling target description than usual:

Enemy 88 giving us hell.

We then continued in what was becoming customary procedure in this situation:

Concentration 303 is 100 left, 400 over.

In other words, I told Fire Direction Center that the target, the 88mm artillery piece, was 100 yards to the right and 400 yards short of a fire mission that had been fired earlier and to which Fire Direction Center had given the designation "concentration number 303." It apparently was a good piece of work. In the margin of the Message

DATE: 7 Aug

LEGEND

T - TELEPHONE
M - MESSENGER
R - RADIO
M.C. - MESSAGE CENTER

DA - DIV. ARTY
FO - FORWARD OBSER.
O.P - OBSERVATION POST
INF - SUPPORTED INF. UNIT.

MSG NO	FROM			TO			MESSAGE	GN NO
65	LN1	1730	R	CUST6	1730	T	CUST6 TO CUST FR6 - GOING INTO POSITION 6 - 118 H88 (5866-1046) - Request No ARTY FIRE	
66	LN	1745	R	FO	1745	T	TYPHOONS STRAFING FT. LINES -	
67	LN1	1745	R				TANK CORNERED BY 4 JERRY TANKS -	
68	B3	1800	R	SR	1825	T	IN POS (603-098) ENEMY N, S, E, W. - REQUEST SUPPLY + SUPPORT IMMEDIATELY. -	
69	B3	1815	R				EN.88 giving us HELL - Conc 303 is 100LL 400 00	
70	B4	1840	R	DA	1850	T	(5709- 1180) Enemy infantry and tanks assembling. Same as above	325
71	S2	1855	T	DA	1855	T	LOCATIONS OF OBSERVERS -	
72	197	1910	T				197th (52.8 - 10.2)	
73	197	1910	T	DA	2150	T	Enemy vehicles (62.7 12.8)	233
74	B3	1920	T	DA	2150	T	EN 88 - (61.33 10.47)	303
75	LN1	1930	M	DA	2150	T	GERMANS dressed in American uniforms have been infiltrating into our lines. Spokesman speak good English.	
76	B3							
77	LN3	1945	R				No chg. in pos - will use same code tomorrow	
78	C4	2025	R	DA	2150	T	TANKS NS & 87 (5755-1262)	330
79	CG	2045	T	DA	2100	T	FR. CIVILIAN STATES 10 GERMANS COMING IN ON HIS FLANK -	
71	Cox	2100	T	DA	2150	T	F Co. Rd Block (588114) much en wh. traffic coyds up rd.	
72	B3	2100	R	DA	2150	T	N85 (6039-1029) in SOB 1805 - large # en wh -	331
73	Cox	2100	T	C3	2130	R	Enemy vehicles (58.8 - 12.8)	
74	B3	2145	R				(60.3 - 09.9) Same position	
75	DA	2150	T				ATKD TODAY BY EST. 5BN. INF, 4BN TANKS, 4BN. ARTY.	
76	Cox	2200	T				35 DIV COMING INTO MORTAIN - UP RED RD. - TDs got 7 TANKS TODAY	
77	B4	2200	B				No chg in pos. nothing new.	
78	C4	2210	R	DA	2400	T	TANKS MOVING N5 635 G 47 (Rdcenter (570 - 1247) hear by sound - (5704-1247)	341
79	S5	2230	P	DA	2400	T	FR. CIV. REPORTS 100 GERMANS + 1 TANK IN ROMAGNY	
80	B4	2235	R	DA	2400	T	(5766-1202) EN INF ASSEMBLING IN FARM YARD BELIEVED TO BE COUNTER ATK.	
81	B2	2245	R	197	2245	T	(645 - 103) Enemy activity - tanks on Road - possible counter attack	342
82	B4	2258	R					
83	Cox	2300	T	DA	2400	T	Inf. DIGGING IN + ASSEMBLING (5868 - 1210)	
84	LN1	2300	T				FT LINES A Co N6, I75, J4, I22 - B Co, N6, J11, D9, D37, D26, D45	
85	Cox	2300	T				Crun rd blk 581-110) to (584-114) F Co RD Blk from (579 to 583) and (118 to 122)	
86	B3	2350	R	DA	2400	T	Running low - ammunition - E Co. -	
87	C3	2300	R	DA				

Continuation of Message Log for August 7, 1944

Log of the Fire Direction Center opposite this message is a check mark. I had aimed and squeezed the trigger carefully.

Throughout the rest of that second day on the Hill and into the night, the Germans continued to press us hard with artillery fire from the 88s and with tanks and infantry that threatened E Company's roadblock at the road junction on the left flank. The troops then dug in for the night, every man exactly where Kerley had put him. A network of listening posts guarded the perimeter, and runners were assigned who would communicate directly to Kerley and to me.

I fired in a normal artillery barrage and important defensive concentrations designed to protect us from a night attack. The method I developed was to adjust fire with one gun, gradually bringing the shell bursts in toward our lines until they were so close that they disappeared from view below the curvature of the hillside. Then a concentration number would be assigned 400 yards closer, or even, in some locations, nearer than that. This became a defensive barrage which I could call up very quickly by number in case of a night attack. This method put the protective fires close-in, near to the troops, but it also set a ring of exploding steel around our position to the east and south. The enemy occasionally tested it, but was reluctant to cross. I did not dare to target protective concentrations on enemy positions to the rear, because of the extreme likelihood that incoming shells would land in our midst.

G and K Companies were to our north. We believed the infantry's Cannon Company was active, shooting into the area to our south and preventing the enemy from doing any more damage on that flank.

Just before midnight, at Kerley's request, I sent a last message for the day:

Running low—ammunition—E Company.

That message was shorthand for our situation, which in fact was already stretched beyond imagination. E Company had no food or water and had received none since the day before. Nor was there any prospect. Snipers to the rear neutralized our movements to a considerable extent. The right flank was open, and the enemy could have moved in or out without great restraint or difficulty. The infantry was running low on rifle ammunition, as the message had stated. Most of the ammunition for the machine guns was in the valley to our rear. From H Company we had scooped up one 81mm mortar, but it could fire at only one elevation and had no ammunition. E Company had two 60mm mortars but only a few rounds of ammunition. One of the mortars could not be traversed, in any case. There were no anti-tank guns. There were no mines. The men who made up the road-block facing the enemy to the front had only one bazooka and nine rounds of ammunition.

A few days after the battle ended, Major General Leland Hobbs, the 30th Division commander, gave his assessment of the situation that first day of encirclement:

> With a heavy onion breath that day, the Germans would have achieve their objective.[4]

To the front, enemy tanks continued to growl and thrash through the fields and orchards, down the country lanes and past French farmyards. We waited, hardly daring to breathe the night air that clung gently to the hillsides. As they crouched in the dark and flattened themselves ever lower between the rocks and dirt of their fox-holes, perhaps some soldiers did think of the girl back home, a cold beer, apple pie. But nighttime was a time for listening, not for thinking. Most strained their ears in the night, reaching out for every little sound, every sign of movement, concentrating on interpreting the slightest noise that came through the blackness and over the Hill. A soldier would touch his throat, feel the dryness in it and be-grudge himself the water that he had drunk the day before. He would weigh the cold steel of his rifle sighted into the dark as it touched his palm. Would it work when he pulled the trigger? Would he keep his nerve and shoot straight in the dark? What if the Jerries broke through the outposts? Where could he run? Every living moment clutched us in the night, each one an eternity.

Back at higher headquarters the strategy was to hold the Hill "at all costs."[5] Although we did not know this, we would not have considered any other course. We were up against the racially elite SS, whom Hitler believed were the most perfect examples of living men. We considered no alternatives but to fight on. Some, no doubt, touched crosses or medallions around their necks. For me, it was my shirt, a woolen talisman of sorts in the thickening, cooling night. Some prayed.

Just Before the Battle, Mother is an old song, a ballad dating back to the Civil War. It was a performance piece, one that could be sung from the vaudeville stage. The lyrics convey a sentimental message for the folks back home, to let them know that the soldier's last thoughts were of home and mother. A nice bit of tearful verse by a lyricist far from the front. Surely not what most men felt that night.

All such notions had vanished from my mind, crowded out by thoughts of the desperate situation that had shaped up: "How long would the radio batteries last? I had been lucky that day, very lucky. Would my luck run out? Don't count on luck, man. Use your head."

I wished for a better weapon. When the Germans came at us next, would it be with tanks or infantry or carefully selected snipers and SS fanatics? What would I do with the Colt .45 that was my sidearm? Fire both clips and then throw it at the enemy? The defensive artillery concentrations that I had fired in so carefully—I reviewed the numbers, the locations: 303, 310, 319, 317. They all ran through my head. "Be ready. Don't doze. What if they come across the valley from the rear?" Survival was the only thing worth thinking about. Home and apple pie could come later—if there was a later.

In the gathering chill of another August night, the first blows of a mighty drop forge were already leaving marks on us that would remain for all time, different for each of us and yet the same. If we survived this battle, we would surely own the Hill, but it would also own a part of each of us.

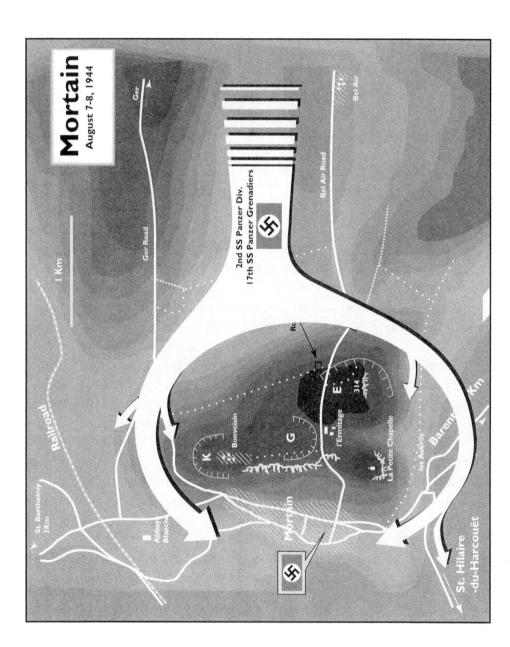

Mortain
August 7-8, 1944

Ger

Ger Road

1 Km

Railroad

St. Barthelmy
3 Km

Abbaye
Blanche

Mortain

2nd SS Panzer Div.
17th SS Panzer Grenadiers

Bel Air

Bel Air Road

Ro

Bonvoisin

K

G

l'Ermitage

E

314

La Petite Chapelle

les Aubris

Barent Km

St. Hilaire
-du-Harcouët

10 *Hand-Me-Down*

Almost 50 years later, Dan Garrott drawled, "Do you still have your daddy's shirt?"

Of course I have it, neatly folded in a plastic bag, a cedar block inside to ward off enemy moths. At more than 75 years of age it is not a museum piece like a Betsy Ross flag or a Civil War sword or bayonet. As an old shirt, however, considerably older than average, it might qualify as a "collectible" in the inventory of one of those marginal antique stores that now overrun the country. It certainly would find a place in a small town or country museum, the kind that without claim or pretense displays housewares, tools, clothes and photographs from other times, giving a partial view of what life was like before the modern age.

Nonetheless, the shirt is a relic, something special, maybe unique. Its history gives it cachet. When I put my hand on the wool sleeve of the shirt that first night on the Hill, I gathered energy from a different time and a different war. My father had worn it in World War I. Professional military men, like Marshall, MacArthur, Eisenhower, and a few gifted patriots saw service in both world wars. But how many shirts can make the same claim?

Why was I wearing a hand-me-down at Mortain? Aiding the war effort by economizing and saving wool was not it. No talisman was intended, either. Charms, rabbits' feet, amulets do not suit me. The suggestion would have embarrassed me. I wore it not as a curiosity, not to be different, not for show. It is true that it clothed me with a sense of family pride. But there was more to it than that.

When my father was 16 years old, he saved a woman's life. Although not very tall, he was a powerful man and even at that age was an exceptionally strong swimmer. One summer evening while hanging around a beach near New York City, he heard screams coming from out in the water. A newspaper account reported: "With twenty men who feared to brave the tide standing on the shore...[he]...leaped into the water...and rescued a drowning woman...." As my father jokingly described the event to me when I was a boy, he dove into the water, swam to the drowning woman, socked her when she tried to sink him and hauled her back to shore. Others apparently thought it was no joke, and my father was awarded a Carnegie Hero Medal. His name and a few details in tiny letters are specially cast in bronze on one side of a large, handsome medal to record the event.

In addition to the medal, the award carried with it limited funds for education, a boon because his dead mother had left nothing, and the aunts who raised him after her death barely scraped by. With these funds, a small scholarship, and his own industry he went on to college. In 1913 Cornell graduated him as a civil engineer, and he went to work for the Pennsylvania Railroad where he learned about railroading: surveying, bridge building, track laying, roadbed maintenance and the management of large numbers of men who heaved long-handled crowbars against the rails, spiked tie-plates and dug the roadbed with picks and shovels.

During the period after his graduation prior to World War I, my father was in the Army Corps of Engineers reserves. With the outbreak of war against Germany and the Austro-Hungarian Empire in 1917, he was among the first to enter service. My father had been brought to America from Hungary by his mother only months after his birth in 1891, and his overseas birth at first singled him out for scrutiny by the military. Suspicions about his loyalty were in due course put to rest, but the experience was difficult for him to endure because he was a man of passionate patriotism for America.

As a railroader, and as a captain in the Corps of Engineers, his expertise and energy moved war-winning supplies and troops across France. American troops in World War I often were transported by rail in "40 or 8s," as the French freight cars were known.[1] Interestingly, the

French maintained the stock of these small, cramped, forlorn bits of rolling stock after the peace. Once I rode aboard one through part of France during World War II. Once was enough.

My father always considered service in World War I as one of the high points of his life. Nonetheless, he regretted never having served in a line outfit with combat engineers, where there was real action. A line from *Henry V*, I suspect, would say it all:

...And gentlemen in England now a-bed shall think themselves accursed they were not here...

He had no need for such thoughts, of course, because he already was a hero, had proved his courage.

Once he showed me a medal that he said was a French Croix de Guerre. As any boy would do, I gawked in wonder and respect until he said jeeringly that he had traded a pack of cigarettes for it. Without doubt, disappointment at not having earned the medal cut him deeply.

And the shirt? One of my father's friends, a consultant in clothing procurement to the army's Quartermaster Corps during World War I, concocted it. Nothing but the best would do. Through connections in the garment business, the friend, eventually my uncle, arranged for the shirt to be cut and tailored specially for my father, of the finest wool serge, not too heavy, with regulation epaulets and first-rate needlework. One could speculate whether the two of them had in mind that the shirt would advance my dad's military career or improve his chances with the ladies. In any case, it must have been sensational in World War I. Twenty-five years later it was still snappy.

The shirt, of course, never went into combat in World War I. When World War II came my way, wearing it in combat was a natural thing to do and seemed to create a spiritual bridge to my father. It was a patriot's shirt, a hero's shirt. What better badge or symbol could a soldier wear? And even more important, wearing it was doing something for him. If he had not seen action in a war, at least his shirt would.

On Hill 314, as apprehension swelled with the deepening shadows and my palm brushed across the sleeve of the shirt, my dirty fingers seemed to touch time past. Was there a connection reaching across time zones into the yet bright sunlight of a hot, Indiana summer day, nudging him gently? Some bit of spirit surely pressed against him quietly and signaled closure to the unfulfilled ambition within.

Hell Fire

Tomorrow and yesterday. When events stream on in endless sequence, at what point do days begin and end? Which is tomorrow? Which was yesterday? Light and dark become different shades of the same wash when the pigment is unceasing, raging violence. Then, only calendar dates are good for counting.

So it was that we began our third calendar day on the Hill long before sunrise on Tuesday, August 8. At two in the morning, enemy tanks milled around below the roadblock on the Bel-Air Road. A barrage at one of the preestablished concentration points kept them away, except one tank which came through into E Company territory, sniffing the dark like a nearsighted dragon. No other tanks followed. The infantry lay motionless, not a breath, not a sound. In the dark the tank found nobody to fight. It turned and went back to its lair.

Meanwhile, under pressure from the attacking Germans who had overrun Mortain and then attacked the southwest knob of the Hill, G Company moved north across the Bel-Air Road along the western ridge—but not before first annihilating the *Heil Hitler* screaming Germans that had infiltrated their position that first night after the counterattack had begun.[1] Once across the Bel-Air Road, the men of G Company took up a position just south of K Company. G Company and K Company were then able to set up a consolidated perimeter defense.[2] The two companies communicated with E Company only by runner, a long run at that, across the top of the Hill or down along the eastern ridge from K Company.

Lieutenant Bartz, the forward observer from C Battery of the 230th Field Artillery, was dug in with K Company. Early that morning, after sunup, he reported that enemy vehicles broke through the roadblock in that sector. He called for artillery fire. The shelling must have driven off the enemy intrusion. It was the last communication that Bartz made from the Hill. His radio had gasped its last, either shot out or the victim of dead batteries.[3] Our forward observer party had not been in touch with Bartz. It was just as well. We had our hands full and needed no added burden of responsibility. For Bartz and his crew, it must have been a time of utter frustration, trapped without a radio, suddenly become infantry with no proper weapons, only carbines and .45-caliber pistols. I suspect that as he sat there on the Hill, Bartz thought a great deal about death and dying. I did not know him well, basing my understanding of him only on fleeting impressions, a quick summing up now and then. He seemed to me always to be looking over his shoulder, and I could already see the pale stamp of death on his face. This gave me an uncomfortable feeling, and I could not look him in the eyes or study his face for long. I never had the opportunity to ask Bartz what had transpired after his radio went out. Not long after Mortain, he was killed in action.

The fact was, however, that when his radio had ceased to function, the artillery defense of Hill 314 fell essentially into our hands. The lives of the men on the Hill were now linked, for better or for worse, to the continued operation of our radio. At the time we did not know that. Ignorance shored up courage and hope. Half a century later, when he learned that with four days still to go on the Hill, Bartz had lost radio contact, Dan Garrott shook his head in astonishment, "You mean it was just our radio between us and the Germans?"[4]

Enemy preparations went on to assault the Hill. By that time, the Hill had taken on a symbolic, as well as a strategic importance. This was true on both sides. For the German command, however, the implication of the stubborn American defense of the Hill must have generated a hysterical thrust, a strange blend of pride, fear and Prussian arrogance. The *Führer* would never accept failure of an elite division with tanks, self-propelled 88s, *nebelwerfer* rockets and other heavy weapons to take the Hill from a handful of Americans with rifles.

Beginning a little after 8:00 a.m., as the sun warmed the earth to receive a gorgeous summer day, enemy infantry, at least a platoon of those gray-green uniforms, assembled to the front for an attack. I called out "Fire Mission" to Sasser, gave him coordinates to transmit, and took them under fire before they had a chance of making a move. A pall of exploding shells and smoke covered the German infantry, blackening the area around them. Dust and debris shot skyward. To them, something awful had happened, but for us it was a scene of distant destruction. We did not hear the screams of pain and terror as shell fragments cut up the air, nor did we smell the acrid smoke of exploding shells, or see the torn, bleeding bodies. It was another "mission accomplished." When the shelling was complete, Sasser at the radio sent on my assessment to Fire Direction Center:

Effect excellent.

For those at the command center, cooped up in a tent, sightless and with no video to show them the war play-by-play, with only maps, dividers and firing tables, it was something to cheer about. When they heard that the shells had hit the target, they put another check mark in the margin of the Message Log.

Then tanks. More infantry. Artillery fire brought all of these intended onslaughts to a standstill. After an hour and a half, the enemy tried a new tactic. A single 88, the first of many to come that day, opened up on our position. Artillery under our direction shot back and silenced it—for awhile.

The German efforts were now coming in bursts at short intervals, like a boxer's jabs and combinations. Not long after 10:00 a.m., Kerley had me send a message to be relayed to his regimental headquarters:

Still holding original position. Elements of H are with me. In contact with G and K. Point marked with white cross. Need batteries

300 and 610, medical supplies and food, basic load ammo for rifle company and 60 and 80mm [*sic*] mortars. Captured enemy jeep 0830. English-speaking officer captured, wounded. His battery is at Ger.

At noon (somewhere, someone was having lunch) enemy infantry began to break out in the open at several locations to the front. An attack shaped up. Again, accurate fire from our 105s smashed the intended assault before it could get under way. The situation was not getting any better. I followed up Kerley's message with an encoded inquiry:

Are we getting reinforcements?

It seemed like a logical question at the time. Of course, as I now know, there was no way that reinforcements could possibly have reached us. Mortain was in enemy hands and the 2d SS Panzer Division had both flanks in its grip. It never hurts to ask.

Our only reply came from the Germans. Infantry and tank assaults had been stopped time and again. They had been repeatedly frustrated, but they began again, this time trying to blast us off the Hill.

Their 88s bludgeoned and tore at the rocks with armor-piercing shells. These shells differed from high-explosive shells that detonated on impact. Although armor-piercing shells were unlikely to be as effective against troops as high-explosive rounds which burst into hundreds or thousands of jagged, body-severing chunks and slivers, the impact of each armor-piercing round conveyed a sense of brute power, unstoppable strength and deep malice. It was not a time to be wandering around in the open. Big iron cut through the air, shattered boulders into sharp splinters, then bounced erratically over our heads.

We crouched down behind the crags, on the face of the cliff to the rear, uncomfortably sheltered, listening for the detonation of guns in the valley to the front. Each incoming shell whistled and screamed and then struck a hammer blow that shook the earth as if someone were pounding it with a giant sledge. After a round struck the rocky promontory, it bounced off and roared into the valley beyond, residual vibrations singing in the air, leaving us shaken but whole.

Sergeant Sasser now maintained with unwavering conviction that the Germans had locked onto our radio.[5] It could have been that. It also may have been that they regarded the crags as a logical target, the intelligent place for an enemy to set up an observation post. Whichever it was, they were determined that day to soften us up or wear us down by pulverizing the ground to which we clung. We felt the frustration, the anger, the hate they had for us as each shell pounded and splintered the rocks.

If the gun was aimed too high, the shell rushed over into the valley or onto the promontory behind. We took consolation in the thought that the Germans might be shooting their own troops.

And it was hot. We hunched down below the back edge of the covering crags and wiped the sweat from our faces. Throats grew dusty, as hot and rough as the rocks we pressed against beneath the overhead sun. We had no water, maybe a sip here and there sucked up from almost empty canteens.

A rumor went around that men on the left flank, to the north, were getting water from a farmhouse, but we had none. Food also was almost gone for most. The only food I had was stowed in my gas mask carrier, along with matches, water-purifying tablets and louse powder. It was against army regulations to carry them there, but where else? By that time, men had started to search the dead for any rations that might turn up. I scrounged up a K-ration from the innards of my gas mask carrier. Should I eat it? It was my last. There would be no other to replace it. I wolfed it down and threw the trash down the cliff into the valley below.

Savage as the blows against the Hill were, the Germans could not afford to waste armor-piercing rounds, intended to destroy tanks, against a hilltop. Soon they shifted to high-explosive shells, and artillery and 88mm self-propelled guns pounded us again and again. We huddled down close to the radio. Shells exploded out front or rushed overhead into the valley behind. The repetitive bursting nearby of numberless shells, pounding on our helmets and in our

ears was mind-numbing, and it exhausted us. We stopped counting
them.

Then, British Typhoons shot across from the left, flying so low
they seemed just barely above the tops of the hedgerows. As they
made one pass after another, they dipped their noses for a fraction of
a second, fired what looked like rockets at tanks or self-propelled
guns hidden behind the hedgerows, and then snapped back to level
flight and streaked away, leaving clouds of oily smoke where their
projectiles had hit. As suddenly as they arrived, they were gone, never
to return again.[6]

As we bunched together, burrowing next to the rocky cliffs, a
shell exploded somewhere on top, but not the same sort of violent
explosion as the other shells. An instant later we were caught in a
snowstorm of small, white particles that floated down upon us. We
looked in amazement, and eyes filled with instant terror. Where the
particles landed on shirts and trousers they sizzled and burned. White
phosphorus! We brushed our clothing frantically, pushed shirt collars up. If any of the stuff touched the skin, it could inflict a horrible
burn, increasing in intensity as it burrowed into a man's flesh. What
would we do if a particle drifted down inside our shirt collars? Suppose an undetected fleck of phosphorus burned through the back of a
shirt and floated against the skin inside? Except for training exer-
cises, none of us artillerymen had seen white phosphorus close up
before. Probably there were very few infantry who had even heard of
it, but this new weapon burst upon us with vicious fury, and the first
shell taught us all we needed to know about it.

At one o'clock I reported:

Observer's position being smoked by enemy.

Another shell. Another missile from hell. A flurry of tiny, burning white fragments smoking like brimstone. Fiery snow! I saw panic
gathering on the faces of men nearby. Sweat began to bead up furiously under helmets and drizzle across unshaven faces. My dirty,
sweaty face matched the others. I remember thinking that if the white

phosphorus shelling kept up for long, it would be more than most men could endure. There was nowhere to hide, no place that was safe. The burning white fragments spun down in search of targets, making hundreds of twirling, smoking arcs that drenched the air. We had to wait it out, hope that it would stop. Would the men panic? I wanted to shout: "Jesus Christ, don't run. Not now," but the words were muffled within me. Over and over again, the words died in my parched throat: "Don't run. For Christ's sake, don't run." If one man ran, more might do the same. There would be no way to stop the flight if it ever started. I pushed my shoulders up under my helmet and waited for the next explosion of hell fire.

As suddenly as the blizzard had begun, it ceased. There had been only three or four, maybe five of the smoking demons. White phosphorus normally was used as an incendiary or to mark a position or a target with smoke. In volume, its terrible torching power might bring enemy troops to heel. The Germans, however, must have had a limited supply of such shells. We looked at one another, hardly believing what had just happened.

No one smiled, but we could breathe easily again.

12

High Noon

The enemy had thrown almost every conceivable type of shell in its arsenal at us. Each type of shell had its own special demonic characteristic. The bombardment took a toll in blood and flesh. Yet the harder the enemy tried to grind us down and obliterate us, the more that they shook us and pounded us, the more determined we became. It was clearly survival or nothing. We all knew that.

The sun was just barely reaching its zenith. After the white phosphorus, there was a lull in the firing. Were the Germans taking a break in the shade, snacking? It was time to do something.

The previous day I'd had a good opportunity to observe the accuracy of the German shelling when I had waited alone at the high crags for Sasser to return from his search for Corn and Garrott. The artillery, other than the 88s, was effective against a relatively large target, a hillside or a major landmark or a building. With longer barrels and higher velocity shells, the 88s were better than the other German artillery, deadly accurate, a weapon to be feared, one of the very best the enemy had. But after my experience the day before, it was clear to me that even an 88 was not accurate in the way that a rifle was. At 1,500 or 2,000 yards, moreover, it was unlikely that an 88 could hit a small target, except by chance, and certainly not with consistency.

As I shouldered against the rough edges of the rocky escarpment that fell off below me into trees and down into the steep little valley at the bottom, I tried to recall what I knew about "range probable error." That term describes a statistical estimate or measure of how far a shell will probably land from and miss its intended target. The degree of error varies, of course, with the distance from the target and other factors, such as the elevation or angle of the gun from the horizontal and the powder charge, the weather and the type of gun itself, low-muzzle velocity or high-muzzle velocity. There were many variables, too many to try to puzzle it out in my head with any accuracy.

What I did know was that the concept of "range probable error" reflected an inherent inaccuracy in artillery fire. If an object the size of a small watermelon or a helmet, for example, was the target, it was highly probable that the shell would miss it. That was reassuring, because under my own helmet I had begun to work up a tactic for confronting the enemy shelling. I assessed risks, weighed probabilities and then considered possibilities.

The very top of the crags presented a difficult target for artillery. Mortars with their high trajectory could have targeted it, but it was unlikely for fieldpieces and 88s. As I pondered all of this, it seemed clear to me that an 88 aiming at a target on the crags would—because of the factor of "range probable error"—either fall short or go over the top.

This would be true even if its direction were exactly right on. That, of course, was also unlikely, because all ballistic missiles also exhibit inherent error in direction. But even if there were no deviation in direction, I reasoned that a shell falling short would hit in front of and below the top surface of the crags. The noise and dust and debris would be unpleasant to anyone up on the very dome, but the explosion would be mostly to the sides and overhead. What little might come directly forward, hopefully would only chip away the front lip of the rough, but somewhat flat, surface of the dome. If the trajectory of the shell was too high, even the slightest little bit, it would pass over and burst in the valley or on the promontory behind us which was in enemy hands.

By that time I had directed so many fire missions that when I saw a new target, I could immediately fix its coordinates with a high degree of accuracy. In many cases it was by relation to a previous target or numbered concentration. The course of action seemed clear. It was our turn.

I told Sergeant Sasser to switch on the radio. We had to be quick. For what I had in mind, the fire missions had to come with almost the speed of the shooting in a quick-draw western—and with comparable accuracy.

Sergeant Sasser turned on the radio.

"Ready, lieutenant."

I motioned for Sergeant Corn to move up beside me. When I moved farther up, he would become a relay between me and Sasser.

I scrambled up the precipice and out on top of the crags into the open, under the glaring sun. Head low, my body flattened into the surface of the dome, elbows stretched far apart and resting on the rocky table, binoculars in front, eyes barely above the top of the binoculars, I searched and waited. It seemed a certainty that I would not have to wait long. If the Germans were looking, they would have seen me.

My body was stretched out in the direction of fire. At that angle they would see only my helmet. They would have to hit me right between the eyes with an 88. It was not a rash, impulsive gamble with death but a carefully calculated risk. At least that's what I thought.

The apple was on my head.

The seconds ticked off, each one longer than the last. When I had worked this out, it had not been my intention to stand up and wave. Were the krauts munching sausage and black bread? I had to lie still. I dared not move. If I did, I might miss an opportunity or foolishly expose myself.

And then it came. They opened up to our direct front. Shells whirled and whined our way. The glasses came up. I saw smoke from the muzzles of the guns, wreathing their position like smoke rings from a cigar. I shouted over my shoulder to Corn behind and below me:

Fire Mission. Enemy battery.

Corn relayed the message to Sasser. No time was lost with the usual salutation or waiting for a response to it.

Crow this is Crow Baker 3. *Fire Mission.* Enemy battery.

By the time Sasser heard back from the battalion Fire Direction Center, the gun position of the enemy had been relayed from on top to Corn to Garrott who was next to Sasser by the radio. Garrott gave it to Sasser and he put it through. Only a few moments went by, but up on top I thought time was stuck. Who would fire next, us or them? I watched the enemy guns through my binoculars, now a gun sight. From down below, seemingly miles away, I caught the sound of Sasser's soft voice as if from a megaphone, and then closer and louder from Corn:

On the way.

A freight train roared by from the left side, from over toward the northwest. Almost instantly, clouds of smoke broke around the German position and only a few yards to one side. It was devastating. The whole battalion must have fired. I shouted an adjusting command to Corn who passed it quickly to Sasser at the radio and on to battalion. Through my binoculars, I saw the next salvos obliterate the target. The German battery closed down, all fight gone out of it.

Six enemy self-propelled guns, about 500 yards closer to the Hill but almost 1,000 yards to the north, now fired. The sequence repeated: glasses up, muzzle blast in view, a quick estimate of the location. Over my shoulder to Sergeant Corn:

Fire Mission. Enemy self-propelled guns. Six guns. Not moving. Throwing fire this way.

Again, the quick response from our battalion's guns, again the first rounds exploding close by the target within eighty to a hundred yards, shattering the enemy unexpectedly. Another command blanketed the enemy with a rain of shells. Those guns stood silent.

Meanwhile a tank and another battery fired on us. The tank was south, in a totally different location, along one of the trails below the cliffs where the Germans had rolled through at the start of their counterattack. The battery was off to the left side, shooting from a position north of and beyond the battery we had just knocked out. One thing at a time: we took out the tank first, then ripped into the new gun battery. Using as a reference point the last rounds fired at the self-propelleds, I shouted at Corn:

Fire Mission. Enemy battery. Four or six guns. Last concentration is 500 right, 300 short.

The first salvos exploded directly in line between that "last concentration" and the German guns—but disappointingly far short. I shouted an adjustment over the noise of the enemy shells bursting around us on the Hill. Corn picked it up, passed it on. Tinkers-to-Evers-to-Chance. Smoke and debris rose from the field where the enemy battery fired at us. Our artillery blistered their position, and their guns ceased. The enemy, as the military says, had been neutralized.

I took a breath, looked around, put my binoculars up and like a bird-watcher quickly peered up and down the hedgerows and at the fields. Then I put them down. "Range probable error" was a statistical formulation, not a gift of eternal protection. I slithered backward off the rough surface of the dome of the crags and scrambled down below before somebody got lucky.

It was almost three o'clock. I was hot and dry, but no longer feeling the least bit humble. The pounding had been intense, and the area around the high crags had been thoroughly thrashed.

But we were shooting back.

13 Notes for Company Commanders

August 8, still Tuesday, the second day of the attack, the third calendar day on the Hill.

For supper we took another hitch in our belts while the long-range shells of a gun bigger than an 88 burst savagely about us, making the ground shudder underneath. Flying steel splinters overlaid with dust and fragments of rock stormed at us. We guessed that it was a 150mm firing from 8,000–10,000 yards, somewhere in the vicinity of Ger, almost six miles away to the east and a bit north. The more massive shell blasts that shook the earth immediately enabled us to identify heavier guns. Smaller field pieces fired more rapidly. The bigger ones fired fewer rounds, but on detonation each one shredded into many more, whirling, jagged, killing bits of steel.

Ger was beyond the reach of the 230th Field Artillery and other direct support 105s. When we gathered our senses, we took a bearing and reported an approximate azimuth to the Fire Direction Center, hoping that an airplane spotter might pick up the exact location and bring in longer range, more powerful weapons, like the destructive 155mm "Long Toms." We wanted that gun destroyed.

The shelling continued to kill, wound and shake up our troops. The enemy's main action had now become one of attrition, picking away at us with their artillery, self-propelled 88s and tanks. All targets within reasonable rifle shot had vanished, and our troops hunkered down in foxholes, scratched their shrinking stomachs and said a prayer now and then. The 2d Battalion stayed dug in, the only thing it could do, hanging on to the high, rocky ground as the fire of the 230th Field Artillery and other supporting artillery battalions became increasingly punishing to the enemy.

The 230th alone was now shooting nearly two thousand 105mm shells during every 24-hour period, night and day, most of it in defense of the Hill.[1] That tallies up to roughly one round per gun every 10 minutes, 24 hours a day. Of course the gun crews fired at irregular intervals, but they were on duty around the clock, waiting to hustle into action when we called for fire missions on specific targets. Those times called for short, intense bursts of energy. The care with which the gun crews fired their howitzers, making sure the powder charges were correct, adjusting elevation and deflection with extreme accuracy, taking up "lost motion" as they made the settings, made the accuracy superb. The number of fire missions and rounds shot off would have been nothing if the men at the guns had not been infinitely precise. The automatic nightly defensive fires laid down around our positions and supporting shelling of other artillery battalions augmented the fire missions on specific targets that I called in to the 230th Field Artillery, and created an explosive, violent, increasingly deadly threat to the Germans.

Night movement was touchy, dangerous. Daytime was a time for dozing, if there was such a time. Nighttime was the time for listening. Each slight sound posed a single question: *Who* is it? There were no crickets on the Hill.

Continued German fire had made observation from the high crags at the southern end very spotty. We anticipated a night attack down the Bel-Air Road on the left flank, with tanks leading the way to push through the roadblock there. Before darkness put us at risk that night, we packed up the radio and moved near to E Company headquarters, closer to this expected action.

Lieutenant Kerley continued to use the high crags for his observation and personal command post. With rare exceptions, he directed E Company from there during the entire battle. He seemed not to give a damn, despite the danger from enemy artillery and the exposure to mortar and sniper fire from the promontory across the valley to the west. Kerley's presence worked magic, buoying up spirits and encouraging everyone. Jagged as a fragment from a German 88, his lean frame became an increasingly rough and inspiring image. Much as we preferred to stick with him, staying there would not work. The high crags were 300–400 yards farther from the anticipated action at the roadblock than our location near E Company headquarters. In the event of a night attack, the delay while a man with a report of an impending attack "ran" those additional yards in the dark over the rocky hillside might be crucial.

Sasser and Garrott dug in the radio beneath a cover of rocks to shield it from flying shell fragments. E Company headquarters had remained in the draw at the left flank of the company position, generally below where our first OP had been. During the days since the attack had started, this headquarters area had turned into a busy administrative center. It was now the prisoner of war collecting point, the aid station, the supply depot (for water, for example, as canteens were now filled and brought in from a farmhouse by patrol on a regular basis), a communication center and so on. A group of infantrymen always gathered there, some coming and some going, sometimes just hanging around or squatting in the dirt and rocks, hiding their hunger and apprehension, taking comfort from the presence of the others, ready for the next assignment.

That night we established a fire mission call center. After entrenching the radio, I shot in protective artillery fires, alerted the infantry outposts to our new location and established a communication network. As well as runners, short or internal telephone lines of the infantry still connected us to an outpost or two. Hand-cranked field telephones fed the wires. Runners, however, would do most of the work. We were ready.

Around 10:00 p.m., we radioed a day-end status report to the Fire Direction Center. The Message Log contains this entry:

> Captured several prisoners. Bothered by snipers. Tanks in front of them. Have hit some. Need batteries for 300 and 600 series radios. Don't seem too worried. Need medical supplies. Getting hungry. Will report more when possible.

We had confidence in the artillery. We had seen it drive off attack after attack. But, *not worried*? It is difficult to believe we were *that* cocky. More likely, it was the interpretation of the radio operator who made the entry in the Message Log. Over the radio he had heard only our voices trying to sound cheerful, giving the best tone that we could to a situation that had edged to the brink of deterioration. Morale was still "fair" and had not yet pitched into a rapid decline.[2] The radio operator saw no drawn, sleepless faces, no wounded bodies, and did not feel the pinch of hunger. By the time they relayed the message to the next higher headquarters, 30th Division Artillery, the radio operators had embellished the log entry, given it an interpretation, and then entered it into the journal of that headquarters as:

Not too worried about situation as long as artillery fire continues.

Division Artillery then sent the enhanced "message" on to 30th Division Headquarters. As an unconnected fragment of information, it sounded positive. At the division level of command it was just another bit of intelligence, a scrap of information which those in charge would interpret and factor into the overall situation along with all of the other reports. If division headquarters took it literally, it would see our situation through the wrong end of the telescope.

By 11:00 p.m., tanks and other vehicles began persistent attempts to run the roadblock. These were now determined, deliberate efforts to force an opening into our position, not casual, probing thrusts.

Men clustered around the radio, relaying enemy movement in hushed voices as runners brought in reports. I evaluated these descriptions of the enemy's agitated starts and stops, converted them into targets and locations, translated their excited, breathy whispers in the night into the language of fire missions. The first three fire missions came in rapid order before midnight. We sent shells hurtling east down the Bel-Air Road, past where our infantry had dug in, blasting tanks and enemy vehicles.

As each separate enemy onslaught crumbled, another took its place. Tanks rumbled toward the roadblock and then retreated when the shelling drove them off. They regrouped and returned, again and again. If the Germans believed that antitank guns and tanks on the Hill were firing directly at them, it might account for their hesitation to punch through the handful of infantry with rifles on the Bel-Air Road and flood across the top of the Hill. But one can only speculate why they ultimately faltered.

After midnight, another barrage, Concentration 360, sent shells screaming by, breaking the summer's soft night air, striking at a gathering of tanks that was probing down a dirt road, hardly more than a trail, that connected the main Ger Road to the north with the Bel-Air Road. This dirt road ran almost straight south past the front of K Company's position on the left flank. If the tanks had rolled on, just another 500 yards, they would have pushed into E Company's perimeter astride the Bel-Air Road. From there the tanks easily could have fanned out on the flat fields on top of the Hill and come in behind the positions of all three infantry companies, effectively strangling and overrunning the entire 2d Battalion.

The fire mission call center that we had cobbled together with the help of the infantry, shored up by telephone communication and runners, enabled us to respond quickly with artillery to the frontal lunges of the enemy. The shelling was unbelievably effective, particularly considering that it was night and no one could see very far or clearly identify a target. In fact, we used sound for much of the "sighting." All artillery battalions in the division fired intermittently during the night at designated locations in front of our positions. This random shelling, when coupled with my own specific fire missions, laid down a ring of steel that tore at the panzers and prevented an attack on our front from ever getting under way, let alone gathering momentum. Concentration 360, typical of the fire missions which I called in, staved off what might have turned into a deathblow from the north, where we had limited observation, even in daylight. The night, long and sleepless, filled us with deep apprehension.

Later on, at daybreak, we would report:

Enemy attempted to overrun observer's position three times during night but was driven back by artillery fire.

We did not know, of course, that elsewhere American troops had stopped von Kluge's lightning attack. On the Hill, the night crept on under constant enemy pressure, hour after hour, relentless, without any letup.

E Company Headquarters close by our new OP did not occupy a very defensible position in case of attack from the rear, that is, from the west. To the immediate rear, a wide field south of the Bel-Air Road, a cow pasture, extended some 600 yards west to the next ridge, which was occupied by the Germans, just above the town. At the southern end of the pasture, the land fell off sharply into a steep valley between the eastern ridge of the Hill, which E Company held, and the promontory to the west at the southern end of the enemy position. In the draw against the rocky slopes of the Hill, E Company headquarters had a slight advantage of elevation in case of attack across the pasture.

But there it ended. It was not the same as being on top of the ridge shooting down from a cover of rocks and entrenchments. Except for rocky outcroppings, almost cliff-like behind us, there was little shelter. An assault from the rear would back us against a rock wall with the enemy between us and our own artillery. Our own artillery would have been a last resort option because of the risk that "friendly fire" which passed over the enemy's heads would hit us.

At night, German shelling invariably stopped. In bombarding us during the preceding two days at the high crags, the German artillery had visually sighted individual guns, particularly the 88s and other self-propelled weapons. But visual sighting was not feasible at night, and firing blindly in the dark, using map coordinates or similar techniques, would have risked hitting their own tanks which maneuvered close to our lines.

Still, they had other weapons, more suitable to the cover of night. An onslaught burst unexpectedly out of the blackness. As we lay in our shallow, rocky foxholes, waiting for the next assault of tanks from the front, foot soldiers charged from the rear across the pasture, automatic weapons blazing randomly. Short, flat arcs of light, sliced madly through the night. Tracer bullets showered across the pasture. Our shoulders hunched and eyes blinked at the eruption of sound, at the flashes and at the many sparks of light.

There is always light at night, however faint. Although the enemy couldn't see us, the ridge line and lumps of rock at our backs stood out against the black screen of night, and they had spotted our general location. They clearly knew where we were.

Enemy bullets sprayed our position erratically. Most bullets went wide, but many came close, lashed the rocks at our backs, splattered our faces with lead and rock splinters as bullets ricocheted in all directions. Tiny particles sprinkled and tickled dirty cheeks, noses and ears, mingling with the sweaty gatherings of fear, not painful but cutting deep in memory.

These automatic weapons played the law of averages. The Germans did not have to sight them accurately. If they fired enough bullets in our general direction, a few would hit targets. If they fired a very large number of rounds, the damage might be considerable. One postulate of machine-age technology, volume and chance, not necessarily accuracy, hit us head-on.

The infantry fired their rifles back at the sparks that exposed the enemy. Incoming bullets shattered against the boulders and chipped out minute, dust-like flecks of rock. The spray of bullets and rock chips hummed like angry bees. Everyone flinched and huddled down to get out of the storm, and the infantry rifles spoke back harshly again and again to the faceless, unseen enemy. Sasser, Garrott, Corn and I clutched pistols and carbines, ready if the enemy came within range.

The Germans wounded and killed many that night. The man next to me—within easy reach—lying tight against the base of the rocky hillside, was shot through the leg and head. We shouted "Medico, medico." When at last the aid man crawled to us, he had no morphine, no bandages, almost no medical supplies of any kind. There was no shelter, no light, no aid facility—just the rocky ground where he knelt beside the wounded soldier. The aid man inspected the damage, but could do no more and crawled back into the night, his aid bag hanging limply across his shoulders. The wounded man lay beside me groaning from pain through the rest of the long night—a low, sobbing sound that faded before morning.

The Germans had launched a wild, disorganized attack. Strangers tried to kill each other anonymously in the blackness. Men fired their weapons at random, struck out blindly against an enemy they could not see. And almost as suddenly as they began shooting at us, the Germans stopped and vanished from the pasture into the night.

By the time the early light of day spread shadows across the backside of the Hill, the soldier lying near me had died, a sheet of shadows drawn close, covering his body. Sometime later that day the dead man disappeared, somehow faded away as had his sobbing in the night.

Except against tanks on the Bel-Air Road, where our fire mission call center came into play using reports from runners and sound, at night we could not see enemy movements and call for artillery fire. Nonetheless, three battalions of 105mm howitzers, one battalion of 155mm howitzers and two field artillery groups with heavier weapons up to eight-inch howitzers pounded selected targets, such as crossroads, intersections and likely assembly areas, with heavy defensive concentrations fired according to prearranged schedules at intervals throughout the night. The artillery fired these concentrations at battalion strength, not merely single guns or even a four-gun battery of a battalion.[3] The magnitude of the shellfire sent a brutal warning that kept the Germans off balance to the front. But the simple fact was that we had been unable to unleash artillery against the attack across the pasture from our rear.

The troops that had lunged from the rear with automatic weapons significantly outgunned our infantry, whose firepower consisted essentially of riflemen spread out across the eastern rise of the Hill in little clusters and groups, without walkie-talkie radios or any means of coordination except runners. A concerted attack of enemy infantry with automatic weapons from the rear could easily have stopped our infantry runners from communicating with my field artillery group. Without knowledge of what was happening at the roadblock, our capability to call in artillery fire would have been effectively neutralized. If, at the same time tanks had pushed past the roadblock, the enemy could easily have overrun the Hill and scooped us up. But they never coordinated any attacks at night.

Perhaps the enemy did not know our situation or perceive the fragile lines of our communication. The heavy and constant incoming shells from our artillery bespoke strength and power belying the unfortified, virtually weaponless position that we held.

When it finally came, dawn lit up smudged and dirty faces, now creased with lines of anxiety that stretched through gathering stubble. We remained in possession of the Hill, a limited triumph.

The 230th Field Artillery Battalion Log for August 8 summed it up as follows:

> 2d Battalion of 120th Infantry still cut off. Lieutenant Weiss still communicates to us the shortage of food, supplies, ammunition and batteries.

But the 30th Division Headquarters, someplace to the rear, was not worried. The G-2, or intelligence, report for August 8, made at 30th Infantry Division Headquarters on the following morning of August 9, stated:[4]

...4. ENEMY CAPABILITIES
a. The enemy can:
   (1) Withdraw bulk of his forces...
   (2) Execute limited attacks
   (3) Defend in present position
b. Discussion
   Capability 4a(1) is considered of high probability. Enemy's attack of 7 August now seems to have been a major effort...There is no evidence...to sustain the belief that he will counterattack in strength again...He is unlikely to defend in present position

because...*he has not attempted a strong attack on the commanding ground held by 2d Bn 120th Infantry just east of MORTAIN*...Limited counterattacks may be expected at any time. [Emphasis added]

HALL

G-2

Lieutenant Colonel Hall's statement no doubt reflected a further reading of "Don't seem too worried." His was the big picture, different from our microperspective, seen at eye level, down in the dirt, under constant attack by tanks and automatic weapons, short of ammunition, food, water, medical supplies and with only one radio between us and oblivion. No enemy tanks groaned close to division headquarters, and no shells exploded in their faces back there.

When he prepared the intelligence report, Lieutenant Colonel Hall also distributed "Notes for Company Commanders" dated August 9 in which he commented:

It is hard to say what would have happened if the Germans had succeeded in their determined attempt during the last two days to drive through us to the sea at Avranches. The battle you waged and are still fighting will probably rate as one of the critical battles of the West, possibly the last attempt of the Wehrmacht to prevent the battle of Normandy...from turning into the battle of France....The attack, launched with elements of four panzer divisions,...was yesterday described by BBC as the most serious attack made by the Germans along the entire front since the first days of the beachhead...The attack is not over by any means...Berlin radio provided the news that eight high German officers had been hanged for conspiring against their beloved Führer...

Kerley would have to wait for his copy of these "Notes." As Hall correctly observed, the battle was not over yet. We waited without the comfort of his comments as the new dawn reached across the sky.

14 Meanwhile, Back at the Chateau...

Wednesday, August 9, the fourth day on the Hill, dawned clear. The stark light quickly purged the air of the residue of the terrible night just past. Early sunshine was just beginning to chase the dew off the ridge-line grasses when my forward observer party crawled up to the crest above E Company Headquarters and set up our third, and last, observation post. It was more centrally located but still on the north, or left flank, of E Company's position.

No mist clouded the light spreading across fields, hedgerows and fruit trees, and the earth warmed quickly to the sun's even touch. Here and there, the stone side of a farmhouse or the horizontal stroke of a roof line intruded into the landscape. The rolling countryside dozed peacefully before us.

Back at division headquarters, Lieutenant Colonel Hall would soon be sitting down at his desk in the Chateau de la Bozage with a cup of hot coffee, writing his assessment that everything was going well, that the Germans had not made a strong attack on our position, and that he considered it "of high probability" that the enemy would withdraw. That was what he had heard and knew. What we knew was what we had heard and seen in the days gone by, the missiles that sucked up the air as they screamed and rushed at us, the explosions, the wounded and the dying. If Lieutenant Colonel Hall's battle summary had been in hand, it would not have consoled us. The Germans still surrounded the 2d Battalion which badly needed food, medical supplies, batteries, ammunition and antitank weapons.

We now obtained sufficient water from the farmhouse to our rear along the Bel-Air Road, closer to the enemy's position than to ours. Our map showed only two or three structures there, leaving them unnamed. In fact, the farm was known locally as "l'Ermitage." Regularly a couple of the infantrymen would gather up six or eight canteens from others, string them around their necks and over their shoulders, as many as they could carry, and sneak off to l'Ermitage. Sometimes sniper fire halted them and delayed the procurement of water. No one cared whose filled canteen he got back.

The Germans systematically attacked the forces on the Hill with artillery, mortars, machine gun and small arms fire. Except for night-time, the never-ending pounding was punctuated only by short periods of waiting for the next assault. Rifles shot against tanks, and rifles turned back rapid-fire assault weapons. A few exhausted men stood against a juggernaut. The lifeline continued to be our one radio with dying batteries. It called down curtain after curtain of exploding steel shells on the enemy, but was incapable of ringing down the final curtain that would end the show. Only reinforcements and joining up with other troops would accomplish that.

Each day crawled more slowly than the last toward the next, marking an end only as light faded and darkness veiled the landscape. Yet, despite this sameness, at least one exceptional event marked each day with a special brand and separated it from all of the others. The sunny cover of this day gave no clue of what was to come.

The previous occupants of the Hill had clawed a large dugout, a rough pit, out of the rocky hillside near the crest of the ridge, removing more rock than soil. It provided a good spot for observation and for the radio. The shallow depth of this pit barely gave cover, but that was true of most foxholes on the Hill. Its larger size, covering two to three times the area of most narrow entrenchments, brought to it a feeling of being exposed and out in the open. The extra space diminished the hidden, protective, cocoon-like feeling of a tighter burrow. But there was no time and little choice, except to dig another one or try to excavate this one deeper. We took occupancy and entrenched our radio securely.

Not far to the left, a large outcropping of rocks, another promontory but a minor one compared to the high crags at the southern end, perched near the crest of the ridge which ran south and which generally defined the eastern line of E Company's position. A few scrub trees and bushes broke the line of tall grass on the crest.

Behind the new OP, perhaps 10 or 20 paces as the hillside sloped away from the top, Sasser, Garrott and Corn immediately began digging two foxholes in a line parallel to the ridge and perpendicular to the direction of attack, as deep as they could go. Fortune favored the effort. Their small, folding shovels—"entrenching tools," as army jargon put it—by chance struck a seam of dirt and loose rock. They excavated deeply enough to give cover to two men, sharing a single foxhole, sitting hunched over and bending as far forward as possible. Limited as they were, the two foxholes protected better than most

**L'Ermitage, where the troops on Hill 314 obtained water.
The eastern ridge of the Hill shows in the background.**

entrenchments on the Hill. We would stay here until the battle was over.

Once the radio had been set up and protected in the OP foxhole, and while the shoveling went on, my work began. I scanned each field and hedgerow, each shady clump of trees, looking for the straight, man-made lines that would betray some part of a tank or truck or the protruding muzzle of an 88. The enemy still lurked out there somewhere. I had yet to see the enemy withdraw and fade away as Lieutenant Colonel Hall had concluded was highly probable.

The Bel-Air Road running off into enemy territory came into sharp focus in my binoculars. Dry grasses, weeds and the dusty leaves of bushes hung over the edge of the empty beige clay and gravel surface of the road. I searched up and down the verges into the bordering hedgerows and past the fences. Nothing intruded.

Then, just a few minutes past 7:00, the first tanks of the day cruised up to the roadblock. The enemy had not gone away. But its "work schedule," the late, almost civilized start, puzzled me. It had been light for hours. Surely the work rules of state socialism did not apply out here. Undoubtedly, the previous night's shelling of the enemy by our artillery still acted as a deterrent. The Germans seemed reluctant to advance, and each tank waited for the others to go first and test the water. Their tanks could have swept through if they had made a frontal assault in broad daylight when they could see the origin of fire and the location of the troops who directed it. But they must have suspected that there was an observer at the roadblock, dug in with binoculars and radio, watching for them to come on.

Like the morning call of a rooster announcing that another day had begun, our first fire mission focused the Fire Direction Center's attention on us once more. It would be Concentration 359. This concentration marked a target area that was rapidly becoming "No. 1" on the list. The tanks were clearly visible straight down the Bel-Air Road, less than a mile from our OP and much closer to the roadblock. As the tanks moved up the road toward the roadblock, the imperative of our fire mission rent the airwaves. At the first explosions, the tanks wheeled and ran off the road into brush and disappeared from sight. Not even a gun muzzle peeked cautiously between the leaves.

No sooner had we beaten back this first run at the roadblock than a platoon of infantry appeared, making a sweep up the road to envelop the roadblock. Another fire mission brought a dose of high-explosive shells in an almost instantaneous response. Black smoke and dust gathered into a low cloud and then slowly floated away. When it cleared, the enemy platoon had scattered from sight. Somewhere in the tall grasses below the trees men lay as still as they could, panting at the quick escape from death.

Then three light tanks came up the road. I called for Concentration 359 again. It lashed and scattered them.

It had been a busy time before breakfast that morning, but, of course, there was no breakfast. The assaults continued.

After the second run by the three light tanks, I spotted a new threat: bicycle troops, the first bit of astonishment for the day. Each day brought something new, but juxtaposed against the growl, the armor, the guns of the panzers, the bicycles floated a surrealistic image into view. For a moment the scene projected innocence itself, the men on bikes, rifles across their backs, pedaling along the country road as if on an outing or a picnic, the road stretching away behind them. I called for time fire. Showers of torn steel rained down and blackened the air, shattering the image. Another assault by tanks followed, aimed at punching through the roadblock. The scoresheet showed five attacks in that first hour.

Not much after 9:00, a platoon of infantry marched up the road. There was no end to it. Again, we called for time fire. A concentration exploded over and around the enemy and blistered their approach. The bursting shells blotted out the landscape with a massive, black smudge and a hell of whirling, knife-like pieces of steel. The barrage drove the enemy troops into hiding. Minutes later, I reported by radio to the Fire Direction Center at battalion headquarters that a prisoner taken at the roadblock had informed us that a "new panzer division was on our front, that things were cooling off, resistance to the southeast was lessening, German resistance decreasing."[1] We did not believe the story. This prisoner was a plant, just a clever *ruse de guerre* to make us less vigilant. We kept our guard up.

The unending succession of fire missions squeezed a large dose of adrenaline into my system as I observed and adjusted shell bursts through the binoculars, my gun sight. Sasser's soft radio voice belied the undercurrent of tension and excitement at the OP. The stream of activity, of shooting up enemy tanks, troops, guns and vehicles—even bicycles—cut through the enveloping fatigue, and masked it. The fierce power of our artillery, blasting away tirelessly day and night, and the threats from the enemy that lurked in the brush and behind the hedgerows below, now and then coming out to lunge and roar at us, gave an edge of excitement that buoyed my spirits, made me feel that I was making a difference.

The next day—August 10—after shooting up an enemy column of vehicles, I sent this message:

> As sleepy, tired, and hungry as I am, I never felt so good as I feel right now.[2]

Our infantry, however, out along the Bel-Air Road, and also north on the trail that connected with the road to Ger, sticking into hostile space like the proverbial sore thumb, alone, isolated, also experienced surges of adrenaline but hardly laced with the exhilaration that came over me. Sergeant Joe Zaraza, a 20-year-old, led a squad of 14 men at the roadblock where they had dug shallow foxholes along the gravelly Bel-Air Road and in the fields that bordered the trail. Bushes and trees provided some obscurity, but no cover. Later his squad of 14 would be augmented by another 16 or so men, some from E Company, others from the small part of H Company that had escaped when the German counterattack had overwhelmed their position below the Hill on the les Aubrils Road.

The .30-caliber M-1 rifles of the infantrymen fired semiautomatically, one shot every time the trigger was pulled, a fine, hard-hitting, killing weapon against other infantry, but of no value against armor. They had a bazooka, but no other antitank weapons. By this fourth day, the reserve of ammunition for the bazooka had dwindled to not more than a round or two, if there was any left at all.

Theirs was only visual resistance against an armored attack, at best a token, one of spirit only. When the Germans attacked, the infantry at the roadblock would wait for the rescuing artillery, for a wall of exploding steel just beyond them down the road, at times bewilderingly close. If, despite the shelling, the tanks rolled forward, they would pick up from their positions at the roadblock, scramble into the high grass and scrub and take cover behind the hedgerows in the adjacent fields. They maintained a presence, waited, listened for the rumble of tanks; and when the tanks had gone, they came back and waited. Time and again. Brave men manned the roadblock and held on with virtually nothing. The days for them were beyond counting, as exhaustion grew and hope diminished.

These brave men were prepared to die. Joe would say later: "I know that I would have been killed. It is not in my nature to surrender." Two decorations for battlefield valor, three Purple Hearts, part of one hand blown away, make evident that his words were not a boastful afterthought. But there was more to Joe Zaraza than mere stubbornness. In another battle, Joe's squad forced enemy soldiers, hands held high in surrender, out of their snipers' nest in a battered building. One of his squad wanted to execute the prisoners on the spot. Joe turned to his men and put the matter to rest simply: "We can't shoot 'em. We'd be just like them."

Within the hour after the enemy infantry platoon had attacked and retreated as artillery fire thundered down on it, a large number of enemy vehicles drove up the Bel-Air Road a few hundred yards east of the roadblock. I called in the artillery. High-explosive shells found their targets easily. Like the tanks, they pulled hard off the road and into cover. By this time there were many troops, tanks and vehicles—not counting the two-wheelers—hiding in the brush.

The vehicles that we had just forced off the Bel-Air Road were not out for a drive and could only be bringing up infantry for an assault. We soon found that out. Sometime during the morning, the enemy overran the roadblock and occupied it. Artillery fire smashed down and drove them off. Our infantry rushed back and reoccupied their former position, ready once more for the next assault—with only their rifles, for which they now had almost no bullets.

The Germans had attacked the men at the roadblock unceasingly during the morning. I had drawn in the ring of protective artillery fire, ever closer, as the assaults came on, now almost in waves. We felt the noose tighten.

Americans in position behind a hedgerow near Mortain, August 9, 1944

National Archives

15   *"Surrender or Die"*

Shortly before 2:30 the afternoon of that fourth day, a convoy of enemy trucks and other vehicles drove up the Bel-Air Road and slowly pulled to a stop 600 or 700 yards below the roadblock. Hordes of infantry in gray-green uniforms poured out of the vehicles and quickly formed a skirmish line stretching across the road and into the adjacent fields and behind hedgerows. Then they waited for a signal to advance. The trucks slowly backed and turned on the road to move off to the rear.

Fire Mission. Infantry forming skirmish line.

The officer at the Fire Direction Center must have sensed that, coming on top of all of the other assaults that day, this one was significant, intended as a clincher. He requested support from other artillery. Within moments three battalions of artillery, "Crow," "Curtis" and "Crunch,"[1] showered down an impenetrable and punishing bombardment. Twenty-four 105mm howitzers and a battalion of 155mm howitzers lashed out together, stopping the attack before it got under way, and leaving the area torn and smoking. The powerful impact of all those guns firing together scattered the enemy infantry and bruised them badly.

But it brought us no relief. Within minutes our radio called out to artillery headquarters:

Need supplies badly.

A quarter of an hour later, I made it more specific:

Need medical supplies. Wounded are dying.[2]

The enemy shelled us again, this time from a large gun some-place to the east. The frightful boom of its exploding shells was alien, full of evil and of such immensity that it shivered the rock and dirt beneath us. We suspected that it was the same gun that had tried to get the range when our OP was at the high crags. Our hopes continued that an airplane spotter could pick up its location and that our bigger guns would destroy it.

As the afternoon wore on into early evening we spotted more vehicles and then motorcycles withdrawing wounded in front of K Company along the trail that connected the Bel-Air Road with the Ger Road. Concentration 359 did its job once more on the Bel-Air Road, and its brother, Concentration 360, scattered the enemy in front of K Company. Our fire had taken a bloody toll on the enemy.

Tank and infantry attacks and the crushing fire of our artillery had followed one another in never-ending sequence, like cat-and-mouse gambits and countermoves. The Germans had not gained a yard. They changed tactics.

Early that evening, sometime after 6:00 p.m., a little parade filed across the field from the tree-covered ridge to the rear into the E Company perimeter. It consisted of one German officer preceded by a single soldier carrying a white flag.

One of Lieutenant Kerley's platoon leaders met the officer and his flag bearer. Speaking in English with great formality, he stated that he was an officer of the SS and offered honorable conditions of surrender. The Germans, he said, knew they had surrounded the 2d Battalion, 120th Infantry, 30th Infantry Division. They had taken many prisoners, and he alluded to several officers whom they had captured, including a Lieutenant Pike. He professed that he personally admired the stand the battalion had made, but the American position was hopeless; and it would not be a disgrace to surrender under the circumstances. The German officer then promised that the men would be well cared for and that the wounded would be given all possible aid. He added that if the battalion did not surrender by eight o'clock, it would be "blown to bits."

The platoon officer refused to surrender. The little parade turned about and marched back into the trees to the west. The platoon leader dispatched a runner with the German officer's message to Kerley at his command post.[3]

What did Kerley know that would affect his decision?

First, American forces had failed to fight through the encircling enemy and clear a path to the battalion. Rations were gone. Men now foraged for cabbages, rutabagas, turnips, anything that might drive off the dangerous weakness that came with hunger and the void that followed hunger, a state of numb disarray as if one were shuffling in and out of consciousness.

As for the rest of it, Kerley would later recall:[4]

The wounded were collected in each company and placed in slit-trenches. They were made as comfortable as possible; however, there was no medical aid available.

Presence of the dead did not serve to raise morale. Since most of the dead were in exposed positions, it was necessary to wait until dark to collect them. They, too, were placed in a central location in each company area, out of sight. Although the men knew the bodies had not been evacuated from the Hill, they couldn't see them, and the same purpose was served as if they had been evacuated.

The ammunition supply had dwindled to practically nothing. Several of the severely wounded died during the night. The bodies of the dead, both our own and the enemy, were deteriorating fast in the warm August sun, and the stench on the Hill was nauseating. The future looked anything but bright, and morale was on a rapid decline.

The enemy had no doubt been monitoring our radio and knew the existing situation....

That is what Kerley knew.

His answer was short, to the point and in those days "very un-printable."[5] The exact words have been lost, but it matched the fire in Kerley's belly.

The battalion would stand its ground.

That day, five of us shared some bits of chocolate and one K-ration, normally a single meal for one person. Later on, a caring rifleman shoved a rutabaga at me. It was an act of special kindness for which I was grateful. I cut the thing into large chunks and slowly ate the moist, tasteless cellulose, filling some of the empty spots in my gut, but not relieving my hunger. I have never eaten another.

Not long after the surrender demand, at 7:15 p.m., I again radioed our need for help—for ambulances—for the wounded.

That night, each man gripped his gun, ready for a final fight. The numerous daylight attacks had come one after the other with no appreciable letup. After the threat from the SS officer, we waited for darkness to bring more.

As the last rays of twilight slanted through the trees across the rocks, approximately at 9:45, I alerted the Fire Direction Center to shoot along a designated line to the front that straddled the directions by which the enemy might come at us in the night. What we requested was:

> ...fire...throughout night—at least one gun every five minutes.[6]

Again, almost at midnight, I radioed:

> Germans building up strong reserves on all sides. Request you fire immediately. Heavy for first hour.[7]

There was only a chance that all of this shelling would hold off the enemy. We had not given up as demanded. The German officer had promised to blow us to bits if we did not surrender. The earth and rocks into which we burrowed sucked up heat from our bodies, and we shivered in the night air. In the darkness, we hunched down nervously below the crest, listened to the explosions of our own, unrelenting artillery. Nobody spoke. Nobody needed to. We all knew that in the black of night we would make our stand. We waited.

While we lay there, I carefully sighted along the barrel of a .30-caliber carbine that I had picked up from someone who no longer needed it, aiming at the crest looming in the dark, black against black, a few yards away. My Colt .45 was on a flat rock where I could reach it quickly with my right hand. Unless the enemy came from the rear again, I was ready. For whatever reason, we expected an attack down the Bel-Air Road and across the crest of the ridge. Perhaps we thought this because all of the attacks during the day had come from that direction. Perhaps we reasoned that because the German officer with the surrender demand had come from the rear, their main force would come at us another way. With so little information we could believe almost anything in the dead of night.

I was glad that I had the carbine. The Colt .45 was not sufficient for the job. I gripped the stock, squeezed the wood, wiggled the butt-end against my shoulder. But something wasn't right. At times as I scrambled about on the rocks and scraped at the soil, and at night for warmth, I wore a pair of lightweight leather gloves. Now they came between me and the gun and interfered with a close feel of it. We had to be prepared to shoot fast, no delays, no getting ready. The gloves were useful, but wearing them gave me too many fingers and thumbs when survival was at stake. I took off the gloves, removed the lineman's knife from the leather case on my belt and hacked off the ends of the fingers of the gloves, down close to the palms. My fingers now protruded through the grimy, scarred remnants, touching steel and wood. It was a good feeling. I fussed with the carbine, worked the mechanism softly. With the cut-down gloves, I could now handle the gun comfortably—load it, shoot it and clear it if it jammed. I folded the knife blade and replaced it in the case. The longest night ticked on.

We expected waves of enveloping infantry with automatic weapons and rifles like the night before, only more of them. We had seen infantry ready to attack several times during daylight. In the night we would not be able to see them until they were on top of us. The air cooled rapidly in the darkness as night pressed down. Men fussed with their rifles. Ears strained at every scrape and sound. But no enemy infantry attacked. I had needlessly mutilated a pair of L.L. Bean deerskin gloves. Instead, tanks assaulted us repeatedly. Artillery fire drove them off. The ring of exploding steel held.

As the night wore on, each second seemed slower than the last. Attacks came, and artillery blasted away, holding them off. But if tanks ever smashed through into our position, artillery would be useless.

Then it happened.

A tank crashed through the incoming shells, brushed past the roadblock and rumbled south off the road into our position, stopping less than 50 yards away on the crest of the ridge above us. We crouched low behind the black rocks, helmets sliding down over our necks, throats dry, palms moist. It was his move.

Men held their guns at the ready. The tank fired first, two or three rounds over our heads to get our attention, as if that were needed. The muzzle blasts lit up the rocks and brush in front of the tank, throwing long shadows down the slope toward us. We stayed down, as low as possible, scarcely daring to breathe. The turret banged open. A helmeted figure pushed part way up through the opening and looked around. He shouted demandingly at us in plain English, "Surrender or die!"

No one moved. The tank commander hesitated. Rifles took aim, ready to fire. Then one man threw down his gun, ran up the slope and climbed onto the tank. The rest of us stood fast and held our breaths. No one else surrendered. And no one died, either. The turret slammed angrily shut like a hammer on an anvil. The tank backed and drove off, treads clanking and slapping against the rock and loose stones on the ridge.

A lone prisoner clung to the side.

16 Remembrance

It is 1995 again.

A friend of mine who has read an early draft of this book has asked me what I said when that rifleman gave up to save his skin, and I am trying to remember. What would you have said? I suppose I cursed him. That's what the unwritten rules of war and human conduct suggest. But, as I write, I am not sure. Perhaps, I only heaved a sigh of relief, glad that the tank had banged off across the top of the ridge and disappeared down the Bel-Air Road. Just as easily, I could have cursed, but in pity, "The poor, miserable, son of a bitch." Or, squeezed the stock of my carbine all the harder, hunkered down in my foxhole and waited—for the next tank, for the next shelling, for the next assault.

And for death.

The story of the men on the Hill is about not giving up, but not all men will stay and fight to the death. When that man threw down his rifle and quit the fight, he surrendered openly to the fear that the rest of us bottled up. I won't pretend to remember *now* how I felt about him *then* or what I said. It would have been pointless then to waste dwindling reserves of energy on the disappearing rifleman, a small event that didn't count for much when measured against all the others. We turned away from him with foreboding of what might yet come, and quivered for ourselves in the uncertain dark of that night.

But, there is a clue about what must have been in the minds of most as we held tightly to the barest fingerhold of survival. In a box of old letters and notes, some dated before the war, I recently found a black, pocket-sized notebook, edges and spine carefully bound with tape to prevent fraying. Inside the front and back covers I had long ago neatly printed my name, now only slightly faded, along with rank and army serial number. Just below my name on the inside front cover, the date "Feb 14," boldly inked, slants up to the right.

A collection of my writings or jottings, most apparently written during lulls in actual combat, almost fills the notebook. There is a short essay on industrial production, economics, social goals and needs. Serious poetry. The beginning of a romantic short story takes up many pages, at first neatly printed in ink—before the ballpoint had been invented, and as the ink obviously ran out, in pencil with the printing turning into a rapidly scribbled scrawl that runs on and on. Hung here and there between the more serious bits are lots of little quips and sayings that I must have thought were funny or pertinent at the time, like "The only way I'll ever get shellshocked will be eating too many peanuts," or "I may be dumb, but you must admit there is a certain quality about it," or "It was a wonderful feeling. We were going home." There is a brief sketch for another short story and a scenario for a play—about war and hate.

And I came across a longer outline for a story about war and battle and the kind of morality that binds men together at such times. In the outline I called for scenes like Mortain. I wrote:

> ...Casualties mount til they are around 1 in 4....[Forward observer] contemplates this and reaches the conclusion that somebody in his party of 4 should be about due. Also as the dead average 1 in 4 or 5...there should be a dead man in the next few casualties. The thought should be developed until it bears down on the reader with the same horrible weight and moment that it squeezes down on the [Forward observer]....Who will it be? Leave that to the reader.

As I leafed through the little notebook, a folded slip of paper fell out. I opened it carefully, mindful that it was fragile with age. On the inside were four lines of neatly penned rhymed verse, about a darkened, ebbing sea and stars beyond sight. I turned the slip over. It was from a German desk calendar, the kind with a single small sheet for each day and holes punched at the side for a ringed mounting so that each day a new sheet could be turned into place. It bore the date, in German, of March 27. At the upper left in very small print was "1945."

February, March 1945—when I wrote those lines calling up memories of Mortain, barely six months had passed since the rifleman had scrambled onto the tank and vanished into enemy hands.

17 Sunshine and Other Military Technology

Request fire all defensive concentrations. Unable to contact after this message.

This message was an unequivocal call for help. We took cover. It was midmorning, August 10, our fifth day on the Hill. Our fourth fire mission of the day ripped across the countryside and left a trail of drifting, black smoke.

But, the situation had become mixed. Beginning before the previous midnight and continuing past 3:00 a.m. into the void of early morning, the sounds of heavy movement of enemy vehicles broke the silence, overlaying the usual tones of nighttime scrapes, snaps and distant booms with new vibrations, deep hums and whines. These noises rose in a crescendo and then softened, falling away for brief instants and then starting up again as many trucks got under way. We also recognized the special sounds of tanks and other track-laying vehicles.

Daylight lit up clouds of dust that glowered angrily in the sun, stirred up by columns that moved east. We reported enemy troops retreating in "large numbers." The movement continued all day. We adjusted artillery fire shooting up trucks and tanks in what appeared to be retreat. In late afternoon one fire mission began:

Fire Mission. Two tanks, two guns and infantry. Ambulance towing one of the guns.

At one point, we observed friendly troops to the south and to the east. A hopeful sign, but not enough to convince us that the enemy really was retreating. If the Germans were giving up the attack, they had an unusual way of showing it. All day long heavy artillery and *nebelwerfers*, those multibarreled rocket launchers known as "screaming meemies," pummeled the Hill. Enemy infantry and tanks hovered in our front yard. We tore at them with high-explosive shells.

Despite an early optimism that the enemy was retreating, as the day moved on it appeared to us on the Hill that he may instead have been realigning his position or concentrating his forces elsewhere. In the small window to the immediate east, we saw enemy infantry and tanks not in retreat. Throughout the day, shells and rockets exploded around the E Company position. In the waning light of "double British summertime,"[1] we shot at enemy tanks and then at tanks and infantry prowling within 1,000 yards of E Company. As late as 8:45 that evening, our artillery destroyed two platoons of enemy infantry, as close to the roadblock as any infantry had come at any time during the siege. The German presence was too intimate for comfort. We swallowed hard and reluctantly accepted that we had been mistaken in believing that the Germans were now in retreat.

Batteries for the radio were our main and critical concern. As long as the siege continued to batter us regularly with artillery and rockets, as long as there were infantry and tanks to our immediate front, as long as no relief came, maintenance of the defense, which only communication by radio made possible, was paramount.

For several days now we had been using two sets of batteries in relays. After the initial encirclement, during those hours of mounting uncertainty when the Germans were first coming on with infantry and bedeviling us with sniper fire, Dan Garrott, putting his life on the line, made the first of several runs that he would make to the jeep. He brought back the extra set of radio batteries that we carried with us. Armon Sasser, like everyone else, had been accustomed to operating with as many batteries as were needed, readily available through normal supply channels. When the first set was no longer at full power, he had followed the usual procedure, disassembled the batterypack and replaced the batteries inside with the second set that Garrott had rescued from the jeep. At that point, no one expected that we would be without supplies for long. But when the second set grew weak and the Germans continued to pummel us, Sasser invented a new procedure.

The first, discarded set of batteries had been lying close by, warming in the sun. Sasser disassembled the radio from the batterypack and removed the second set of batteries. He laid them carefully in a protected space surrounded by rocks where the direct rays of the sun would strike and heat them. A warm battery works better than a cold one as anybody knows who has tried to start a car on a cold winter morning. Sasser was determined to squeeze every last bit of power that he could out of the two sets of batteries that we had.

"Let's hope that this will work," he said to us.

Now he put the first set of batteries to work for the second time, batteries that had been "resting" from the day before—a discarded set under normal conditions. They seemed adequate. The Fire Direction Center could receive us clearly.

Sasser then began a little cooking operation, giving the batteries an intravenous injection of energy from the sun. No army training manual listed sunshine as an item of materiel, but there was plenty of it. Sasser put it to use effectively. What he did was to disassemble the batterypack several times a day, switching from one set of batteries to the other, never using one set so long that it was in danger of running down to the point of no return. The set that was not in use was placed in direct sunlight, soaking up the sun's warmth. He tried to gauge the alternation so that at night we would have two sets of batteries, each with some reserve power. Rotation and energizing of the batteries in the sun became a serious ritual. No one, however, thought to gather them up at night and hold them close and warm them with body heat, like eggs under a hen.

Care and nurturing of the batteries had buzzed through Sasser's head almost from the beginning. Since the second day, when the Germans began the attack, he had routinely switched the radio off except when transmitting. It was improbable that he would be able to keep the batteries alive much longer.

Meanwhile, our division headquarters had been negotiating with the Army Air Corps trying to cajole it into dropping supplies to us. Communication between the services was not easy. The Army Air Corps bureaucracy had its own set of problems and objectives and its own tangle of red tape. It first needed to make reconnaissance flights, and its procedures for scheduling such flights were slow-moving. Our division headquarters requested air supply to us through dual channels of communication at least four times before there was a positive response.[2] On the Hill we had no knowledge of these efforts or that they had at last been successful.

Late in the afternoon, on August 10, American fighter planes unexpectedly burst out of the skies and strafed and dive-bombed several areas in front of us. Then the planes circled and streaked across the battalion's position at low altitude. Men jumped for cover, fearing that our position had been mistaken for the enemy's, but the planes roared by. In 30 minutes they roared by again, this time escorting low-flying cargo planes displaying U.S. insignia on their wings and fuselages, and gliding in from the west low over our heads. It was a glorious sight! We stood up and cheered! Clouds of blue and orange parachutes floated down, little bundles from heaven, swinging gently in the late afternoon sunlight.

But the bundles from heaven continued to float down in the direction of the glide path of the planes, teasing us with their swinging motions as they drifted eastward. Our hearts had risen into our throats with joy and hope. Now they plummeted into our empty stomachs and congealed into hard lumps of disbelief, as the parachutes settled down and collapsed in enemy territory. Kerley organized patrols quickly and sent them out to try to recover the supplies. It was risky business. The patrols gathered up some food along with ammunition and possibly a few mortar shells. They did not recover any medical supplies or batteries for our radio. German troops recovered most of the bundles.

The Army Air Corps tried a second drop the following morning. The first flawed attempt by comparison was a brilliant success. The second was a complete and total failure.

Each hour of daylight, each little unit of sunpower was now more precious than ever. We clung stubbornly to our lifeline.

Later that evening, after the first airdrop, our artillery battalion began an experiment in an effort to deliver medical supplies by shooting them to us in artillery shells. The same old laws of physics, those of forces and motion, those that kept the earth turning and revolving around the sun, the sun whose heat kept the electrons flowing in our batteries, would also doom this attempt. Simple analysis could have predicted the result.

At headquarters of the 230th Field Artillery, somebody—we don't know who, maybe an officer, maybe a mechanic—opened base ejection smoke shells by unscrewing the baseplates. This in itself was a feat—not only because of the general fear of explosion—but because no special-purpose wrench was immediately available, and he had to loosen the baseplate with a hammer and a screwdriver.

Then he removed smoke canisters and base ejection charges, and placed a steel disc in the nose of the projectiles, replacing the fuse which, if detonated, would have destroyed the contents. Medics then packed each of the empty shells with bandages, cotton, adhesive tape, morphine syrettes and sulpha drugs, all carefully wrapped and padded with cotton. They also inserted mixed plasma into one shell.

Other projectiles were similarly emptied and filled with sand to a weight estimated to approximate that of the "medical shells." Fire Direction Center radioed instructions to us for opening the "medical shells." Of course no one on the Hill had a hammer or screwdriver. The infantry did have bayonets, and rocks covered the hillside. At about 9:00 in the evening the battalion began test firing the sand-loaded projectiles.[3]

A crowd of infantry gathered with us around the rocky promontory to the left of our OP. The Fire Direction Center radioed to us:

"Dud on the way." When we received "on the way" over the radio, we shouted it out for all to hear. The infantry had been instructed and stationed to watch for the shells and report to me where they fell. It was expected that the distribution would be very erratic. Poor communications and ricochets on the reverse slope to our front compounded the effort to adjust these one-of-a-kind shells. Of course, we had to do this without the benefit of the smoke and sound that normally accompanied impact. We were trying to spot shells as they whizzed through the air over us and then struck the ground in front and bounced.

Knowing that the incoming shells were experimental and subject to great error made everyone nervous. It was difficult to keep eyes east and not duck when "on the way" was shouted. Altogether, about an hour of precious radio and battery time was needed to complete the adjustment—as contrasted with the seconds and at most minute or two that targeting of the enemy normally took. The drain on our batteries was tremendous—and no "medical shells" had yet been fired—only sand-filled duds.

The gun that was doing the shooting was nearly three and a half miles to our rear, using a low charge and a compensating elevation of the gun barrel. When the adjustment was finally completed, "Medical round on the way" was radioed to us. Six "medical shells" were fired at five- to ten-minute intervals. At around midnight we reported to Fire Direction Center that none of the shells had been located. The inability of the naked eye to spot a shell going by overhead as well as darkness and enemy sniper fire made recovery impossible. We would have to see in another dawn before determining the results of this bit of technological improvisation.

Back at field artillery battalion headquarters, however, the operations officer continued to stir the pot. He thought he was on to something. At one o'clock in the morning, he awakened the battalion surgeon. The operations officer wanted to fire six additional shells to us as soon as possible after dawn. The surgeon and his aid men lit a lantern in the aid station and went to work. They assembled more supplies and carefully packed them into empty shells. In the meantime, the operations officer had also secured five 155mm-base-ejection shells to be filled with medical supplies, also to be fired in the morning by a "Long Tom" unit. The surgeon and his men worked busily for hours.

By eight o'clock on the morning of August 11, battalion had fired six more shells.[4] At 10:15 a.m. that morning we reported that a total of five shells had been recovered, whether fresh off the vine or from the previous vintage we did not know. Somehow the infantry unscrewed the baseplates, despite having no tools other than bayonets, knives, rocks and similar implements. The infantry aid man crowded his way into the front row, anxious to get his hands on the promised medical supplies. What came out was an almost homogenous lump. The individual medical supplies, so carefully packed inside, had been jammed together and entangled in a solid, heavy mass.

Dan Garrott and I remember looking in amazement at what had once been wide rolls of adhesive tape, now smashed down into flat discs less than half an inch thick. A fine dust of sulpha powder coated the interior of the shell casing and the almost unrecognizable contents. All of the glass morphine syrettes had disintegrated. Perhaps the medic managed to disentangle some little bit of the bandages and gauze and scrape up and salvage some loose sulpha powder. If so, a nominal amount was recovered. Hardly enough to be helpful. When we really were to need it—desperately—there would be none.

It is not hard to envision why this experiment could never have worked. When a "medical shell" was fired, it went from zero velocity to many hundreds of feet per second before it was out of the gun barrel. This tremendous force *to the rear* squashed the contents hard against the baseplate of the shell, just as if it had been jammed there by a piston inside the shell. When the shell landed and the forward motion suddenly stopped, it all worked in reverse. Of course, because the payload had already been compressed at the firing, there was now room for it to travel forward inside the shell, perhaps giving a little extra snap to the impact, which shoved the glass morphine syrettes, the adhesive tape, the packages of sulpha powder and bandages into the nose of the shell. Although the garbage compactor had not then been invented, the contents looked as if they had been run through one.

The battle reports describing this experiment, written by men who were not there on the Hill to see the results, indicate a degree of success. Even those reports, however, are conflicting.[5] At E Company, where the bulk of the shells were targeted, the experiment, like the airdrops, only confirmed how far we were beyond the reach of help.

After the excitement of the airdrop and the diversion brought by the firing of the "medical shells," the night of August 10 was relatively calm.

Shelling of likely avenues of enemy approach increased. After nightfall our artillery fired on a scheduled basis, more heavily than before. We did not know that this was because in other sectors, where the 30th Division had been engaged, the fighting had grown less intense. The ring of explosive fire laid down was too hazardous for the enemy to attempt to breach our positions at night.

With the first airdrop, hope had crested and flooded us with a frothy jubilation which was sucked out a heartbeat later. More than ever, we looked to the radio, husbanded the batteries, refused to abandon the stubborn hope that we created within ourselves. Uncomplicated but intelligent methods *and sunshine* did more for us than any technological expedients. Laying batteries in the sun and carefully rotating them succeeded. By contrast, the prodigious effort needed to carry out the two airdrops and the techno-heroic exertions expended on the "medical shells" accomplished little.

In the final summing up, we looked to simple measures and to ourselves for survival.

18 Last Chance

The abortive airdrop and the firing of the second group of "medical shells" threw the dust of hope into our eyes. When our vision cleared, we confronted tanks and infantry attacking from the east. It was now the morning of August 11, the sixth day on the Hill. Sasser's voice, dry and hoarse, echoed the familiar chant which I began once again:

Fire Mission. Two enemy tanks.

The panzers had butted in, once again, down the dirt trail that connected the Ger Road on the north with the Bel-Air Road. They tried to hustle past the K Company entrenchment around Bonvoisin, but the violent eruption of shells on all sides forced them to retreat, trailing clouds of dust. Had they continued down the trail only 200 or 300 yards—a couple of city blocks at most—they would have broken into the midst of G Company and the northern tip of E Company. If the enemy had resolved to break into our lines, the howitzers' roar melted their resolve. The number of times that the enemy had faltered at a decisive moment grew ever larger.

Again I turned to Sasser:

Fire Mission. Tanks and infantry advancing.

This time the enemy aimed an assault straight at E Company's roadblock on the Bel-Air Road, about 800 yards away. They didn't make it. Artillery drove them into hiding.

Despite these persistent attacks, we developed confidence that aid would reach us by noon, though it is impossible to identify the genesis of this belief. Maybe it flared up from the dry summer grasses, erupting suddenly like a prairie fire. Why noon? A rumor touched off by hunger, raw indignation, visions of food and lunch would focus on noontime. We were certain that we would be relieved by then.

But no relief and no lunch came into our lives that day.

Elsewhere, however, the battle was going better for the American forces. At Fire Direction Center, the keeper of the Message Log made an entry at 12:35, not long after that hoped-for noon, stating that our troops had occupied Hill 285 to the north and: "Not many Germans. Pocket gone." By 3:15 that afternoon, he recorded that "Friendly troops have entered Mortain." Other reports showed the enemy withdrawing.[1]

We knew none of this. On Hill 314, we waged a savage fight to the death.

The Hill continued to be a last point of aggressive action in the Battle of Mortain. The enemy attacked and pounded persistently, brutally punishing the troops on the Hill when the Battle of Mortain was essentially over.

Why did the Germans continue to hammer at us when elsewhere they were pulling out and retreating? Perhaps they believed that if they occupied the Hill their artillery could cover the retreat of their forces better. From the Hill they could have seen American forces to the south and to the east. But if they had been successful in occupying the Hill, they would have put themselves in the same position, and subject to the same risk of destruction we faced.

Violence and malice centered on the Hill without letup, almost like some kind of Wagnerian vengeance, playing itself out as the attack collapsed in catastrophic disorder, costing the enemy the Battle of France and ultimately the war. In the end, the Germans would suffer most from the violence that they had set in motion. It may have been that the troops who originally had the mission of taking the Hill were unable to face the realization that a small force of Americans without tanks or antitank guns had held off a larger, heavily equipped and superior force. Another possibility is that a higher command left them to boil in the juice of failure, enduring the ultimate fate of being unsuccessful. The Greeks put it simply: "If you don't come back with your shield, come back on it."

What is most likely is that the German tank and infantry units which attacked from the front and the rear, encircling the Hill, did not communicate with the rest of von Kluge's task force and believed the Germans were still attacking successfully. A friend and older mentor, a wise man who was meticulous in the use of language, once patiently explained to me that he had spent a lifetime being misunderstood. In a fast-moving, chaotic battlefield situation where communication is not precisely framed and is at best fragmentary, it is very likely that the Germans faced off against us as blind to what was happening elsewhere as we were.

The carnage continued all day.

In the late afternoon I was alone on the crest of the ridge at the large foxhole that was our OP. I have no recollection where Sasser, Garrott and Corn had gone, perhaps for water or to carry a message from me to Kerley. In any case, if Sergeant Sasser had been with me, the story would be incomplete. Nearby a number of infantry, probably five or six, milled around nervously, waiting for rescue, for water, for word that it was over.

Now, from the western ridge of the Hill itself, the Germans brought heavy weapons to bear. First, tanks shelled E Company's position, blasting us from somewhere on the southwest knob of Hill 314, where a tiny, stone chapel, not on our map, "La Petite Chapelle," perched, obscured by trees from our view except for the tip of its spire.

Then, a new explosion ripped the air. Lethal bombs plummeted from the tops of covert arcs, falling nearly straight down, arriving unannounced. Everyone hit the dirt, flattened low in the grass, tried to find shelter against rock outcroppings. Mortar fire! With barely a whisper, the mortar shells dropped out of the sky—one at a time as if from a single mortar—all around the OP. Each exploded with a violent, blistering roar, intensely jarring because it was unexpected. Like the shelling we had just received from the tanks, the enemy had lobbed these shells from our rear, from the west.

U.S. soldiers search the rubble of Mortain for enemy troops.

The fuss with the medical shells the night before and that morning had drawn the enemy's attention to our position. The lookouts, the relays and the general interest in that curious development drew a crowd around the OP and to the rocky promontory close by to the left of it. If the Germans took note of these gatherings of our troops, they would have marked the location as a place of special importance where troops would assemble again. As well, they might have observed me at the OP. Logically, the next step for them was to set up a mortar, ready to fire when the next opportunity came.

The mortar is a remarkable weapon, more remarkable because it is so crude and simple, and at first glance unlikely to hit anything at all. Basically, it is a piece of unrifled steel pipe, a few feet long, with the sealed or bottom end resting on a heavy metal baseplate, and supported closer to the upper end with a metal bipod, usually threaded, so that the barrel can be raised or lowered. The weapon breaks down easily into its separate parts and can be carried by several men and set up anywhere. The projectile, which is shaped somewhat like a little bomb, is dropped down the pipe. As simple as that. When it hits bottom, a charge explodes and propels the little bomb into the air in a very high arc. Because the tube is pointed upward at a high angle, almost no warning sounds when the mortar fires. Gravity and the atmosphere affect the projectile's trajectory, and the shell drops almost straight down from the sky to the target, where it explodes on impact. Despite its crude simplicity, mortar fire is highly accurate. Our light mortars were capable of shooting more than a pound of high explosives approximately one mile. German mortars would have done the same because there is no significant technology involved in the weapon. In any case, the German mortar was half that distance away. We were within easy range.

After the first barrage stopped, one infantryman jumped into the OP foxhole with me. I shouted to the others to lie still.

"Keep down. Don't draw their fire."

Silence lulled us for a moment or two. Some of the infantry raised their heads and looked around. Others huddled down, waiting for the inevitable. One man got up and ran, streaking off into the brush where he disappeared.

The shelling began again with intensive ferocity. Whroom! Whroom! Each shell cracked the air, exploding in waves. The harsh ripples fanned our faces, but the shells hit no one.

Then, a space of tranquil minutes, designed to lure the unwary into the open. The riflemen waited. Nothing. A few moved gingerly, scrambled to other positions behind great chunks of boulders and into depressions in the rocks.

When the shelling and noise abated this second time, it was clear, to me at least, that the enemy could see us if we moved. If a single soldier showed himself, the Germans would believe that others were there, too. Any movement signaled *Fire Mission* to the German mortar. The explosions, the smoke and the dust that filled the air, covered a large area around us. To the enemy it must have looked as if they were devastating us.

I shouted again.

"Don't run. I'll shoot the next man who runs."

I waved my pistol. Another round came in and exploded nearby. Whroom! The enemy was testing. Only one round. Silence. Had they finished? Only the man next to me waited to see, because only in the movies do men take that kind of an order seriously. Like a covey of wild birds, the other men rose and rushed away to the south, disappearing in the dusty sunlight. I shouted again. Nobody paid any attention to my threat. In their haste to leave, I doubt if they heard me. It would have been pointless to shoot frightened, tired, soldiers, my own troops. We were all in the soup together. They knew it, called my bluff and left. The mortar blasted away again, fast on their flying heels.

The man lying in the foxhole with me shook and trembled in the dust. His body rose and fell, vibrating with each exploding round. His terror was extreme. I clearly remember lying next to him and wondering what it would be like if a mortar round came into our foxhole. I could almost hear the explosion even as it blew our eardrums out. I didn't know if we would feel pain, or if we would die instantly and never know what had happened. I could see arms and legs shredded and torn apart while our blood streamed slowly away with our lives to rest in the Hill forever. I lay still, held my breath, shook my head hard and squeezed my brain to shut out those thoughts.

Then the mortar stopped firing. My companion got up and ran, desperately, as fast as his shivering, tired body would take him, off into the brush until he fell gasping behind a rock or bush, wiping the sweat of terror off his brow. I listened. Except for shelling in the distance, no other sounds broke the dusty silence. I reached over cautiously and switched on the radio, gave a minimal report of the shelling to battalion Fire Direction Center, and then switched it off and waited for the next attack.

It never came.

Sergeant Sasser had gone not far away toward the right flank with Lieutenant Kerley and saw why.

One of the riflemen who had been at my OP came panting to Kerley, flung himself into the grass behind a rock and gasped out what had occurred. Kerley had seen the mortar shells bursting and wasted no time.[2] Kerley waved to his redheaded mortar sergeant and moved toward the left flank, out of the trees where the view to the rear was not blocked, but with good cover from boulders, scrub and tall grass. The redheaded sergeant followed, and Sasser came close behind.

On his belly, Kerley searched the fence line across the open pasture and the promontory to the west with his binoculars, swinging them slowly back and forth across the panorama. As he focused carefully, he saw men in gray-green uniforms squatting next to a mortar near the edge of the opposite ridge to the west. He handed the binoculars to his sergeant, pointed. The redheaded sergeant put the binoculars up, swept them from side to side, then steadied.

"Yes, sir. It's a mortar, all right. Several men."

"Sergeant, how many rounds do you have left?"

"One, sir."

"Hmm."

Kerley paused, thought for a moment, weighed the possibility of destroying the mortar across the way with that one round, and considered how valuable it might be against some future target, but as yet unknown and unseen.

"Do you think you can hit the son of a bitch?"

"Yes, sir. I reckon I can."

"Then blow his ass off."

"Yes, sir."

"Set up here, out of sight."

The sergeant mumbled one more "yes, sir" and left on a dead run, bent over, staying as low to the ground as he could. Kerley continued to watch the enemy mortar crew. At length, satisfied with what he had seen, he sat down behind a boulder, unfolded a ragged chunk of paper, the dirty, crumbling remains of his map,[3] and studied it carefully, checking his location, noting the position of the enemy mortar crew, using the end of a knife blade and his gritty thumb nail to measure the distance on the map against the printed scale.

Minutes passed, a quarter of an hour, before the mortar sergeant returned with three men. He and two of them carried a 60mm mortar barrel, the baseplate and the remainder of the assembly. The third man, M-1 slung across his back, carried the last mortar shell, carefully cradling it in his two hands. The infantrymen crouched low as they set up the mortar. The rifleman clutched the mortar shell for dear life against his belly. He squatted next to a rock outcropping, leaning his back against its solid roughness.

Kerley showed the redheaded sergeant the rumpled map, pointed with his dirty finger. The sergeant looked up. Kerley handed him the glasses. He took them from Kerley and peered across at the ridge to the west, then down at the map. Back again to the west. They talked quietly for a while about yards and meters, distances, elevations.

The sergeant crawled on hands and knees over to the mortar, shook the baseplate with both hands, making sure it was as flat and solidly positioned as possible, sighted it ever so carefully, and adjusted the elevation screw. He brought the binoculars to his eyes and examined the target across the fields. Finally, he raised his eyes to the skies, searched for signs of wind in the leaves of the trees and bushes, scanned the clouds for any token. Hardly a breath of air stirred in the August afternoon.

He turned to Kerley, passed the binoculars back to him and nodded his head. Kerley nodded back. The redheaded sergeant held out his hands to the rifleman with the mortar shell. With great care the man stretched his hands out to the sergeant as if passing off a newborn babe. The sergeant took the shell, bent his head, pressed his parched, dusty lips against the metal casing and then lifted it up to the end of the barrel. Once more he turned his head toward Kerley. Then he let it drop and ducked.

"On the way."

The men hunched over as the shell hit bottom and fired. A small puff of smoke and a throaty "chung" sent it skyward. The late afternoon sun shone down gently. Kerley steadied the glasses. To the side of the enemy mortar, less than 10 yards away from it, a puff of black smoke suddenly erupted.

Kerley turned his head. He wasn't given to making wordy speeches. "Nice work, sergeant."

The redheaded mortar sergeant grinned. Kerley continued to watch through the binoculars. The mortar crew disappeared into the brush and trees.

19 "Without Reinforcements Can Hold Til Tomorrow"

The longest day is the day of unfulfilled hopes. How long it is depends on whether you measure in waking hours, by the number of times the Germans attacked, the number of enemy tanks you sighted, the number of mortar shells that exploded around us, how often the roadblock was overrun, the number of fire missions that we shot or by how many wounded went untreated or died. The seconds tick off as the men wait for the battle to end, counting each one, as hopes for rescue rise, fall, fade with twilight, counting on endlessly into the night.

There was no letup even as twilight darkened. Infantry outposts reported a "strong point" and mortar shells came from the left, close in along the trail running south from the Ger Road in front of K Company, little more than a football field's distance away. It looked like another attack, unless the Germans were taunting us, knowing we were incapable of sending out troops in strength sufficient to attack and destroy the intruders. In response to my call, the 105s chimed in with familiar music, and the black threat crumbled.

We teetered on the edge. When the day had started, we had pounded the enemy and driven him off to our front and been sure that rescue would be at hand soon, by noon, four or five hours away at the most. Why noon? It was a groundless rumor touched off by hunger, exhaustion, hope. As we realized our calculations were wrong, a congealing, creeping numbness overlaid all normal emotions.

If rescue was at hand, there would have been no need to attempt the fruitless airdrops or to experiment with "medical shells." The "medical shells," in particular, bespoke an act of desperation conceived from an inability to break through the German lines and relieve us. As morning drifted into afternoon and then passed into dark, the attacks on the Hill had continued: tanks and infantry to the front, tank fire from the rear, the blistering attack by the mortars.

No hopeful signs emerged. We did not know that there were now American troops in Mortain. If someone at Fire Direction Center had said: "The next time Baker 3 calls in, tell him we're in Mortain," it would have given us real cause for hope. But no one did.

On the western side of the Hill, to our rear, palisades of rock rose sharply from the central part of town. Houses and outbuildings straggled up the steep slopes almost to the edge of the small plateau that rested at the top. These houses and outbuildings were within a few yards of the southwestern knob of the Hill from which the mortar and tanks had shelled us so viciously in the afternoon. The shelling belied the fact that there were American troops in Mortain.

We could see no end. A little food from the first airdrop and water from the farmhouse had brought a bit of relief, but not even a flickering hope for the wounded who were dying. Our radio batteries had grown very weak. When they gave out, our principal means of defense would be lost.

No soldier endures so much with so little without becoming obsessed with a sense of ownership. The 2d Battalion had fought the Germans to a standstill for five days, and the Hill belonged to it. If we could hold out through this night....

We had communicated with battalion Fire Direction Center almost entirely for fire missions. As long as we continued to do that actively, as long as we were "shooting back," it was unlikely that they would fully appreciate how bad our situation was. When I reported that the wounded were dying, I had not said how many. We always spoke tersely when giving explanations and making requests for supplies. We radioed reports of attacks, such as the mortar attack that afternoon, in a matter-of-fact way with a minimum of detail and Fire Direction Center noted them briefly without explanatory detail in the Message Log as:

B3 receiving artillery and mortar fire from the west.

"Oh," you might say, "so the Germans are shelling Baker 3." There was nothing that told whether the artillery and mortar fire was light or intense, just a round or two or a devastating barrage. We had never given descriptive details. In the context of a killing war, what are a few shells more or less?

By nature, language is ambiguous, often vague. The speaker says "The wounded are dying." He sees the hundreds who have been hit. At the other end, the listeners hear only the bare words that have been spoken. Wounded men often do die. The listeners do not know from such a statement whether 10 or 100 are lying in pain. They do not see the carnage. They have not counted the dead.

But *two out of five* men on the Hill were dead, wounded, or missing. No message that I sent ever said that. At headquarters our command could not know it.

The element of luck—there is no other way to describe it—had been significant, as with the tank that had rolled through the roadblock and called for our surrender but then failed to follow through and call in additional tanks and troops to overrun our position. But even luck eventually runs out.

The way the men had scattered in the face of the mortar attack that afternoon hung vividly in my mind. The man shaking beside me in the foxhole at the OP was not shaking with patriotism. Creeping terror and desperation had overcome him and filled his heart with undiluted fear. We had no knowledge of what was understood at headquarters. But it seemed unlikely that the commanders to the rear, the battle managers, could visualize the extent of the pounding the Germans were giving us, the persistence of the attacks, the damage that had been inflicted, how fragile was our grip on the Hill.

There seemed little point in conferring with Kerley who was not given to that kind of inquiry and whose methods did not include interpreting nuances or linguistics. In any case, he and I never discussed

LEGEND

T - TELEPHONE
M - MESSENGER
R - RADIO
M.C. - MESSAGE CENTER

DA - DIV. ARTY
FO - FORWARD OBSR.
O.P. - OBSERVATION POST
INF. - SUPPORTED INF. UNIT

DATE: 11 AUG

MSG N°.	FROM			TO			MESSAGE	CN. N°.
	Party	Time	How Rec't	Party	Time	Rec'd		
1		0630	R				EN. INF. AND HALF TRACK	383
2	B3	0850	R	DA	0810	T	Fired six medical shells to B3	387
3	B3	0851	R	DA	0953	T	2 enemy TANKS at (5869 - 1113) also 5964 - 1099	386
4	Custer	0945	T	DA	1010	T	G Co - lines (5948 - 1028)(5945 - 1094)	
5	B3	0953	R	DA	0953	T	TANKS - INFANTRY - (6101 - 1081) advancing	378
6	Cox	1035	T	DA	1033	T	Shell rep# 123 — Con sending fragments	
7	B3	1015	R	DA	1145	T	Recovered 5 of our med. shells - Morphine broken. Curtis now firing medical shells	✓
8	Custer	1215	T				50% of morphine broken — in chemical shells	
9	24-1	1235	T	DA	1335	T	We have 285 Hill - Not many Germans - Pocket gone	
10	OA2	1255	T	Custer	1255	T	PW report Co. Germans with orders to hold until last man. Went down from Hill 285 into bottom - location unknown (30 MG - 3 tanks)	
11	Cox	1305	T	DA	1510	T	Possible En. Cp. held by 2 ant tank guns (5949 - 1209)	377
12	A4	1330	R				In position TN6 - ✓3 ✓ (5694 - 1223)	
13	Goo	1505	R	DA	1520	T	Knocked out 1 AT. gun on adjustment (5781 - 1283) Adjusted	377A
14	Cox	1515	T	DA	1520	T	A patrol in contact (radio) with E Co. tanks on way to get wounded.	
15	Cox	1516	T	DA	1520	T	Friendly troops have entered Mortain	
16	S3	1512		DA	1545	T	20 rounds of propaganda - sending out white flag demanding surrender	
17	A4	1600	R	DA	1615	T	Position (56.82 - 11.50) N6 - 0251 reports Rocket suspected AA. 1250 - range	
18	Cox	1640	T	DA	1640	T	Enemy withdrawn from AREAS 573 - 1119 (572 - 1115). Arty barrages called off	
19	B3	1650	R	DA	1720	T	Tanks and vehicles 6180 - 1100 Adjusted	3881
20	Cox	1658	T	DA	1712	T	Bandages and sulphur recovered from 3 medical shells (1653 - 1551) Rest of supplies scattered	✓
21	Cox	1658	T	DA	1712	T	Troops not in Mortain - near stream west of town	
22	Cox	1712	T	DA	1712	T	Cupboard moving in on their mission	
23	Cox	1725		DA	1816	T	B. Co. has taken first woods.	
24	B3	1735	R	DA	1816	T	TANKS - 58. 50. 10.60	
25	Cox	1745	T				Request for medical shells for K. Co. — More later	
26	B3	1815	R	DA	1815	T	B3 Receiving Arty and mortar fire from the west	✓

Portion of Message Log for August 11, 1944

tactics. I was the attached artillery observer. He was in charge. My job was to call in fire missions, not to consult on management. Besides, he was at the high crags on the right flank. As night drew closer, I was not inclined to wander around on the Hill searching for him and exposing myself to guns of the nervous, unpredictable men with too many nerves scraped raw. One of them might pull the trigger in the dark without asking first.

As I sat alone and considered all of this, I realized that a finger inside my head was pointing at me. If anything was to be done, only I would do it. I hesitated as other thoughts pressured me. Any serious description of the situation that I might radio could easily be misunderstood and taken by my superiors as a sign of weakness. The old adage about killing the messenger who bears bad news hung in my mind. The men on the Hill, including my forward observer party, had stood up to the Germans, taken their best and given it back to them. If I now reported that our position was perilous, I could imagine that I might be considered gutless. That would be a hell of a conclusion to the many days of siege. Better dead on the Hill than misunderstood and marked as a coward.

I mulled over it for a long, long time. Maybe I was being overly dramatic. The mortar attack might have unhinged me. It could be that I had lost faith in our forces—and in myself. I did not think so. Determination to fight on was still there aplenty, but expectation of rescue had dwindled in the face of the German attacks, coming on again and again. The number of dying and dead was growing rapidly, and "rescue" efforts by airdrops and hastily invented medical shells had failed miserably. We clung to the Hill by our fingernails. What the reaction might be if I reported it made me apprehensive.

Finally, after much agony, I decided to focus attention on the battered remnants of the 2d Battalion. Hundreds of lives might depend on getting the word back. Doing that seemed more important than personal considerations. If headquarters knew the facts, we might hope for continued survival. The explanations, if any, could come later.

The forward observer party gathered around me in the gloom. The message had to be in code. The primitive cryptographic device which we carried had a limited vocabulary. The message must be attention-getting and brief, yet tell the story. But it could exhibit no sign of quitting. We worked the words, fumbled with the language, crossed out and rearranged. At last the message sounded as right as it could be. Sasser switched on the radio and sent the encoded message.

When he completed the transmission, Sasser flicked off the radio. It was 9:50 p.m. At the other end, in the Fire Direction Center, a tired noncom, nearly as sleepless as we were, brought out a code device and laid it on a table. The device consisted of two grids, one containing code words and the other corresponding message words. When correctly superimposed, decoding was not much more complex than using the Little Orphan Annie decoder that we had gotten with box tops years before. The noncom began the decoding process and scribbled the real message on a scrap of paper, after which he entered it in the Message Log:

> Without reinforcements can hold til tomorrow. Request message
> be sent to highest headquarters available.

Fire Direction Center honored my request and forwarded the message to both Division Artillery and 120th Infantry Regiment Headquarters.

Barely 30 minutes later, the inevitable happened.

Five enemy tanks charged through from the rear, from the direction of Mortain, and roared up the Bel-Air Road scattering the men holding down the roadblock. Once past the roadblock, the tanks slowed and moved cautiously. If these tanks joined up with the enemy to the front, they would split the 2d Battalion position in two and isolate E Company. E Company still communicated tenuously with G and K Companies by runner. If German tanks destroyed runner communication with G and K Companies, we would then have no means of knowing when and where the enemy threatened them, and we would lose the capability of protecting them with artillery called in by our radio.

Once that circle closed, the Germans could strangle E Company quickly. Protective artillery fire would not be an option because it would expose E Company to destruction along with the Germans. A dirt road, just east of the crest and roughly parallel to it, hardly more than a trail, ran off from the Bel-Air Road to the south and then curled past the high, gray crags. To our immediate rear was the trail down which Dan Garrott had driven the jeep before parking and camouflaging it. If the Germans hustled tanks and troops down both of those trails for 500 or 600 yards, they would squeeze E Company into a narrow corridor along the crest.

The riflemen at the roadblock withdrew a safe distance.

Fire Mission. Enemy tanks.

Wavering batteries struggled to push the message past the ragged tip of the antenna into the blackened skies. We could still transmit. It was 10:22 p.m.

Artillery fire knocked out one of the tanks. The others turned and ran *west*, back through the roadblock toward Mortain, leaving one smoking carcass off the road in the weeds. The riflemen slowly came up from the brush, from behind rocks and hedgerows, and wearily crawled out of the dirt to take up their vigil once more.

Amazingly, unbelievably, almost impossible to imagine, the five tanks appeared to have made no effort to contact their own forces to the front. In retrospect—we had no such thought at the time—it is possible that they were reconnoitering an exit, a way out of the losing battle back in town. When they saw the infantry at the roadblock, they had slowed down, perhaps wary that there were more Americans ahead. The artillery shells that searched them out in the night and destroyed one of them would have been a sign of trouble ahead. *They probably believed they had picked the wrong road out.* Although the tanks withdrew to the rear almost as unexpectedly as they had come, from our perspective we had been overrun.

Shooting tanks in the night was a feeble distraction from the mounting worry in my head. I continued to struggle with myself over the message that I had sent, fancying that it had been a futile gesture and that if I ever got off the Hill alive, I would receive a rebuke.

In a sense, I had usurped Kerley's authority. Maybe I shouldn't have done it. It might have been wrong. Those thoughts ran through my mind over and over, closed in on me tighter than any night on the Hill had ever done.

The message had been my decision alone. I brooded in the dark. It was a lonely night, and I fidgeted restlessly.

Unknown to me, while I was busy with the five tanks at the road-block, a response to my message had come in from General Hobbs, the division commander.

The general had sent his response by telephone, not radio, through channels that went from Division Headquarters to Division Artillery Headquarters to the 230th Field Artillery Battalion where the Fire Direction Center telephone operator received it at 10:20 p.m. At 10:22 we had turned on our radio briefly, but only long enough to shell the five tanks which had broken through the roadblock from the rear on the Bel-Air Road. I completed that fire mission and went off the air immediately to conserve battery strength. Fire Direction Center did not pass on the general's response during that brief interval.

After receiving the general's response at 10:20, the telephone operator had handed it to the officer in charge at the Fire Direction Center who then gave it to a radio operator to send to me. But by then it was 10:24, and we had already switched off our radio after shooting the five tanks at 10:22. We shot several fire missions later that night, but at no time during any one of them did anyone ask me: "Did you get the message from General Hobbs?"

The keeper of the unit log of the 230th Field Artillery Battalion made the following entry for August 11:

2d Battalion still surrounded—additional medical supplies fired
into the 2d Battalion area by our artillery and 743rd Armored

Battalion. C-47's were again unsuccessful in trying to drop supplies to the isolated battalion. 45 missions, 545 rounds fired.

At division headquarters Lieutenant Colonel Hall was his usual terse self in assessing enemy operations for the day:[1]

Enemy resistance lighter but still present, especially in MORTAIN area. Possible enemy attempts to regain high ground east of MORTAIN broken up by artillery fire. Tanks continue to be used in support of infantry. Local withdrawals took place.

Over the years I often had reflected about what the reaction to my message had been. When the battle ended, no one commented to me about it, and I did not ask. There was no point in looking for trouble when there seemed to be none.

Moreover, with the passage of time, my recollection of the message that I had sent grew faulty. I came to believe that I had radioed: "Without reinforcements can*not* hold till tomorrow," rather than that we could, as I actually had done. The negative implications of this faulty recollection tormented me for many years.

When researching for this book in the National Archives, I stumbled across the truth. I found the message that I had sent and was immediately reprieved from the recurring torment of false memory. But even more important, while I had lived those many years without knowing whether I had done right or wrong in sending that message, the general's response, relayed to me at 10:24 that night, had lain silently, little pencil marks on a sheet of paper, keeping its secret for fifty years:

Reinforcements on the way. Hold out. Hobbs.

31	X3	2000	R	DA	2115	T	... West ...	
31	X3	2000	R	DA	2115	T	MG - West 19.8.4 (r.e.c.)	391
32	B3	2036	R	DA	2157	T	(by r4 - N co.) Enemy strong point - mortars - ✓	384
33	A5	2120	R	DA	2135	T	MGuns - (3.4.5 - 13.5)	
34	41CAN	2135	R	DA	2135	T	En Artillery - GUN position (5979 - 1369) adj COBQIE # 15	
35	B3	0150	R	2A	2500 / 2000	T	"Without REINforcements CAN hold Til tomorrow." message in Code sent in by B3 - ("Requested to be sent to higher headquarters available."	✓
36	X3	2210	R	DA	2215	T	Enemy mortar in vicinity (5.6.8 - 10.91)	
37	DA5	2220	T	B3	2224	R	Reinforcements on the way, hold out "Hibbs" T5 2215 - 2224	✓
38	B3	2222	R	DA	1030	T	(6160 - 1634) - Tan 5@ (6880 / 6101 1806 / 1041)	359 / 215

Continuation of Message Log for August 11, 1944

20 *Tattoo of Death*

That longest day slowly withered. The ring of defensive artillery fire scattered the night at intervals and broke it into pieces, giving us security to the east. As on previous nights, the shelling proceeded in accordance with a schedule, targeted on landmarks and road junctions intuitively selected at Division Artillery Headquarters, which was located some six miles to the west at la Bozage.

At 2:15 in the morning, now Saturday, August 12, the seventh calendar day on the Hill, I fired blind at tanks moving east beyond the roadblock, not far away. Heavy enemy movement, that of a very considerable force, congested the Bel-Air Road. It had been hiding up and down the trails and among the buildings of the farm settlements adjacent to the road except when coming out from time to time to probe and feint and lunge at the roadblock. With such a force, the Germans could easily have overrun our positions on the Hill instead of lurking in the brush and in deserted farmyards.

Fifteen minutes later, more vehicular traffic brought the artillery into action again. Exploding shells and jagged chunks of steel beat down mercilessly and destroyed German tanks, troops and vehicles, creating a junkyard collection of military iron along the way.

My men were exhausted. That night and in those early morning hours I did not ask them for assistance with the fire missions. From time to time, I shook myself up from the foxhole and went forward to the OP. The radio was dug in there, well protected and readily accessible. Alone, I ran the radio, sent the messages, called for artillery fire. I could press the "send" button on the microphone as well as the

145

next soldier. In the dark there were no other interfering tasks, such as spotting the enemy through binoculars, which required me to use both hands.

Below the crest of the ridge, Sergeant Corn and I still shared the same foxhole which he had dug when we last moved the OP. The foxhole was not very deep and barely long enough for both of us to crowd into it. We sat at opposite ends and faced each other with our legs overlapping. I was a tad over six feet tall, and Corn was even bigger. By leaning forward and bending from the waist, a man could lower his profile and protect upper body and head. It was a tight fit. Sergeant Sasser and Corporal Garrott were holed up in a similar entrenchment a few feet to the left, that is to the north, in line with the foxhole that Corn and I shared. Somewhat smaller men, they had more room and, arguably, more protection in equivalent space.

Sometime after five o'clock that morning, I struggled out of the foxhole, left Corn, and went forward the 30 or 40 feet to the OP. There was considerable movement to the front. Dust rose along the Bel-Air Road and billowed up in the early morning light, swirling and spilling into golden clouds. I crouched in the oversized foxhole. Through binoculars, in the faint light, I strained for glimpses of the commotion to the front and of the Germans, who now were clearly retreating.

From behind, a terrific explosion jolted me.

Dirt, rocks and a fog of dirt spattered Garrott and Sasser. Their ears and heads rang as if inside them a mighty bell swung and clanged beyond all restraint, again and again. Garrott was shaken, but unhurt. In a quavering voice he questioned Sasser. Sasser at first was unable to speak and just nodded his head that he was uninjured. He sat shuddering in the foxhole, his knees knocking together, the bones, like chattering teeth, banging out a tattoo. Garrott listened for a moment, then turned his head to the foxhole behind and shouted.

"Corn?"

"I think I've been hit."

Garrott scrambled out of his foxhole, hustled up to the OP.

"Lieutenant. Corn's been hit."

I shut down the radio and ran back to the foxhole with Garrott. A large shell from the rear, presumably shot by a German tank, had hit the foxhole where I had been sitting with Corn minutes before. If I had been there, it would have taken off my head as I leaned forward in the foxhole.

Fragments of steel from the exploding shell had torn into Corn's right leg above the knee, almost severing it. His body was bleeding in many places. Unable to move, he lay calmly in the foxhole and seemed quite aware of what had happened to him, as if he had reached down and touched the shattered limb that now hung together with a few sinews and threads of muscle, felt the blood oozing from the other wounds, made his own diagnosis. He exhibited no sign of pain, no anguish. A wound like his often produces no immediate sensation of pain. That comes later. Nonetheless, he was remarkably composed and seemed already to have reached an understanding about his body— and the future.

Corn asked us to help him up. We hesitated. The fumes of the explosion lingered. Boxed into that shallow foxhole, now more like an open grave, he surely felt again and again the hideous blast, the moment of terror. As we stood there watching, uncertain, his feelings ran through us, agitated our blood, made us tremble for him.

It would be chancy to move Corn and risk worsening the damage. It was also too great a risk to leave him there. We could see that he wouldn't remain in that foxhole long. He had two husky arms, and with some dogged, terrible burst of desperate energy we feared he would wrench himself out onto the rocky hillside. Besides, even if it were possible to treat his wounds, to staunch the flow of blood, somehow to save him, it was not reasonable to try to administer aid down into that foxhole on the back slope of the Hill. Somehow together, silently, Garrott and I decided that he must be moved to be helped.

Garrott ran down to the infantry headquarters nearby and came back breathless with several riflemen. One man brought a blanket which they managed to roll under Corn. Then, with all hands pulling and gently sliding the blanket over the rocky sides, they carefully heaved him up out of the foxhole, keeping his big body as nearly horizontal as possible. Once he was settled on the ground above the foxhole, they loosed their hold on the blanket and stood back. Corn seemed relieved to be out in the open.

Again he asked to be helped up. Several of the infantry grabbed him under his arms. With their help and using his left leg, he stood almost upright. Sasser, still scrunched down in the foxhole, watched from a few feet away. Blood gushed from Corn's right leg for an instant. Sasser gasped in horror. The men picked Corn up and carried him to the OP, where he would have protection in case of further shelling. I knelt down, and they laid him on the blanket next to me.

Corn wouldn't be needing his web belt. I pulled it through the loops of his trousers, took it off and wrapped it around his right leg above the knee and buckled it. It was all there was for a tourniquet.

I then turned on the radio. It was 5:45. Tanks came into view, about 1,000 yards east of our OP, not much over a half-mile away off the Bel-Air Road, and still very close and dangerous. They seemed to be avoiding the congestion on the Bel-Air Road by driving east along trails which were south of the road and which led past farmers' fields and out into the Forêt de Mortain. I sent in a fire mission and blasted away, raising a storm of smoke and dust.

But it all took time, almost 10 precious minutes to shoot the retreating tanks before they disappeared into the woods. I frantically shouted a second message into space:

> Urgent message. Must have ambulances immediately to evacuate wounded.

Had they heard me? At this point I was unable to receive anything on the radio, and it appeared to be dead. But could I still transmit? Was it possible that the batteries had enough juice to send but not to receive? I had a feeling, deep down, something intuitive, that they heard.[1]

The Germans still surrounded us. I didn't really expect an ambulance to get through for Sergeant Corn. But in those moments of desperation, I didn't give it a thought.

MESSAGE LOG

LEGEND

T - TELEPHONE
M - MESSENGER
R - RADIO
M.C. - MESSAGE CENTER

DIV - DIV. HDTS
F.O. - FORWARD OBSR.
O.P. - OBSERVATION POST
INF. - SUPPORTED INF. UNIT.

DATE: Aug 12

MSG No	FROM Party	Time	When Sent/Rec'd	TO Party	Time	When Rec'd	MESSAGE	CN NB
1	B3	0215	R	DA	220	T	Tanks on road (6160 - 10.39) 359 (6101 - 10.41) 378	
2	B3	0200	R	DA	0235	T	Heavy traffic on east-west road 6160-10.39	378
3	Custer	0520	R	DA	0525	T	Custer reports German tanks firing at each other near R Junction 314	
4	B3	0645	R	DA	0605	T	(59.79 - 10.18) Tanks (6119 - 10.17)	378 375
5	B3	0855	R	Custer	0855	T	Urgent message - must have ambulances immediately	
				DA	905	T	to evacuate wounded.	
6	B3	0615	R	Custer	0615	T	MESSAGE "Must have medical supplies flown in at earliest possible moment"	
				DA	0525	T		
7	DA	0635	T				No fire line - Nothing west at Highway 3	
8	B3	0655	R	DA	0700	T	Enemy Infantry tanks (6160-10.39)	359
9	B3	0801	R	DA	0807	T	Platoon of EN infantry (6215-10.36)	396
10	B3	0805	R	DA	0807	T	Heavy tanks (6160-10.39) Effect good some tanks are burning (50 tanks Rept 0835)	359
11	Custer	0853	T	DA	0851	T	Panzer Regt at least 30 tanks, horse drawn arty and inf. withdrawing along highway 4 6 BNs firing having excellent effect -	
12	Custer	0905	T	DA	0905	T	Inf obs report Germans in disorganized retreat along highway 4 and nearby fields -	
13	B3	0915	R	DA	0916	T	reinforcements have arrived	
14	Crew	0941	T	Cmnd	0942	T	No Fire south of 10 grid line west of 60 grid (58.5 - 10.7) Friendly fire falls on church. Crew requests cease fire	
15	Custer	0955	T	DA	0957	T	French women 1P1 men report no Germans in Mortain - Friendly troops entering town	
16		1050	R				EN vehicles on road near 62-12 grid intersection	
17	DA	1107	T	Brig	1108	T	Be on lookout for butterfly bombs dropped by EN last night	
18	Cox	1113	T	DA	1114	T	EN CPs at (6315-1313) and (6212-1234)	
19	B3	1140	R	DA	1155	T	Armored vehicles vic (6215-10.36)	396
20	A4	1400	R	DA	1270	T	In pos NG 522	
21	LN4	1213	T	DA	1220	T	Johnson Ft lines N8 D69 D96 on hill are (6098-0953)(6108-0908) Evac wounded 12th hrs contacted CCB Crew + Crop in Mortain	
22	Cox	1185	T	DA	1240	T	When relieved 120th will occupy defensive positions from (5426-1170) to (5832-1388) Johnson will occupy our present positions	
23	Cox	1413	T	DA	NG	T	50-100 vehicles knocked out on highway 4 between 2400-4000	
24	N4	1525	T				LN 2 Lt Lee and Sgt Bushnell were captured some time in past 4 days -	
25	O3	1530	T				Lt Bartz + party reported in	

Portion of Message Log for August 12, 1944

National Archives

Corporal Garrott again ran for help. After a time he returned with an infantry aid man. The medic looked at Corn's leg. His aid bag was nearly empty and contained no bandages, no morphine, nothing that would help. He shook his head helplessly and left. I looked at Garrott. He looked at me. There must be something that we could do for a dying man.

"Lieutenant, there's a bottle of calvados under the back seat of the jeep. It's a mighty good painkiller. Would that help?"

I agreed. "Go ahead. But watch out, Dan. The Germans are behind us." He nodded and left at a run.

It was 6:15, an hour since Corn had been hit. Time was running by quickly, much too fast. The morning sun shone into my eyes, filtered through great clouds of dust to the east. At times a tank or a truck came out of the haze for an instant or two, and then disappeared into the dirty air. The enemy was scattering in front, a profusion of tanks, infantry, vehicles. Corn was the first concern. I turned on the radio again. Oh, God, if they could only hear me!

Crow this is Crow Baker 3. Must have medical supplies flown in at earliest possible moment.

No one was going to do that. The first attempt at flying in supplies had been made days ago and was a flop, and, in any case, airplanes loaded with supplies and parachutes were not available on call. I might as well have asked for Florence Nightingale in a chauffeured Rolls Royce.

Garrott returned empty-handed, shaken. "Lieutenant, the Jerries cleaned me out. They took everything." He went on bitterly as if he had uncovered a new category of war crime. "The sons of bitches even got my jelly and crackers."

Garrott went back to the foxhole where Sasser still sat, almost in a trance. What Garrott wanted most was to get as far away from this scene as possible. Nor was it a time to be standing around in the open. He crawled into the foxhole with Sasser, his head still shaken from the shell blast and visions of the helpless Corn, and buried himself in the sheltering ground. The two of them sat together for many minutes, silently healing from that terrible blast, hanging on, gathering strength for whatever would come next.

I turned to Corn, loosened the belt on his leg, waited five minutes, tightened it again. I tried hard to remember the procedure with a tourniquet. That was it, wasn't it? Bitter hate pumped through my veins. I looked at Corn, swore bitterly about the Germans, flicked on the radio.

'Crow. This is Crow Baker 3.' There was no answer. The radio was not receiving. 'God damn it, answer!'

I wanted to shoot everything that I could see, to kill everything out there in retribution for Corn. I wanted to kill.

This is Crow Baker 3. *Fire Mission.* Enemy infantry. Tanks.

I knew they heard me. They must. I shouted into the microphone, instinctively responding to weak batteries by yelling. "Concentration 359." The enemy poured out of the fields onto the Bel-Air Road, still very close to our position. Moments later black smoke from exploding shells blanketed the target. They had heard me! The radio still transmitted!

I took a deep breath and checked my watch. It was nearly an hour since my silly message demanding an ambulance. It was almost 7:00 a.m., and it was time to tend to Corn again. I leaned over to my right and loosened the makeshift tourniquet. "Want to shoot some Jerries?" Corn's innocent question six days before rang through my head. In my rage, I wanted to shoot and kill them all.

Fire Mission. Platoon of enemy infantry.

They could hear me! That's all that mattered now. At the top of my lungs, I bellowed the target location at the microphone. These infantry were farther out, a mile and a half down the Bel-Air Road, but still close enough to be a threat.

Guns roared and a torrent of shells burst across the landscape. Black splotches marked the explosions, but over the din of the enemy's retreat I could hear only an occasional muffled bang. I shouted hoarsely, but the flood of noise from the front drowned my curses. Death and devastation enveloped the enemy.

The sun rose higher. I took off my helmet, wiped the sweat on my forehead, stuck the helmet loosely back on top. My heavy growth of beard was moist. I wanted to hold back the rise of the sun toward its zenith. Unlike the previous days that had stretched slowly from one second to the next, this one raced onward, eating up hours while Corn's strength ebbed with each flying second, and death moved closer.

He lay there serenely listening to the fire missions, nodding his head ever so slightly in approval, his strength nearly gone. I tightened the belt on his leg once more. It was now after 8:00.

Fire Mission. Heavy tanks.

Concentration 359 again. There was no end to the German tanks hidden off the Bel-Air Road. Clouds of dust billowed up from the fleeing enemy. Artillery exploded to the front. I saw black smoke, confusion, wreckage.

This is Crow Baker 3. Effect good. Some tanks are burning.

Once again I loosened the tourniquet, waited five minutes, tightened it again. I talked to Corn. He was coherent, weak. What was that he said? The noise to the front was deafening. I bent close over him, tried to hear what he said as his lips moved and parted briefly. Inside me, hate, rage and grief ran together in a stream of violence.

I wanted a power that I did not have. I wanted to smash with a giant fist the tanks, trucks, troops that I saw now running away. The realization that I was too feeble to do that enraged me further.

Several riflemen had now gathered around the OP, watching Corn silently. They said nothing. Nor did I. With my binoculars, I continued to observe the destruction and commotion as the Germans withdrew to the east. Almost in a daze, mechanically, I tended the belt on Corn's leg.

Gradually, the rage subsided into deep fatigue. Corn was dying, and I couldn't do a damned thing about it. I could blow tanks and men off the landscape, but I couldn't save him. I sat sorrowfully in the dust, the sunlight now grown harsh.

Sasser and Garrott by this time had joined the circle of watchers at the OP. Corn always carried a nickel-plated pistol. Where he had gotten it would be anyone's guess. Maybe he "liberated" it, or bought it. Perhaps he had won it in a poker game. Neither Sasser nor Garrott knew. Corn was a stranger, much as I was. He had come from C Battery and joined B Battery as chief of the survey section filling a vacancy at the same time as I had joined B Battery. One survey section chief after another from B Battery had been wounded or killed at the front with the artillery forward observers. Corn had filled the most recent vacancy.

Now Corn beckoned weakly to one of the riflemen. The man stepped forward cautiously. Corn motioned to take his pistol. It was a choice possession. Sasser and Garrott would have been pleased to have had it, but he did not offer it to them. They stood by, puzzled as Corn gave the pistol to a stranger. And again with his watch and whatever else he had of value. He gave it all to infantrymen who were there by chance, to strangers whose names he did not know. He offered nothing to his friends. The moment was bewildering.

We come into this world as strangers. Many often travel the world as outsiders, alienated. Some live their entire lives that way, unknown even to those close by who are their husbands, wives, lovers, children, parents. As a stranger, Corn had come to B Battery, and almost as a stranger he had climbed into the jeep with us days before to ride to an unknown destiny at Hill 314. Should it be baffling that as death came close, Corn would turn to strangers? Of all those who ringed the foxhole where Corn lay, only death, which had slipped silently in among us, was not a stranger.

Reinforcements had fought their way through the Germans to the rear and first appeared on the Hill around 9:15. By that time, Corn was beyond help. Death came imperceptibly. Half an hour later his pulse was gone.

But the carnage continued. At 11:40 I went on the air again:

Crow. This is Crow Baker 3. *Fire Mission*. Armored vehicles.

This was the last of the 193 fire missions that I shot during the German counterattack at Mortain. For hours afterward, smoke from burning vehicles and dust rose along the Bel-Air Road on the slopes to the front. The 2d Platoon of E Company sent patrols to investigate, and reported turrets and other portions of enemy tanks and destroyed vehicles throughout the area. Tank and vehicle tracks ran together in utter confusion and disarray, showing how frantically the enemy had sought to avoid our fire.

It was not until 2:30 that afternoon that one battalion of the 119th Infantry, from our own division, and elements of the 35th Infantry Division finally relieved us.

Abruptly, the siege broke off.

No line on a chart had plotted the battle for us, so that we could see that each attack and each retreat, each up and down, trended toward the conclusion of the battle. Death struck at us until the very end. Then, without a cue, the play ended, the curtain rang down, the house lights went up and we left.

We turned Corn's body over to an obscure army unit known as "Graves Registration." The three of us gathered the radio and equipment and walked wearily down to the jeep. I flopped into my seat, exhausted, all strength and emotion wrung out, left lying there beside Corn in the dirt.

The afternoon turned hot, parching, metallic bright. Garrott started up the jeep easily, and we bumped up the trail to the Bel-Air Road and swung west through the wreckage that had once been the pleasant little town of Mortain. The fighting had trashed the town, leaving only shattered walls and piles of rubble.

No tanks growled and lunged at us. The pounding of the 88s had stopped. The mortars stood silent. For the moment, we had left danger behind. But no notes of triumph, no cheers of victory welled up within us. We drove somberly back to B Battery, each of us wrapped in his own thoughts. We had lost something, left it behind on the Hill.

A German staff car and its driver were caught by shellfire at a crossroads near Mortain. A French farmer and a little girl inspect the wreckage.

The intensity of the struggle is shown by the ruins of Mortain, August 13, 1944.

**The church at Mortain, one of two buildings that survived. The
other was the Hotel de Ville, or City Hall, which dates to the 1600s.**

Courtesy of Dr. Gilles Buisson

21   *Poison, My Dear Field Marshal?*

In the end, the counterattack had floundered and would cost the enemy the Battle of France.[1]

Although the Germans achieved some initial surprise, they encountered stiff and determined resistance on the ground in all directions. From the air, the enemy columns were easy targets, and Allied airplanes blasted their tanks and armored vehicles. Moreover, the "...Germans failed to use the first hours of the attack, the hours when darkness and surprise were on their side, to seize the high ground overlooking Mortain. That would be a fatal mistake."[2] The stout defense of the Hill by the 2d Battalion[3] buttressed by artillery fire which prevented the American forces on the Hill from being destroyed or captured[4] had been a major factor in preventing the Germans from driving through to Avranches and the sea.[5]

The collapse of the counterattack discredited von Kluge in Hitler's eyes, and under menacing circumstances, he was stripped of his command and ordered to return to Supreme Headquarters. When he recalled the savage fury that had been unleashed on entire families of the conspirators, on so many who were innocent, how could there be hope for him who had fumbled the *Führer*'s supposedly brilliant plan to break the American forces in two? From the roads that lay ahead, he could still choose. He did. Before the airplane that carried him to the Wolf's Lair touched down, he swallowed poison.

Responsibility for the failure of the counterstroke was now clearly established. The armchair general had a scapegoat.

 **22** **_Bunnies, Chickens and Ducks_**

At B Battery, the luxury of a helmet bath, clean clothes and food awaited us. Dan Garrott had worn the same shirt and pants since before he landed in France on D plus 2, June 8. The collar of the shirt and the edges of the pants pockets by now looked as if they were trimmed with black leather. He had clean socks and underwear. Army supply lines, however, were not yet able to provide him with a clean uniform. He dressed again in the veteran shirt and pants to finish the Battle of France. I was more fortunate, able to change into clean clothes from head to foot. I carefully packed away my dad's shirt.

Our work on the Hill had ended. Chance had favored the three of us, the other artillery observers and 370 infantry who had come off the Hill at battle's end. There were 277 dead, wounded and missing infantrymen who did not.[1] At the 230th Field Artillery Battalion Headquarters, the clerk had made the following entry in the Battalion Log for August 12:

> ...Sgt. Corn fatally wounded and Lt. Weiss returned safely after sending in 193 missions in the six day period that the 2d Battalion was surrounded....

The battalion surgeon gave us sleeping pills, and we rested. With a solid night's sleep at last, Sasser, Garrott and I perked up. What did the troops at B Battery have to say to us? What did they ask us about our days of entrapment on the Hill? Not much. On August 10, the Germans had directly threatened the 230th Field Artillery Battalion.

The artillerymen, normally in position with 105mm howitzers well back from the front lines, had grabbed carbines, manned jeep-mounted machine guns and readied themselves to fight as infantry. They were still caught up in the excitement of this brief incident, and we listened with interest.

On August 13, the day after our return from the Hill, the intelligence officer summoned me to battalion headquarters, gave me a portable typewriter and directed me to write a report. I typed out not quite 10 pages, double-spaced, a precious contemporaneous record of the battle. Had I at the time had any sense of history, I would have written five times as much. I did not know then that I would continue to write it in my mind the rest of my life.

The same day I wrote to my dad:

Well, here I am; or to put it another way, we got back—some of us. We were out my forward observer party and I, for 7 days & 6 nights. It was pretty rough. As a matter of fact there was nothing that didn't happen to us....Did a good job and everybody was pleased. We were pleased to get back and find fried chicken and french fries waiting....

It is very pleasant here. We are in position near a farmyard; little bunnies, chickens, ducks, etc. hop around and play all over the place. Everywhere we go the place is full of tame rabbits. Some of the men have picked them up for pets.

Not much to write about from here; you know more about what goes on than we do....

Not much to say? Mail censorship regulations restricted what we could write home. No high-fives, no shouts of victory, no boasting— just "Did a good job and everybody was pleased."

How quickly it might appear that we return to normal.

Although the battle around Mortain was crucial to victory in the battle for France, Allied troops never quite tightened the noose that General Bradley had fashioned for the Germans to the east past Mortain near Falaise. Bradley thought he had bottled up at least 19 German divisions, but tens of thousands of German soldiers and valuable German armor and equipment escaped Bradley's trap through the "Falaise Gap" to fight another day. Nevertheless, as many as 10,000 may have been killed there and five times that number were taken prisoner. Many enemy divisions were completely destroyed.

Within two weeks after we had climbed so wearily into the jeep and driven down off the Hill, the Allies were able to tally almost a quarter of a million Germans dead or wounded and almost that many taken prisoner in the fight for Normandy. They had chewed up and put out of action thousands upon thousands of enemy vehicles, aircraft, tanks and artillery pieces, and dead horses were beyond counting. By then the Allies had landed over two million men in Normandy and substantial vehicles, armament and stores. The cost, however, had been nearly as great as that paid by the Germans, 210,000 casualties of which nearly 37,000 were dead.

But the fight for Normandy had ended.

After those days in Normandy in August 1944, the war rushed on to endless other maneuvers, skirmishes and battles, and we charged through the rest of France and raced across Belgium in hot pursuit of the retreating Germans. At the Albert Canal on the border with Holland, I stood too close to an incoming 88 shell and had to take time out. But again I was lucky. One man with me was killed, and the shell put 96 holes in Dan Garrott's jeep. Both the jeep and I would return to fight another day—in snow and freezing cold in the Battle of the Bulge, on past the Roer River where the Germans successfully stalemated a U.S. crossing until after the Bulge, crossing the Rhine River in a U.S. Navy skiff with an outboard motor just ahead of German shells, and then the long push across Germany to the Elbe River and convergence with the Russians. Finally, in May 1945, the hot war in Europe was over, and I went on to a new assignment farther east in Germany, where I witnessed unmistakable signs that the cold war had begun, although no one had yet announced its beginning.

Afterword

Just days after the battle at Mortain ended, an artilleryman, one who was not on the Hill, wrote: "This battle was an artilleryman's dream come true...."[1] But what does an artilleryman dream when the battle has passed? Are his conceptions those of glory and victory, of pride at having won? Does he dream of shooting soldiers and tanks as if they were on a make-believe battlefield?

Or, as I have, does he hear the scream and whine of shells, see men huddled against the earth shaking with fear? In my dream I sat alone in a foxhole with a dying man, alternately loosening and then tightening a belt on the remains of a leg nearly blown off by an enemy shell, vainly trying to stop the flow of blood and life, powerless to quiet the pain or to do more. I shouted out in hate and dreamed tears of rage and grief.

For a long time after the battle ended, I searched for meaning within a shadowy circle that looped around me, seeking to quiet the violent core of anger, the red world within, to find peace. But now, I see the battle like a rerun of an old movie, no longer a living experience.

In writing about Hill 314, I have felt a nagging concern that this scrap of action may idealize war as high drama. Viewed this way, the horror and destruction of battle disappear in the smoke of dramatic violence. Stories such as this allow the reader to experience other lives, but they can also create sentimental fantasy that obscures the scream and hammer blows of incoming shells, the darting, unfocused

161

eyes sprung wide with terror, the men who lie stunned in their beds for a lifetime after. Jagged iron cutting the air seeking a thigh, a chest or an arm, a man shaking violently with fear under incoming mortar shells, a soldier with a bullet through his head moaning softly in the darkness, the stench of bodies rotting in August sunlight define the larger significance of war. The irony is that we ennoble such malice and misery. War's complicated madness demands that men shoot blindly into the black of night, trying to kill other men whom they cannot see and do not know. This reverberates in exploding theaters of battle and also in the pounding beat of young rockers, like those in chapter one who fight their enemies with music.

Some have said that Hill 314 was the pivot point of the biggest German counterattack in France during World War II, but the quick thrust of the German panzers around Mortain and the beleaguered battalion on Hill 314 have been largely forgotten. Almost no one remembers it, except historians and the few remaining survivors who were there.

Twice I have gone back to Mortain in search, to the Hill itself.

On my first return visit in 1983, I had arranged to meet Dr. Gilles Buisson, the honorary mayor and historian of Mortain, at the top of a street that traverses the cliffs east of the town where it turns into the Bel-Air Road, now Route D 487. I arrived early and walked south up a tree-covered ridge, growing quite excited as I neared a high point at the end. Almost at the top of the ridge, I came upon a small chapel with a small sign stating that it was "La Petite Chapelle." Down below, the road to Domfront ran off to the southeast. A vast plain stretched to the south and to the west. Dimly, in the far west, some 25 miles away, the outlines of Mont St. Michel were barely discernible. The town of Mortain lay immediately below us. But there had been no chapel on *our* Hill. We had never seen Mont St. Michel. I shook my head in confusion and walked back to the car.

Dr. Buisson was waiting. He smiled expansively and pointed proudly across the road to a simple, white sign with black, painted letters near the edge: "La Montjoie. Cote 314."

"Here you are," said Dr. Buisson. "Hill 314."

I shook my head negatively and tried to explain that E Company and my forward observer group had not fought the Germans here. The mayor insisted that this was Hill 314. I had no detailed contour map, only a Michelin road map. Dr. Buisson did not need a map. The sign told him where he was.

The images in my mind had been crystal clear. The struggle on the Hill was perhaps the single most significant event in my life and in the lives of most men who where there. How could bright remembrance be so erroneous, unless recollection and imagination had traded places? Uncertainty would nag at me for years.

On the second visit to Mortain in 1994, I came prepared with a copy of the contour map we had used as a firing chart during the battle in 1944.

Dr. Buisson and René Langlois, the deputy mayor of Mortain, met me at the hotel and we drove up a steep slope out of town, taking the same streets that Dan Garrott had followed 50 years earlier. At the top, we pulled off into a small parking lot that was adjacent to the entrance to "La Petite Chapelle." We got out of the car, and Dr. Buisson and Mr. Langlois walked across the road to a white sign. It read: "La Montjoie. Cote 314." They both beamed.

"Here you are," said Dr. Buisson. "Hill 314."

I brought out my copy of the battle map and indicated our location on it. We were on the western edge of Hill 314. I pointed to a long ridge some 600 yards or so to the east, then back to the map.

"It was over there." My hosts were skeptical, but agreed to humor me. We drove down Route D 487 to the top of the east ridge where we parked the car. A dirt road still curves off to the south.

For some time we tramped across the ridge and traversed its slopes through brush and dead bracken, picking our way slowly between trees and saplings. At length we came to the southern edge of the ridge, to a massive pile of rocks, fractured by time and weather into huge, gray chunks, torn from the Hill and pushed up into a jagged

The sign on Hill 314

heap. The sides fell away in steep cliffs to the south and west. Broken pieces of rock strewed the ridge, and trees and brush grew out of the cracks and on little patches of turf. Was this where an enemy shell had snipped the antenna off the radio, where white phosphorus had drenched and blistered us, where the Germans had dueled us with 88s? It seemed likely. But a study of several maps showed that there also *had been* another high point 150 or 200 yards farther east. That high point was now gone, completely demolished, the target of a deep quarry whose stone had been cut out and crushed for use on roads until the 1970s. Which place was it, the high, gray crags on which we now stood or the hole in the ground? My French friends grew impatient. I settled for the one that I could see. We returned to the car and drove off.

The next day I returned by myself, feeling that I had such ownership of the place that I was entitled to walk about freely, despite the signs that said *Entre Interdit*. For some time, I stumbled through thick undergrowth along the east ridge of the Hill, south of the Bel-Air Road, seeking for some sign of remembrance. For a while I saw nothing but the tangle of brush which enveloped the landscape. Then I came upon what appeared to be a sunken area, small, uneven, perhaps six to eight feet across. Dead, stiff bracken, scrub, a host of little trees, had overgrown the uncertain crater. The shape and size were about those of the last OP, where Sergeant Corn had died. Vegetation that rose up partially obscured the true depth and gave the hole the appearance of being relatively shallow. Still it would have been deep enough for protection from shell fire. I wandered a short distance. Not far below was a major outcropping, a jumbled mass of large rocks, cracked and gray. We had dug in our radio at the last OP, up the ridge from such a rocky mound.

It fit as well as I might expect with landmarks uncertain and the ground overlaid by such a heavy cover. If it was not the precise place, I would find none that resembled it more. I walked back up the slope and stood a long time at the edge of that ragged hole, my head bowed in memory. For a fleeting moment anguish flooded through me, and once again I knelt down there beside the dying Corn. Then the vision cut out. I saw only a shallow pit, an uncertain outline obscured by scruffy vegetation and little trees reaching up for light. All fragments of flesh and bone had returned to earth. Not a cartridge case, not even a buckle or a button remained. I saluted and walked on.

The visit to Mortain now was at an end. I put my frustrations aside, realizing that it is not possible to go back except in spirit and as a reflection of other images. More important, I had learned that one should tread the path back with caution.

For the French, the visit produced a time of exuberance, warm welcome and champagne freely offered. It was also a time to reflect upon something that I was too young to know in 1944, that freedom is not secured by a single event, no matter how momentous.

Just as I have returned to the Hill to pay tribute and to search for meaning in my own life, others also go there. Some perhaps make the journey out of curiosity. Most are spurred by deep anguish and the need to walk the ground, to absorb a feeling of time, to try to make contact with a loved one who was there—or with someone they never knew. They pay tribute and search for some remnant, the tiniest scrap, a trace from the past that will let them discover the loved one and which will help them define or understand themselves. Curiously, the lives of those who join the search often come together, and it becomes a common quest.

When I visited Mortain in 1983, my son Charlie photographed Dr. Buisson and me standing together. When Dr. Buisson published his book the following year, he included the photograph with a legend, in French of course, that said that I was a lawyer in Portland, Oregon. With that information, anyone who wanted to could easily track me down. They have. I was as close as the white pages.

Several years ago I received a telephone call that began:

"Are you the Robert Weiss who was at Mortain?"

Stunned silence followed while I tried to recover from this unexpected question from a stranger.

"Yes, I was. Why do you want to know?"

"My uncle was killed there. Did you know him?"

As it turned out, I had not known him. The uncle, Joe Maciejewski, was an infantryman, a rifleman, with another of the 30th Division's regiments, and was killed near St. Barthélemy, approximately three or four kilometers north of Hill 314 on the first day of von Kluge's counterattack. The casualties were heavy there, and his battalion lost 350 men that day.

Joe was six or seven years older than Jim Sobieski, my caller, and was more like a big brother than an uncle. For a time while growing up in Detroit, he had even lived with Jim and his family. Joe owned a bike, and the two of them used to pal around together, riding here, going there, cruising the city. Joe was only 19 when he was drafted. He gave Jim the bike to keep for him until he came back from the war. Jim used to hang around the house waiting for the mailman and word from his uncle, but Joe wasn't good at writing, and word never came. One day Jim's mother said that she'd received a letter. Joe wouldn't be coming back.

"What about his bike?"

"I guess it's yours now."

The kid took the bike and rushed outside, rode it around for a while, turning tight circles and jumping it over curbs, but it wasn't the same.

Joe must have been a pretty swell uncle if the kid was still trying to find out about him 40 years later. Of course, Jim Sobieski was no longer a kid except in his heart, still riding the streets of Detroit in front of his uncle balancing between the handlebars, and then riding the bike solo after his uncle went away to war, and on and on through all the years, pedaling the bike alone.

Not long after he called, we met and talked, and I told him a little bit about what I knew. Of course, he had been to Mortain and read everything that had been written about the battle, and my information was superfluous. But, that wasn't the point. I believe that what he wanted was to be there on the battlefield with his beloved uncle, to touch and to hold onto him as death came near. It made no difference that I hadn't known Joe. Just talking with me was enough, as if by talking with someone who had been there he could reach the past, lift the haze that obscured the years and come into the smoke and dust of the battlefield with his uncle when he faced the enemy and death.

Psychologists have many theories and speculations about searches which the living make for the dead and the missing. No one really knows. The matter is complex and deep-seated. At the core is a need to know what can never be known, and a longing that somehow seems to find relief, if not deliverance, in touching someone who was there.

More recently, I received a letter from a judge in Minnesota, Bernard Boland, who also found the picture in Dr. Buisson's book while visiting Mortain. Sometimes a mystery or a secret lies between the covers of a book, and an unexpected event will occur when some-one opens the book and turns the pages.

Boland's father, a lieutenant, had joined the 30th Infantry Division as an officer in H Company of the 120th Infantry Regiment about the same time I was assigned to the 230th Field Artillery. H Company was on the right flank of Hill 314 when the Germans counterattacked after midnight on August 6. The Germans brushed H Company aside in their first move to reach Avranches, and those men of H Company who were not killed or captured moved up the Hill and were absorbed by E Company, where I was.

His father, he believes, was killed on August 9, 1944, a day of unceasing attacks on the Hill and the day the enemy demanded that the 2d Battalion surrender or be blown to bits. I said he "believes" his father died that day because he has a telegram from the War Department that says so. But he also has a telegram from the War Department dated seven days earlier that reports his father missing in action since August 11. Which is the truth? What really happened? When and how did his father die? For Bernie Boland, like for Jim Sobieski, the search has never been put aside permanently. Bernie wrote me: "...eventually, I always return. This is how it has been all of my life...."

In Bernie's case, his father was a man he never knew. He was less than a year old when his father died, and his mother "to this day is unable to talk about him or about the war." The pain is deep, and the need for him to know remains. "...many times, I have given up looking and asking questions only to be moved by a magazine article or a book to do a little more research or to write another letter...."

So he sought me out. Bernie feels that I was "as close to where... [his] father fell as anyone...[he'd] found—probably within 100 yards." Possibly he is right. As with Sobieski, Bernie already knew everything that I could tell him about the battle. What he most wanted to hear was something that would help him make contact with the father he never knew, something that would help him reach out and know his dad, the smallest fragment that would help him define himself as his father's son.

But I had not known his father, or how he had died. I could only offer the simple thought that no one can go back to that other time, and then sadly, leave him to rummage for his lifetime through the parcel of his father's personal effects that the War Department had sent years ago, forever in search of what he can never know. Except for scraps, some letters, the change from his pockets, a battered wristwatch, grief is all that remains.

Bernie has since written me that in his lifetime and in the course of his many visits to Mortain he has seen "the scarred earth, the shellpocked ridges, the torn and skeletal trees..." around Hill 314 restored. Not so with the human heart. As he has reflected, "Perhaps only the landscape can be healed."

In making the two trips back to the Hill, and in writing this account, a search for meaning in a larger sense became inevitable. As I resurrected the bitter fighting and searched through the minute-by-minute entries in the Message Log, the same questions pushed to the front again and again.

Why was I, of all soldiers, given that role in that battle? Why did some men survive? Why did others die? How did American foot soldiers hold out against German tanks? Why didn't the German tanks storm through and overwhelm our position? What enabled the civilian GI to give as good or better than the professionals of the Wehrmacht? Why did the dying Corn give away his nickel-plated pistol to a stranger? Is courage a fixed, finite quantity, each soldier having just so much? Is courage expendable, or is it renewable? And what about fear? Does any soldier go into battle without fear? Was

The author and Dr. Gilles Buisson at the 30th Infantry Division Memorial on the western ridge of Hill 314.

there a collective intelligence, some kind of group consciousness or linkage, at work on the Hill that gave special strength to our meager forces? If so, why or how did it happen? Answer if you will. There may be many answers or no answer at all to these questions.

I also have pondered many aspects of a more personal and intimate nature. For those six days, surrounded as we were, events had spun out of control. For myself, and for some others, the imprint of this experience has been to plan and to try to live the rest of our lives in control. When I have not been in control, I have often raged at persons or events that have upset my schemes, expectations and visions. When I have relied on luck, I have felt dangerously out of control.

Memories of such an experience remain in varied hue and degree, different for each man who was there. Some events have stuck and others are totally blank. How to explain this? Some part may be the result of subconscious repression of memory, subduing events that one may not wish to remember. But that is hardly an adequate explanation because the siege at the Hill deeply imprinted us, with lines as sharp and vivid as if it were yesterday.

Maybe it is because some facets of the action have been replayed, consciously or unconsciously, thousands of times in the years since. As clearly as if it had just happened, I can hear Corn saying: "Want to shoot some Jerries, Lieutenant?" and then my seeing the gray-green uniforms of enemy troops. Other events have for me become obscure or have disappeared entirely.

What were Kerley's words of disdain at the German surrender offer? My mind is empty. Neither Sasser nor Garrott had any recollection. Yet we were all present, and these events were the stuff of high drama.

What kind of a miracle was it that enabled our radio to transmit when it could not receive? Suppose it had been the other way around?

It is impossible not to reflect on what chance called me a few yards away to the OP just minutes before the shell struck the foxhole which Corn and I shared. Why had Corn and I shared the same foxhole? We were the two biggest men. Logically, to even up the fit, a big man should have been paired with one of the smaller men in each of the foxholes. Garrott should have been where Corn was. Garrott would say of this, "I'm glad you didn't think of that until 50 years later." Mysteriously, many events and circumstances work together.

The failure of the 88mm shell to explode that day at the high crags, the so-called round of "Polish" ammunition, may have been chance. On the other hand, perhaps the enslaved Polish worker in the ammunition factory was playing a part in anticipation long before the Germans struck at Mortain. How did Sasser "know" to heat the radio batteries in the sun and to rotate them? There is no technical explanation of the continuous sunshine that warmed the life that barely flickered in our radio batteries. The sun does not always shine in August, even in France. Fifty years later at Mortain in August 1994, fog and rain greeted the official celebration of the Battle.

And who can explain the role that fate or nature or peculiar circumstance—some might even say "providence"—played in opening a "curtain of visibility" for the field artillery forward observers? Had the forward observers not had commanding views of the area, particularly of the terrain immediately to the east and below the Hill where the Germans marshaled their assaulting infantry, tanks, assault guns and artillery, the American guns would have been of little effect. Without the aid of front-line visibility, and because the artillery, some six miles to the rear, could not see the targets, they would have had no clue as to where to point the tubes.

Fire missions would have been limited to those observed by spotter aircraft and interdicting fire on targets selected randomly from a map, such as road intersections. That would not have saved the battalion.

But, wouldn't good visibility be inherent in a position like Hill 314, some thousand feet above sea level and higher than the surrounding countryside? Not always. Visitors to the Hill today find the views obstructed and closed off by a dense growth of pines and are unable to see the landscape from which German infantry, tanks and guns besieged the American battalion a half century ago. These trees, a part of the large area of the Forêt de Mortain, or Forest of Mortain, to the south, have blocked observation for at least a decade. Lucky, you might say, that the Forest of Mortain had not spread across

Hill 314 in August 1944. Yes, lucky perhaps, but fate or nature or peculiar circumstance, even "providence," fit better.

A 1909 map of the area shows the Hill blanketed with trees, then labeled as part of the Forêt de Mortain. Had the battle been fought at that time, 35 years earlier, a curtain of trees would have cut off visibility to the front. Thirty-five or so years later, the pines have again obscured observation. What happened in the interval between 1909 and 1944? No one can say with certainty. It was not disease, because the principal territory of the forest to the south was extensive in 1944 as shown by the map which the American forces used. The same map shows Hill 314 without trees. Another more likely speculation is that during the tough years after World War I, especially during the depression years of the '30s, hard-pressed French farmers cut the trees for firewood. Whatever the reason, no trees blocked the attacking Germans from view in August 1944.

Nature's screen fell away and gave victory and relief to beleaguered men of the battalion. Then it grew back, again obliterating and shutting out all visual perception of the horrendous events of August 1944. Occasionally today, someone, usually with a metal detector, will discover a bit of residue from the battle, a casing for a .30-caliber bullet or a chunk of rusting iron ripped from an exploding German artillery shell. Apart from such lingering remnants, there is nothing else to find or see. The curtain has again closed.

Finally, who can explain the ultimate irony of my role in that battle? I know now that, with my heritage, if Hitler's panzers had overrun the Hill, they would have shot me summarily. The thought that someone, born into the race he so despised, turned back his elite forces surely keeps Hitler squirming and twisting above the fires which roast him eternally.

Dan Garrott has told me that every year when August comes around, his thoughts go back to those days so long ago. Even to think about those days is to journey there. Most living things, birds, animals, fish, even insects, respond instinctively to the seasons. Some rush to meet winds or tides or cry to a full moon some bit of history or tribal custom cached in the genes. It must be the same with other veterans of Hill 314. When early August splits the summer, the clockwork in their minds rewinds to 1944, and the events stored there automatically rerun in a catharsis of time and self. In making the pilgrimages to Mortain, I discovered that I could not find the Hill as I remembered it. My search for meaning revealed no bright-line images, but it broke the fifty-year siege in my mind, rescuing me from the iron grip of the past.

The author, ten days after the Battle, at a captured German airfield near Gauciel

30th Infantry Division Memorial on Hill 314

Appendix A

Post-battle Report

This report was typed by the author on August 13, 1944. The handwritten interlineations in most cases were made by others.

Duri ng the morning of Sunday,6 August, my party moved forward
to occupy an OP in the vicinity of Mortain. After consulting Lt. Lee,
the liaiso n officer,in the town itself,we decided to move on ahead
and occupy a position on the very high ground about 1000 yards east
of the tow n altho our own supported infantry had not yet arrived to
take up po sitions in that area. At that time elements of the 18th
infantry were holding the hill with A Company in the position which
we occupie d. On arriving at the hill we contacted Lt. Walsh of the
32d FA who was the Fwd Obsr of the artillery our battalion was
relieving. He pointed out possible OP's and in particular showed
us one which gave a view straight down the east-west road which ran
over our h ill and into Mortain. This road paralleled another road
1500 yards to the north which was a main highway and represented the
principal avenue of escape for the German units which we believed were
trapped in front of us.The road to the north connected with the road
to our fro nt by numerous trails which were hidden from observation
by hedgero ws and foliage. It was pointed out to us that shooting the
retreating Germans on these roads was a regular picnic and that all
we had to do was knock them out when they showed themselves. This was
easy in ou r zone of observation as any enemy movement was always
revealed by a cloud of dust. We also learned that the 18th had been
supported by the 5th FA which had an OP on our hill,AT units,and
TD's who h ad even fired from the top of the hill not 50yards from
the artill ery OP;their discarded shell cases are still visible on
top of the hill. The situation,then,was a matter of our merely

holding th e high ground which we occupied, shooting the Germans
and
which our e nveloping troops flushed out of the hedgerows, making
use of the excellent observation which our OP afforded. In this
respect it   must be noted our hill is one of the highest points in
N ᴼrmandy 80808830.80 and dominated the land to our front, to the
northeast and north, and in the south. In the latter direction
we had obs ervation for perhaps 15 miles, but at first we didn't
bother wit h this sector as it was supposedly a friendly flank,
and the be st information we had on taking over was to watch to
the front, the south representing the zone of action of our own
troops. Th e observation to the north altho considerable did not
permit us a view of the roads, and, hence, our most important missions
would lie to east or the direct front, which, in fact, they did.

    Seve ral hours after we moved in E Company, 120th Inf, occupied
the hill with the same holding mission. It was evident at first, and
much more so later, that this high point we occupied was a pivot on
which eith er one army or the other could be turned, depending on who
occupied i t.

    That first after noon we set up our BC Scope and observed the
hill to ou r front very carefully. MOvement was negligible and we
were able to fire only three or four missions during daylight hours,
these targ ets being principally foot troops. Enemy attack aviation
was active over us that afternoon.

    That night we moved into the draw behind the hill and bedded
down for a quiet night inthe well dug in fox-holes which the #2d rA

had been thoughtful enough to prepare for us. By this time we had wire communicat ion and our plan of defensive fires from Lt. Lee. This, incidentally, was the last we heard from or about 24-2. We gave K Co. cmdr, Lt. C urley, a copy of the defensive fires and also informed him of the pre sence of an obsr from the 980th FA, a 155 outfit. We also never saw him after the first evening. As we bedded down everything was quiet, and we anticipated that ~~asixafxkba~~ any action we would see in our pos tion would be slight indeed.

Rati ons that day which the FA obsr consumed had been regular breakfast with the btry, K for lunch, and hot B ration with the infantry tha t night. This ration record over the period of time is included i n this reprt; the FA obsr without a doubt ate more and better than anyone else on the hill because of the rations he carried wi th him and because of the solicitude of the infantry for he artille ry, which later proved to be a lifesaver.

That first night, like five others which followed, we get no sleep. Bri efly, German aviation was over us, tanks were active to the font, and, f inally, German troops came around our right flank thru H Co. whi ch was attached to us. In that minor envelopment they captured 1 9 out of 20 jeeps, the 57mm AT gun which was the only such prote ction on the road which bordered the right flank, and brought in horse-drawn artillery. We were kept awake firing missions from the p lan of defenseive fires we had, the basis of our missions being repo rts of infantry listening posts and patrols. We also fired a fe w missions by sound in the area in which the Germans had cut thr u our flank. Some artillery fire lit a trifle close,

but injured nome of our own troops and probably actually beat off the
        of
German men ance, which we were not aware but which most have been there.
T his state ment is based on the regular night attacks which the enemy
made on ou r postion thereafter,and of which we were more that aware.
We were al so harassed by sniper fire that first night.

    The morning of Aug 7 was very misty,and it was 0930 or 1000
hours befo re we could observe much to the front. When the mist
did clear it left us facing a German Attack. Machine gun fire which
snipped th e bushes all around the rock in front of our OP forced us
to abandon it quickly.Sgt. Corn and Cpl. Garret had gone to investigate
the possib ilty of getting back to 24-2 for batteries around the left
flank as o ur rear was in enemy hands. Sgt. Sasser and I crawled off
the OP with the BC scope,triped,radio and btry pack,and one telephone
between us. When we got back to our foxholes we found a runner from
Lt. Curle y waiting for us. We which disposed of the excess equipment
in our jee p which was right there and left for the south end of the
hill wher e Lt. Curley was directing the defense of his postion. This
was the hi ghest point on the hill,and probably furnished the best
all-around observation. The attack in front of us was mostly infantry
advancing across the fidld toward us;we took most of the fight out
of them wi th a few concentrations of tire fire. By 1400 the situation
was well i n hand and Sgt. Sasser went to find the rest of our party
         s till
which was which unheard of since they had gone to look into the pos-
sibilitye of getting back for supplies. Shortly after this an 88mm

opened up on this second OP of ours. It made a good target being
a very pro minet outcropping of rock. Fortunately,its fire was more
annoying th at anything else,altho there a few uncomfortable close
rounds tha t bounced off the rocks beside us. One in particular never
exploded un til it was well into the valley to our rear;the only
explanatio n to be made was that the Germans were using Polish
ammunition. During the late afternoon sniper fire from the hill to
our rear m ade the valley in between untenable;we moved up on top
and became the pocket. G and K Co.'s were also in the pocket;we
did not f orm a consolidated force,however,as our only contact
with these companies was by patrol. Before darkness we had received sev eral casualties and our position looked critical. First
platoon pu t in a road block at the RJ on our left flank and we
fired the a normal barrage and some important concentrations for
our defens e that night. Our party established itself well behind
he high ro ck outcropping on the OP after having had the top of our
antenna s hot off during the afternoon firing. Our situation was
this: the company had no food nd water since the day before and
no prospec t of receiving any;we were surrounded;snipers to the rear
neutralize d us to some extent;our right flank was open,and the enemy
could move in our out withouth much trouble(Cannon Co. fire in this
area was e xcellent and its constancy probably discouraged the enemy
enough to prevent his th establishing positions on our
right flan k): we had one 81mm mortar that could fire at one elevation
nd which h ad no ammunition;we had two 60mm mortars,one of which could
not be tra versed and which had a little ammunition;there were no AT

guns avail able;we had a few rifle grenades;the read block had all
our strong anti-tanks weapons,one bazooka with nine rounds of ammuntion;
we had no mines;most of our machine-gun ammunition was in the valley.
To the front we could hear enemy tanks moving in the darkness. We believed
these were part of the 15th Panzer Div. This information had been received
from a German artillery officer captured early in the day on top of our
hill. He had come up to reconneiter positions for his guns to be used
for direct laying.

Rations that day were two K's adn two squares of a D ration.

That night one tank came into our positions,but for some reason
no others followed him up. We could have been driven off the hill with
ease. Artil ary fire that night as before kept the enemy away and made
the avenue s of approach too dangerous.

Duri ng the day Aug we were under fire from 88's,75's,and one
150 gun. This fire was were heavy and meant to drive us off our
OP. It inc luded HE,AP,and WP. Our artillery was quite attive and we
ffectivel y neutrlized three enemy batteries which were shooting at
us. One go od point of German fire was that everytime he got an over
on our po sition he had a hit on the hill behind us which his troops
occupied.

At o ur OP we still had no water,altho it was rumored that on
our left f lank men were getting water from a farm house which was
still res i ded in by a Frenchmen. Rations for the day: one K ration.

That night we moved towards the left flank as the German fire

had made observation from the réck quite spotty. The inf cmdr continued
to use it for his OP,however,and did so during the entire fight. He didn't
seem to gi ve a damn. We moved in to the Co. CP which was also the PW
collecting pt,aid station,supply depot,and so on●. We established our
own fire d irection denter that night. All protective fires were shot in;
ad at the approach of enemy forces(almc t invariably tanks) from either
flank th e inf would call us by phone from those points,and we would give
them the f ire. We kept our radio# well ~~intrenced~~ entrenched. It was our salvation.
C annon Co . lost theirs that day by needless exposure.

That night the enemy made three very definite attempts to come thru
on our lef t flank,and each time artillery fire drove ~~him~~ them off. An attack
on our pos it ion was also made by foot troops armed with automatic weapons
which was repulsed. Their fire was effective,however, and caused many
casualties . The man lying next to me was shot thru the leg and head,and
we were al 1 splattered with lead and rock splinters from the ricochetting
bulletd.

On t he 9th we moved up on the hill into our third OP.more centrally
located,bu t generally on the left flank. We had good observation down the
road,and s till had communication with the roadblack on the left and the inf
cmdr on th e right. Troops of the enemy occupied our roadblck,but we drove
them off w ith artillery fire adn reoccupied it. The troops to our rear
asked us t o surrender and reported the capture of 16 EM and five officers,
including Lt. Fyke of 2d Bn. We told them "Hell,no". From this information
it looked as if 2d Bn staff had been captured.We believed the hill behind

us to be o ccupied by approximately 35 men who were in a bad way and were
bluffing. (Information from a prisoner). We didn't redlize how many Germans
were behin d us. Things looked very bad that night and we fortunately
were saved by the ring of fire set up the seven battalions of artillery.
We all sle pt with out hands on our guns ready for a final fight. One
tank came within 50 yards of our OP,fired a few rounds,called for us
to surrend er or die,and left. One man surrendered.

Rati ons that day:four squares of a D ration and the appropriate
share of o ne K ration which was split five ways. We now had plenty of
water from the farmhouse,altho sniper fire sometimes prevented its
procuremen t.

On t he tenth we began using discarded batteries for the secnd time.
Our set ha d been off since the sec nd day except when we were actually
transmitti ng. C-47's dropped supp/ies that day,half of which were lost
to the ene my and which contained no batteries or medical supplies. The
mortars ha d plenty of ammunition. That night was quiet,relatively,and
the ring o f fire made appreach by the enemy hazardous. He stayed in
his hole.

Rati ons of the tenth were 4 squares of D ration and two K's.

On t he 11th we continued to drive off the enemy and by this time
were confi dent that aid would reach us by noon,which never happened.
That day w e drew a lot of enemy artillery fire from frnt and rear and
mortar fir e from the hill behind. This lone mortar was knocked out with
our 6dmm. We spotted enemy in our uniforms to the rear and that made us

cautious a bout firing on any troops. That night we again received the
ring of fi re. Five tanks came from the rear and occupied our roadblock.
Our troops with drew and we shot them with artillery,definitely knocking
out one an d scaring them back. They made no attempt to contact their
forces to thefront. Our troops reoccupied the roadblock.

  Rati ons were two K rat ions.

      of 12 Aug

  Earl y in the morning there was lots of movement to the front and we
commenced firing in earnest. At 0915 my chief of detail,Sgt Corn,was
in‡ure by artillery fire from the rear which hit almost in our slit trench.
I had left it not five minutes before. He died quietly four and one
half hours later,showing complete interest,consciousness of the situation,
and good j udgement on decisions up to the end. Visiblity came early and
we stopped large concentrations of enemy troops and tanks to the front.
He began a n attack which never attained momentum because of the devasting
artillery fire laid down on him. He seemed to have vacated the area by
the time t he dust cleared. For hours after we could see smoke in the
draw to th e front from burning vehicles and the east west road was
strewn wit h wreckage. Second platoon sent a patrol to investigate and
reported t urrets and other portions of enemy tanks and vehicles thruout
the area. Tracks were an utter confusion and showed clearly how the enemy
had s ought to avoid our fire.

  We w ere relieved at about 1430 by elements of the 35th div.

  Thru out the entire occupancy of the hill we noticed an apparent
indecision on the part of the enemy to overwhelm our position which he
could have ea-ily done. His radio position locaters picked us up quite

easily. An y wreckage or injured personnel were removed almost as soon as they becam e casualties;to this and he employed every means,including the use of an ambulance as a wrecker and tow vehicle. He fired on us with artillery at hight only once,that being the time Sgt. Cern was hit. Altho quit e often beat back and silenced,at the slightest carelessness in exposin g ourselves thereafter,the enemy would strike back at us. He doesn't qu it .His aggressiveness demands 24 hour observation,whether by sight or sound.

Robert L. Weiss
2d Lt.   FA

Appendix B
Message Log 230th Field Artillery Battalion
for the period August 6–12, 1944

MESSAGE LOG

— LEGEND —

T - TELEPHONE   DA - DIV. ARTY.
M - MESSENGER   FO - FORWARD OBSR.
R - RADIO   OP - OBSERVATION POST
M.C. - MESSAGE CENTER   INF. S - SUPPORTED INF. UNIT.

DATE: 6 AUG

MSG NO	FROM Party	Time	Sig by/Recd	TO Party	Time	how	MESSAGE	COM NO
1	241	0840	R			R	Liaison of 1st C 317A left. Have no maps or know any troops or situation	
2	A-3	1435	R				In Pos. (M5-K:9) (553-108)	
3	DIV ARTY	1530	R				CP. Loc. (509-138)	
4	B3	1550	R	DA	1200	T	I Co Inf Marching (6164 1058)	300
5	—	1230	R	DA	1200	T	ALL LNO's & OBSVRS CALLED IN POSITION SO FAR	
6	C3	1700	R	DA	1700		EN. KIT - N5 J91 (611-119)	301
7	144	1300	T				~~Recent~~ Civilian states EN. Arty. 25 m — on hi ground between La Tourniere & La Grande Bosch 2 guns in BR. cut -200 meters from town — Inf. moving on sunken roads — vic. St. Clement - OP's & bombings on hi ground - EN. consists Paratroopers. 10 Inf. Regts. Rus. front	
8	B3	1245	T	DA	1400	T	Receiving morter fire from Az. 1391 -	✓
9	AA	1245	P	DA	1850	T	AIR PLANES THIS AFTERNOON WERE 12 FW. 190 -	✓
10	DA	1500	T				BAKERY (628-076) - DA CP -	
11	B3	1900	R				EN. Act in Bldg. (614-106)	✓
12	144	2045	R				EN. btry RCP by civilian app (6180-0844)	✓
13	B3	2130	R				(6172-1050) 15 EN. INF. IN VIC	✓
14	DA	2130	T				TANKS ON road between BORENTON AND MORTAIN TANK AND INFANTRY ASSEMBLY AREA (644-060)	
15	DA	2400	T				NO FIRE LINE GRID LINE 57 N-OF 17, 50 TO 10 65	
							7 AUG	
1	LN3	0010	R	DA	0115	T	IN POS P6 K47 (6622-0466)	
2	03	0110	R	DA	0145	T	EN. INF. + Veh. Qan 301 - 304	✓
3	B9	0600	R	DA	0605	T	(5939-0953) 400 EN counter-attacking in this vic	✓
4	DA	0635	T				I+R reported in contact with GERMAN TANKS AT ROMAGNY	
5	LN1	0640	T	DA	0645	T	Column of EN trucks con 330 332 334 (60.04-1890) (6016-1120) (6050-10.86)	
6	C3	0655	R	DA	0659	T	(609-11.9) Armoured Assembly Area 2 observer.	
7	B3	0720	R	DA	0721	T	(6648-0852) EN Vehicles -	✓
8	B4	0800	R				IN position TN6 - J12 (5672-1203)	
9	B4	0800	R	Center	0805	T	Enemy tanks — infantry along road. TN6 J7-J8 R1 (5654-1258) and N. along rd. 600 yds -	
10	LN1	0745	R				2 Tank N6 J60 (565-135) 2 tank N6 D69 (573-117)	
11	DA	0815	T				Counter-attack (54.28 - 20.77)	
12	N6	0845	T	Code	0855	T	Enemy TANKS - N6 J33 J36 (5684-1251)	
13	DA	0900	R				Be PREPARED TO FIRE on 10X MORE TANKS PLUS INF AT CRUNCH "C"	
14	B4	0916	R	Center	0920	T	TANKS - INFANTRY (56.94 - 12.22) - Observed	314
15	LN1	0830	R	DA	1130	T	Front lines. N6-I 66 J96 J21 J34 J33 J39 D37 No change in position	
16	B4	0935	R	Center	6105	T	12 enemy vehicles and infantry (5765 - 1227) 315 No's 3x vehicles - others dispersed (5784 - 1209) Adj	315
17	B3	0950	R				Check fire (enemy vehicles (6)	303
18	LN3	0955	R	East	0955	T	P6 K34 L63 Front lines - 6648-665 - 047	
19	B3	0955	R				Position - N6° W12 - N6 W33	
20	B3	1005	R				303 is 800 short - enemy vehicles	✓

Aug 7—

No		Time				Message	No
21	B4	1025	R			In Pos N6 G42	
22	B3	1025	R			20 Germans MG N8 – J38 (6039-1042)	317
23	B3	1025	R DA	1150	T	Front lines N 8 I 89 N8 J21 – Arty landing cks c	
24	B3	1035	R Custer			Moving under M.G. fire	
25	B4	1040	R Custer			En Tanks moving out (AAA) 314 (5694-1222) 2K0.	
26						2 tanks knocked out	
27	B4	1050	R			Con 314 – 100 Right - 100 over 2 enemy tanks	314
28	B3	1030	R			Enemy vehicles tanks Concentrations 303 —315- 316	
						(6151-1046) 2" (3254-1209) 316 (6142-1055)	
29	C3	1105	R			Check Pt 2" Enemy vehicles (62.1 - 12.0)	304
30	B3	1110	R Custer			T Strong enemy force CON 316 (6142-1055)(6168-103.0)	316
			DA	1120	T	1 vehicle hit—men milling about— large counter-attack	
31	B3	1110	R			Front lines extended –N8 –J24 from last line	
33	A3	1205	R			In position RI V07 (66.32- 0522)	
34	B3	1205	R			Tanks moving across road – 66.72 - 10.52	314
35	B3	1207	R			Tanks in draw - N8 – J47 (60.5 - 09.9)	314
36	S-6	1215	T			Tanks going W. (572-147)	
37	Cav	1215	T DA	1730	T	Shell rep 110	
38	M4	1215	R			In Position (?) N6 – G21 – 11.45	
39	A3	1245	R DA	1545	T	Two scout cars - PS P70 - (6761-0608)	
40	Rad	0125	R DA	1545	T	Tanks in vicinity 58.7 – 10.0 At 10.0.0 "	
41	S-6	1300	P DA	1545	T	Slightly wounded sent back from 3rd BN. – Slightly wounded captured by Germans– serious cases sent in back to our own hosp. –	
42	B3	1320	R DA	1545	T	Conc 308 v 200LL 400 55 – EN. AA WEAPON (6151-1046)	319
43	S-6	1230	T DA	1730	T	Shell rep #111	
44	LN1	1340	T			Ft Line B Co N6 J3, J4, J12, J14, D30 – B Co N6 D23 - B Co N6 D28, D46, D35, D44, D53 -	
45	B3	1350	T DA	1545	T	EN. AUTO. WEAPN N8 K20 (613-107)	320
46	LN1	1350	T			83 rpts E go ft Lines N8 I89, J32	
47	B4	1420	R DA	1545	T	Enemy infantry – tanks vicinity of houses (57.06 – 11.60)	321
48	B4	1420	T			In position T N6 D28 - (56.82 – 11.58)	
49	A8	1435	T			In position M5 J28. - (54.3 – 10.7)	
50	B3	1440	R DA	1545	T	61 M mortar in vicinity (62.2 – 10.8)	
51	B4	1445	R DA	1545	T	Con 321 – 100 over –2 mks + mf	321
52	Verify	1448	T DA	1545	T	Counter battery – 6 rounds Verify 105m	
53	B3	1455	R DA	1545	T	EN MORTARS– (6224-1073)	322
54	V86	1510	T DA	1545	T	Tanks (568-098)	
55	B4	1510	R DA	1545	T	1 TANK N6 J31 (569-119)	
56	B6	1515	T DA	1545	T	5 Rounds 42.18.00 105m · Vic. B Btry	
57	LN1	1630	R DA	1531	T	British plane strafing our front lines	
58	LN1	1600	R LN1	1531	R	MESSAGE FROM CUSTER 6 TO CUFF 6	
59	C4	1605	R			In Position N5 G12 (56.72 – 1203) T– N5 G12	
60	B4	1625	R DA	1730	T	1 Enemy tank TNL J51 - (52.18 – 11.91)	32U
1	LN1	1630	R S-6	1630	I	Message from Cuff6 & Custer 6 "Cannot say quiet– on your imagination"	
2	S-6	1630	T	1630	T	1 tank reported 200 yds from Custer CP– going N	
3	B4	1705	R DA	1730	T	Enemy infantry - mortars vicinity houses 5.00 - 11.40.50	
4		1730	R DA	1730	T	Receiving shellings 88 · 4 guns AZ 18 0 0	

MESSAGE LOG

LEGEND

T - TELEPHONE
M - MESSENGER
R - RADIO
M.C. - MESSAGE CENTER

DA - DIV. ARTY.
FO - FORWARD OBSR.
O.P. - OBSERVATION POST
INF. S - SUPPORTED INF. UNIT.

DATE: 7 Aug.

MSG NO.	FROM Party	Time	By Whom	TO Party	Time	By Whom	MESSAGE	CN. NO.
65	IN1	1730	R	CUSTER	1730	T	CLIFFG TO CUSTERG - GOING INTO POSITION AT N8 H88 (5860-1046) - Request No ARTY FIRE	
66	IN1	1745	R	DA	1745	T	TYPHOONS STRAFING AT LINES -	
67	IN1	1745	R				TANK CORNERED BY 4 ENEMY TANKS -	
68	B3	1800	R	1800	1825	T	IN POS. (603-098) ENEMY N, S, E, W. - REQUEST SUPPLY & SUPPORT IMMEDIATELY. -	✓
69	B3	1815	R				EN. 88 GIVING US HELL - Cans. 303 is 1004L 400 00 -	✓
70	B4	1840	R	DA	1858	T	(5/09'-1180) Enemy infantry and tanks Assembling Same as above	325
71	52	1855	T	DA	1855	T	LOCATIONS of Observers -	
72	197	1910	T				197th (52.8 - 10.2)	
73	197	1910	T	DA	2150	T	Enemy vehicles (60.7 12.8)	330
74	B3	1920	T	DA	2150	T	EN 88 - (61.33 10.47)	303
75	IN1	1930	M	DA	2150	T	GERMANS dressed in AMERICAN uniforms have been infiltrating into our lines. Spokesmen speak good English.	
76	B3							
77	IN3	1945	R				No chg. in pos - will use same code tomorrow	
78	C4	2025	R	DA	2150	T	TANKS N5 & A87 (5755-1262)	330
79	CG	2045	T	637 DA	2100	T	FR. CIVILIAN STATES 10 GERMANS COMING IN ON HIS FLANK -	
71	Cox	2100	T	DA	2150	T	F Co. Rd Block (588 114) much en veh. traffic 60 yds up rd.	
72	B3	2100	R	DA	2150	T	N8 E (6139-1029) in 50R, 100S - large # en veh -	331
73	Cox	2100	T	C3	2130	R	Enemy vehicles (58.8 - 12.8)	
74	B3	2145	R	E			(60.7 - 09.9) Same position	
75	DA	2150	T	*			ATKD TODAY BY EST. 5BN. INF, 4BN TANKS, 4BN. ARTY. -	✓
76	Cox	2200	T				35 DIV COMING INTO MORTAIN - UP RED RD. - TD's got 7 TANKS, TODAY.	
77	B4	2200	R				No chg in pos. - nothing new -	
78	C4	2210	R	DA	2400	L	TANKS MOVING NT 635 G 47 (Roadcenter 570 - 1244) hear by sound - (5704-1247)	341
79	S-5	2230	P	DA	2400	L	FR. CIV. REPORTS 100 GERMANS & 1 TANK IN ROMAGNY	
80	B4	2235	R	DA	2400	L	(5766-1207) EN INF ASSEMBLING IN FARM YARD BELIEVED TO BE COUNTER ATK.	✓
81	B2	2245	R	197	2245	T	(645 - 103) Enemy activity tanks now Napp possible counter attack	327
82	R4	2258	R					
83	Cox	2300	T	DA	2400	L	Inf. DIGGING IN + ASSEMBLING (5868-1210)	
84	IN1	2300	T				Ft LINES A Co N6, I75, I4, I22 - B Co, N6, I14, D9, D37, D26, D45	
85	Cox	2300	T				Crm rd Blk. 581-110) & (584-114) F Co RD Blk from 579 & 583) and (118 & 122)	
86	B3	2350	R	DA	2400	L	Running low Ammunition - E Co. -	
87	C3	2350	R	DA	2400	L	Tanks other vehicles running around -	327 ✓
88							- (5860 - 1240)	
89	B4	2400	R	DA	2400	L	Inf. Ass. - (5730 - 1228)	344

MESSAGE LOG

LEGEND

T - TELEPHONE
M - MESSENGER
R - RADIO
M.C. - MESSAGE CENTER

DIV.A - DIV. ARTY.
FO - FORWARD OBSR.
O.P. - OBSERVATION POST
INF - SUPPORTED INF. UNIT.

DATE: 8 Aug

MSG N°	FROM			TO			MESSAGE	CN. N°
	PARTY	TIME	SENT SAT	PARTY	TIME	SENT SAT		
1	24-1	0020	T	DA	025	T	A Co CP hit by heavy German Artillery - CP party radio knocked. extent of casualties not known. Friendly fire also received in A.C.P. area.	
2	24-1	0050	T				NEED ANOTHER OBSERVER - Lt DEVITT HIT, is now with medics. THINK TROOP WAS KILLED - R.D. KNOCKED OUT -	
3	B3	0210	R	DA	0215	T	Tanks - normal barrage + moving into position (61.39 - 10.29)	✓
4	P4	0330	R				Possible counter attack - (5737 - 1234)	344
5	B4	0600	R	DA	0700	T	Enemy infantry same as above	744
6	A8	0600	R	DA	0700	T	(3) Enemy tanks vicinity 5709 - 11.9 (1 Ko'd	
7	DA	0715	T				Croyden lines (58-1-14.5) (67.4 15.4)	
8	C-3	0658	R	DA	0940	T	(5709 - 11.9) Enemy vehicles going through Road block 6139 - 1029	301
9	B4	0720	R	DA	0940	T	Enemy infantry digging in (57.37 - 1234)	344
10	B4	0720	R	DA	0940	T	In position TN 6 √13 - (56.72 - 1218)	✓
11	B3	0815	R	DA	0940	T	(6159 - 1029) EN INF ASSEMBLING 1 Plat or more	346
12	B3	0810	R	DA	0940	T	5 TANKS 50 MEN Reported 1 1/2 kilometers North of road junction 314 on road. Info from officer P.W. (59.8 - 10.5)	
12	B3	0935	R	DA	0940	T	(6159 - 1029) 1 Plat of EN INF.	✓
13	DA	0950	T				(54 - 16) Do not fire on ARMOR in this AREA it is friendly	
14	B3	0945	R	DA	1040	T	N8 R82 (6213 - 1090) EN 88 MM 60N	348
15	DA	0950	T				Restriction lifted on AREA (54 - 16)	
16	B3	1015	R	CUSTER DA	1020	M	Cuff 6 to Custer 6: still holding oblig. pos - elements of H Co are still with me - still in contact with G + K - Point marked with white cross. Need batterys 300 + 610. med supplies + food. basic load ammo for rifle Co + 60 + 80 morters - Captured EN. jeep 0830 English speak German officer captured wounded - ski. stry is at GER	
17	DA	1040	T				Johnston coming up on Rd. MORTAIN - BARENTON DON'T FIRE W/I 1000 yds. N. of Rd.	
18	B3	1145	R				EN ACTIVITY - INF - (5984 - 1052) (6213 - 1090) (6149 - 1025)	345 ✓
19	NN1	1200	T				A8 is in pos N6 D28 - B4 is with A Co. - Lt NG √13	
20	A8	1201	R	DA	1220	T	EN Road block AND TANK AT (5699 - 11.86)	349
21	B3	1200	R	DA	1220	T	Coded message ABC we Getting Reinforcements?	✓
22	DA	1225	T				EN troops entrenching (5890 - 1284) TOT AT 1230	
23	A8	1245	R	DA	1302	T	EN INF ON Road - (5697 - 11.86) Adj + (5719 - 1203)	351
24	B3	1250	R	DA	1302	T	2 EN TANKS on road (61.20 - 10.70)	352 ✓
25	NN1	1300	T				Lt BEESMER + PARTY HIT - will by morters - will let PAPPAS HANDLE OBSVN	
26	B3	1305	R	DA	1307	T	observers position being smoked by enemy	✓
27	NN1	1305	T				Lt BEESMERS party suffered only slight wounds no info on injuries of Lt BEESMER -	
28	B3	1353	R	DA	1355	T	EN Btry (6238 - 10.04) Adj (6228 - 1008)	354
29	Lu	1345	R	DA	1355	T	shelling √13 -	

MESSAGE LOG

LEGEND:
T - Telephone
M - Messenger
R - Radio Bus
MC - Message Center

CO - Commanding Officer
CO - Command Post
OP - Observation Post
Unit - Supported Unit Unit

DATE:

Msg No.	From	Time			Message	Gn. No.
30	B3	1415	R	DA 1450 T	Conc 346 is 1000 R. RR - En. Self propelled guns - (6170 - 1111) 6 guns - not moving - drawing fire this way - adj cond (6178 - 1103)	355
				DA 1450 T	Cobble #14 +/5 .	
31	B3	1415	R	DA 188 T	1 En. Tank N8C90 (5982 - 0954)	
32	B3	1450	R	DA 1500 T	1 EM BTRY - wider 4 or 6 gun fired about 5 min. ago - say 355 in SW RR 3005s (6211-1142) adj cond (6308 - 1176) - cobble #16	356
33	193R	1420	R	DA 1525 T	Infiltrg Rcn. Reports 6 gun BZRY AT (621-155) Believes Hg. Bivouaced at (620-157) Motor Trans Port & 4 10 Moving S. AT (625-134) 6 gun Heavy Btry. at (626-135) - PW Rpt. Am Dep AT 712 149 just off Road in woods.	
				DA 1550 T	Cobble Report # 14, #15, #16	
34	A6	1645	T	DA 1715 T	Shell Rep #17	
35	B3	1645	R	DA 1650 T	(6335 - 1685) En btry - firing over my head - 357	357
36	A146	1705	R	DA 1705 T	Receiving ARTY FIRE IN CUSTER CP, coming	
37					FROM THE SOUTH - CHECK UNIT ON RIGHT	
37	193	1620	R	DA 1625 T	15 Self propeled guns with UNKNOWN NUMBER of INFANTRY at 626-049 At 1400 SOURCE V2	
38	B3	1810	R	DA 1810 T	150 FIRING ON US. H2 800, 8000 to 10000 yds. in vic GER-	✓
39	CROW	1810	R	PM 1810 T	New Custer CP N9 P31 (5581 - 1074)	
40	M	1830	R	DA 1840 T	(5208 - 1188) 1 EN tank	328
41	DA	1900	T		Notify M3 of EN BTRY DUE E. OF HIM	
42	B6	2020	T	DA 2020 T	ER told some put. that Germans were coming from SE H. Kilo Away	
43	C8	2100	R	DA 2331 T	IN Pos NG J12 (56.73 - 1202)	
44	B3	2230	R	DA 2331 T	(6110 - 1012) EN tanks	359
45	B3	2200	R	DA 2215 T	Captured several prisoners. Bothered by snipers Tanks in front of them (have hit some) Need batteries for 300 +600 series Radios Don't seem to worked Will Report more when possible Getting hungry Need medical supplies -	✓
46	B3	2300	R	DA 2331 T	(61.10 - 10.12) EN tanks	359
47	B3	2330	R	DA 2331 T	(61.10 - 10.12) EN vehicles	319
48	IN1	2400	R	DA 0008 T	Shell Rep #115	

Message Log

LEGEND
T - TELEPHONE
M - MESSENGER
R - RADIO
M.C. - MESSAGE CENTER

DA - DAILY
FC - FORWARD OBSERVER
O.P. - OBSERVATION POST
INF - SUPPORTED INF. UNIT

DATE: 9 Aug

Msg No	From			To			Message	C.N. No
	Oper. Unit	Time	How	Oper. Unit	Time	How		
1	B3	0145	R	DA	0200	T	(5969-11.13) EN TANKS	360
2	B3	0640	R	DA	0715	T	En attempted to overrun observers position 3 times during night but was driven back by Arty fire	
3	B3	0710	R	DA	0745	T	(61.10-10.12) EN tanks (Adj (6112-1036)	359
4	C6	0720	T	DA	0725	T	Shell rep #116	
5	B3	0740	R	DA	0745	T	1 Platoon EN INF (61.59-10.38)	
6	B3	0735	R	DA	0745	T	(6112-1036) 3 light tanks	359
7	24	0800	R				If firing in 18th sector make sure that it is observed and 1st round will be A "good" over	
8	Cox	1800	T	DA	0801	T	A Co received (friendly Arty fire) 56.9-123	
9	B3	0750	R	DA	0810	T	Enemy bike troops - INF. 6139 - 1028	361
10	B3	0805	R	DA	0920		Tanks - (61.10 - 10.12) adj (- 10 36)	359
11	C	0805	R	DA	0850	T	Shelling from btry - A2 1100	
12	+	0900	R				Position - moving N9 P93	
13	C8	0910	R				Position the same -	
14	B3	0915	R	DA	0930	T	Platoon of Enemy infantry coming down Road	361
15	B3	0920	R	DA	0930	T	P W Inform: New Panzer division on our front - things are cooling off, resistance to SE E lessining - German resistance decreasing	
16	B3	0925	R	Cox	1838	T	Our position Now - I 68 I 77 I 88 I 95	
17	C	1000	T	DA	1030		Enemy resistance (5740-1040)	362
18	DA	1002	R	DA	1023	T	Position - N9 Q33 - receiving Arty fire A2 1200 - 105 possible B.N. ((5695-100)	
19	C8	1005	R	DA	1023	T	Receiving Arty fire same as before (B5 1100	
20	B3	1040	R	DA	1045	T	Enemy vehicles (6154-1035)	363
21	WN	1140	T	DA	1045	T	In Pos N9 Q32 (5698-1092) Recon El N9 Q 43 (5708-1092) Sgt PARRAS with 16 M- ER ELISE landed (5706-1074) at 1100 A24500 appr Bn. IV. - Receiving En arty fire A2 1300 - 4 rounds at 1135 - est 105 m.	
22	A8						Position TN9 A33 - same as 24-1	
23	C6	1230	T		1230	T	Germans may have observation from Hill 285 wood (569 118) - warn all to be careful of circulation	
24	B3	1240	R	DA	1240	T	Tanks - 6112 - 1036 1 (Can see 2 possible	359
25	B3	1205	R	DA	1250	T	Tanks near Check Pt #1	
26	B3	1310	R	DA	1350	T	Estimated Co. of Enemy infantry (6149-1025)	248
27	B3	1400	R				1 TANK - PLATOON INF 364 (6130-1045)	
28	Cox	1400	T				3rd Bn. has gone in to NW - obj. TCWE have advanced about 2,000 yds	
29	B3	1430	R	DA	1530	T	forming skirmish line - with 3 Tps. - may be 4th vic (6690-1249) - (we find now - 364 - Crumb 722 - and Curtis 461)	
30	B3	1505	R		1911		NEED SUPPLIES BADLY	
31	B3	1520	R	Custis	1520	T	Medical Needed - Wounded Dying	
32	Arty	1542	R				Curtis has begun smoking	
33	B3	1615	R	DA	1625	T	Being shelled from large gun (150) A2. 1600	
34	Cox	1655	T	DA	1745	A	Enemy Pocket N6 - P42 P61 I48 - B21 #16 J31 J41 J42 J22	
35	Cox	1655	T				appeared A Co front lines J3 J13 J22 J21 - they are cleaning out above pocket	

Msg No.	From	Time			Message	Cn. No.
37	Wolf	1730	R DA	1745	T Shelling # 117	
38	B3	1805	R DA 1820	T	Several enemy vehicles. (61.60 - 1038)	359
39	Wolf	1820	T DA 1820	T	More rounds #717 _ compass 1806	
40	24-1	1830	T DA 1830	T	Position T N9 - R27 (57.98 - 11.46)	
41	Cov	1830	T DA 1830	T	Balls reports shells landed at (56.7-113) Az 24° at 1800 shells 3/4" thick.	
42	Cov	1940	T DA 1940	T	Crew is Balls - more shells from Az 64°	
43	B3	1848	R DA 1840	T	Motorcycles withdrawing wounded personnel (59.22 - 110.8)	36.0
44	B3	1860	R DA 1850	T	Germans request B3 to surrender - have captured 5 officers 16 enlisted men. B3 Answer - "Hell! No"	
45	C8	1855	R C8/1855	T	Request relief badly shaken up - need jeep to tow in Pour jeep	
46	B3	1915	R	1915	T Request Air (or Ambulance) N816 (589 102)	
47	2N1	2000	R		In Pos N9R34	
48	Cov	2010	T DA 2030	T	Cannon Co stru w A Co. reptd 25 men going along RR. Then orchard then on w -N5 J18, I19, P91, P71	
49	240	2040	R		Heard from C3 through Cannon Co	
50	Cov	2035	R	2040	T Shelling # 118	
51	C8	1855	R Cannon 2040	T	(Msg to 24-1) Unit Reorganizing remains - will need big arty prep - am at your yesterdays CP	
52	B3	2145	R		Have 3.49 girl from ckpt to base pt throughout night - at least 1 gun every 3 min.	
53	C8	2150	R		C8 - Same position as this morning 5673-1202) doubtful -	
54	C6	2210	T		C6 hy driver slightly wounded on way to C8 - returned to bty with jeep.	
55	B3	2220	R		Platoon OK at 22,20	
56	B3	2245	R Cannon 2245	T	Germans building up reserves on all files - request you fire immedtly heavy for first hour -	
57	B3	2230	R Cannon 2230	T	Hear many vehicles on east-west rd. (enm. 359) to our front - track laying	

Aug 10

1. B3 0250 R Custer 0250 T 39.73 – 10.93 Vehicles on Road.
2. B3 0300 R Custer 0305 T MANY vehicles on Road – 59.69 – 11.10   Verify
7. B3 0700 R Custer 0700 T Fires successful during night = one fight
   DA 0700 T with a TANK – SKIRMISH –
4. C8 0735 T Custer 0745 T Position the same as last night.
5. S2 1000 P SMOKE drifting over ENTIRE APER
   coming from South east
6. LN4 1000 T DA 1005 T MAP CAPTURED by CROYDEN shows
   EN CPs at N8 P31 (59.27-1020) N8 H37 (5811-1050)
   N8 I 19-29 (59.08-1051) GUNS At N866&69 (5742-10944)
   N8 I 35 (59.25-1008) N8 S 46 (6152-1023) N8 S 48 (6152-1018)
   N8 J 90 (5868-1065) N8 N 71 (5252-1074) ARROWS
   ON Road N8 I 62 to I 3 N8 I61 & I 11 (two dotted
   roads South of les Aubris went to RR
7. A4 1015 R DA 1425 T IN Pos N9 Y91 (5651-1187)
8. A8 1040 R DA 1045 T Reports friendly ARTy falling on our TANKS
   At (5764-1262)
9. B3 1000 R DA 1052 T Requests fire All defensive concentrations unable
   to contact observer After this message
10. A4 1130 R Friendly troops moving in N5 B41
    (5712-1185)
10A. Custer 3 1135 T DA 1140 T (578-128) Obs 25 Inf Captured map inverted
11. Custer 3 1200 T DA 1210 T this may be Inf RESERVE AREA
12. Custer 3 1240 T DA 1241 T ENO Removing mines At 577-112 Recieving
    heavy Small ARMS fire from AREA 528-099 We cannot
    observe Request if anyone in div CAN observe—
13. B3 1245 R DA 1330 T EN troops, (6130-1045)   364
14. A4 1320 T DA 1330 T FN Rocket guns N5T 19 (590-128)
15. DA 1701 T Ft LINES 12 INT 1588 (578-130)(577-132)
    2nd Bn (573-140)(573-144)
16. B3 1325 R DA 1330 T Recieving Heavy ARty – Hn. 16 cm gun   ✓
17. C4 1332 R DA 1339 T 2 AT GUNS A INF Ass Area (3949-1269)   377
18. B3 1415 R DA 1425 T EN Vehicles on Road (6130-1045)   364
19. A4 1420 R DA 1425 T No change in position
    1420 B3 1420 R Msg "TIME FOR SIGNAL -1500" from
    Custer 6 to Easy 6 –
20. LN1 1515 R Ft lines N9 W13 Q10 Q29 Q37 Road blocks
    N9 J 50 V66 L1R OP N9 Q29
21. A8 1517 R 6 Rds landed At (5797-1134) seemed to come from (5798-1203)
22. B3 1520 R DA 1525 T CAN Observe friendly troops to south
    AND EAST of his position
23. B3 1600 R DA 1610 T EN troops Retreating 6160-1039 AND
    IN AREA between Base Point And check
    Point Retreat is in large Numbers
    HEAVY ARTy FIRE AZ 1600 RN 8000-10000 yds
24. B3 1650 R DA 1650 T Two tanks, two guns + INF (6151-1041)   378
    Ambulance was towing one of the guns
25. S2 1715 P Btry 1715 T Notified Batteries of situation
26. 1230 R Custer 1740 T EN Btry (5887-1113) Adj (5918-1112)   379
27. B3 1735 R DA 1735 T Recieving heavy Arty fire AZ 1500 from 7 See open 200 cal

LEGEND
T - TELEPHONE
M - MESSENGER
R - RADIO
M.C. - MESSAGE CENTER

MSG NO	FROM			TO			MESSAGE	Cir. N°
	Unit	Time		Unit	Time			
28	B3	1813	R	DA	1818	T	Nebelwerfer AZ 500 (603-099)	
29	B3	1818	R	DA	1888	T	EN /4FS (6191 1041)	379
							NFL No fire EAST or South of 655-120 North	
							to (655-120) EAST Along 12 grid line	
30	B3	1820	R	DA	1850	T	3 EN cargo trucks (6160-1039) No Med sup on Lon lande	
31	DA	1822	T	BA			(58.9-10.2) En. Guns reported by CAUSWAY	
32	B3	1847	R	DA	1850	T	Receiving fire from nebelwerfers	
33	B3	1850	R	DA	1850	T	PJ (6139-1086) EN battery Tanks (ERUNG)	247
34	A4	1852	R	DA	1852	T	Friendly fire falling 50 yd in front of A4	
35	DA5	1910	T				35 Div has contacted some of our units	
36	X3	2000	R	DA	2030	T	EN INF IN HOUSE (5857-1064)	
37	B3	2015	R	DA	2030	T	INF + Tanks (6801-1040) 500 own more inf.	378
38	A4	2020	R	DA	2030	T	In pos (569-1170) N9 P99	
39	S3	2045	R				2 Plat Inf N9 J19 - (602-104)	340
40	PROP ?		R	DA	?	T	(5910-1084) - En gun	379
41	DA	2045	T				Vendor requests no own fire ? (590-120)	
42	S-4	2110	R	S-3	2110	P	Line 2 1200	
43	B3	2145	R				fire shells packed with medical supplies to N8I88	✓
44	LN4	2155	T	DA	2300	T	Shellreps # 120 AND # 121	
45	LN4	2350	T	DA	2255	T	Shellrep # 122	

MESSAGE LOG

LEGEND

DATE: 11 AUG

T - TELEPHONE
M - MESSENGER
R - RADIO
M.C. - MESSAGE CENTER

DA - DIV. ARTY
FO - FORWARD OBSR.
O.P. - OBSERVATION POST
INF. - SUPPORTED INF. UNIT.

MSG N°	FROM			TO			MESSAGE	C.N. N°
	PARTY	TIME	HOW SENT	PARTY	TIME	HOW SENT		
1		0630	R				EN INF. AND 4 ½ TRACK	383
2	B3	0800	R	DA	0810	T	Fired six medical shells to B3	✓
3	B3	0851	R	DA	0955	T	2 enemy tanks at (5969 - 1113) Adj - 5984 - 1099	376
4	Custer	0945	T	DA	1010	T	G Co lines (5948 - 10.78)(5947 - 1094)	✓
5	B3	0953	R	DA	0954	T	Tanks - Infantry - (6101 - 1041) Advancing	378
6	Cox	1035	T	DA	1035	T	Shell rept 123 - Cox sending fragments -	
7	B3	1015	R	DA	1145	T	Recovered 5 of our med. shells - Morphine broken	✓
8	Custer	1215	T				50% of morphine broken - 2N chemical shells	
9	24-1	1235	T	DA	1235	T	We have 285 Hill - Not many Germans - Pocket gone	
10	OA2	1255	T	Custer	1255	T	PW report 300 Germans with orders to hold on till last man went down Hill 285 into bottom - location unknown (30 MG - 8 tanks)	
11	Cox	1305	T	DA	1310	T	Possible En. Cp. held by 2 anti tank guns (5949 - 1269)	377
12	A4	1330	R				In position TNG - √3 √e (5694 - 1222)	
13	Cox	1505	R	DA	1520	T	Knocked out 1 AT gun on adjustment (5781 - 1282) Adjusted	377A
14	Cox	1515	T	DA	1520	T	A patrol in contact (radio) with E Co - tanks on way to get wounded.	
15	Cox	1516	T	DA	1520	T	Friendly troops have entered Mortain	
16	S3	1512		DA	1515	T	20 rounds of propaganda - sending out white flag demanding surrender -	
17	A4	1600	R	DA	1615	T	Position (56.82 - 11.58) N6 - 0281 reports suspected Pocket A2 12 -	
18	Cox	1640	T	DA	1640	T	Enemy withdrawn from Areas (573 - 11.9)(572 - 11.5) Arty barrages called off	
19	B3	1650	R	DA	1720	T	Tanks and vehicles 6150 - 1100 Adjusted	388
20	Cox	1658	T	DA	1712	T	Bandages and sulphur recovered from s medical shells (1053 - 155) Rest of supplies scattered	✓
21	Cox	1658	T	DA	1712	T	Troops not in Mortain - Near stream west of town	
22	Cox	1712	T	DA	1713	T	Cupboard moving in on their mission	
23	CC			DA	1805		B Co has taken first woods	
24	B3	1725	R	DA	1805		Tanks - 58. 50. 106.0	
25	Cox	1740	T				Request for medical shells for K Co - More later	
26	B3	1815	R	DA	1810	T	B3 Receiving Arty and mortar fire from the west	✓
27	197	1830	T	Custer	1830	T	Enemy infantry 5834 - 1030	
28	S-7	1850	T				(5852 - 1759) to (5860 - 1200) INF MOVING	
29	Cox	1858	T				N5 C26 - Medicals shells - (5914 - 1136)	
30	A8	1930	T				New at b'ry (A sent in by LN1, a.6 one 06 - wooden	
31	X3	2005	R	DA	2115	T	MG west (58.3 - 10.3)	390
31	X3	2005	R	DA	2115	T	MG West 58.4 (10.6)	391
32	B3	2030	R	DA	2157		(5984 - 1100) Enemy strong point - mortars -	384
33	A8	2125	R	DA	2135		MGuns - (59.5 - 13.5)	
34	116AN	2135	R	DA	2135	T	En Artillery - Gun position (59.79 - 1369) adj. Corbie #18	
35	B3	2150	R	Custer 2200 DA 2200			Without Reinforcements can hold Till tomorrow - Message in code sent in by B3 - ("Requested to be sent to highest headquarters available.")	✓
36	X3	2210	R	DA	2215	T	Enemy mortar in vicinity (58.8 - 10.9)	
37	DA5	2220	T	B3	2224	R	Reinforcements on the way, hold out Hobbs" TS 2215 - 2224	✓
38	B3	2222	R	DA	1030	T	(6160 - 10.34) - Tanks (6401 1041)	359 / 378

MESSAGE LOG

LEGEND

T - TELEPHONE
M - MESSENGER
R - RADIO
M.C. - MESSAGE CENTER

REG - DIV. ARTY
CO - FORWARD'S OBSR.
O.P. - OBSERVATION POST
INF - SUPPORTED INF. UNIT

DATE: Aug 12

Msg No	From Party	Time	Sent Cat	To Party	Time	Cat	Message	Cn No
1	B3	0215	R	DA	0220	T	Tanks on road (6160 - 10.39) 359	
							(6101 - 10.41) 378	
2	B3	0220	R	DA	0225	T	Heavy traffic on east-west road 6160-10.39	359
3	Custer	0520	R	DA	0525	T	Custer reports German tanks firing at each other near R junction 314	
4	B3	0645	R	DA	0608	T	(59.79-10.48) Tanks b(6119 - 1017)	324 325
5	B3	0658	R	Custer	0655	T	Urgent message — Must have ambulances immediately	
				DA	0605	T	to evacuate wounded."	
6	B3	0615	R	Custer	0645	T	Message " "Must have medical supplies flown in at earliest possible moment"	
				DA	0525	T		
7	DA	0635	T				No fire line = Nothing west of Highway 3	
8	B3	0655	R	DA	0700	T	Enemy infantry tanks (6160-10.39)	359
9	B3	0801	R	DA	0807	T	Platoon of EN infantry (62.15 - 10.36)	396
10	B3	0805	R	DA	0807	T	Heavy tanks (6160-10.39) tanks are burning (50 tanks kept at 0835	359
11	Custer	0853	T	DA	0851	T	Panzer Regt at front 30 tanks, horse drawn arty and inf withdrawing along highway 4 6 Bns firing having excellent effect	
12	Custer	0905	T	DA	0908	T	Inf obs reports Germans in disorganized retreat along highway 4 and nearby fields	
13	B3	0915	R	DA Custer	0916	T	Reinforcements have arrived	
14	Custer	0947	T	DA Custer	0942	T	No fire south of 10 grid line west of 60 grid (55.5-10.7) Friendly fire adj on church Custer requests cease fire	
15	Custer	0955	T	DA	0952	T	French women 1PL men report no Germans in MORTAIN — friendly troops entering town	
16	MG	1050	R				EN vehicles on road near 63-12 grid intersection	
17	DA	1102	T	Shays	1108	T	Be on lookout for butterfly bombs dropped by EN last night	
18	Cox	1113	T	DA	1117	T	EN CPs at (6315-1313) and (6212-1234)	
19	B3	1140	R	DA	1145	T	Armored vehicles vic (6215-10.36)	396
20	A4	1200	R	DA	1220	T	IN pos N6 522 (6098-0953)(6108-0908)	
21	LN4	1213	T	DA	1220	T	Johnson Ft lines N8 D69 D96 On hill fire evac wounded 12th has contacted CCB Crew + crop in Mortain	
22	Cox	1235	T	DA	1240	T	When relieved 120th will occupy defensive positions from (5926-1170) to (5832-1388) Johnson will occupy our present positions	
23	Cox	1415	T	DA	NO	T	50-100 vehicles knocked out on highway 4 between 2400-1000	
24	N4	1525	T				LN 2 Lt LEE and Sgt Bushnell were captured some time in past 4 days	
25	O3	1530	T				Lt Bartz + party reported in	
26	DA	1530	T				No fire lines. Grid 16 East to 61 North to 17 then East and grid 13 from 61 East to 65.5 North to 15 East to 71 South to 10 East along 10	
27	B5	1600	T	DA	1640	T	IN pos (59.2-10.3)	
28	A4	1600	T	DA	1640	T	Received 12 Rds EN arty from AZ 1400	
29	DA	1730	T				28th Div in Sour Deval loading elements at (59-16) Unconfirmed report 35th at highway 3 (62-12)	

No.	From Phone line			Message	Gr. No.
30	BS/1840R	DA 1845 T		IN Pos N8I86 (59.79-10.23)	
31	BS 2100 R			IN Pos N8576	
32	DA 2124 T			(60.75 1375) TOT 2140	
33	S3 2140 R			IN Pos N8A67	

Notes

Prologue

1. Bradley, *A Soldier's Story* (Henry Holt and Company, 1951), p. 371.

Chapter 2
Three Fourteen

1. For example, in an after-combat interview on August 25, 1944, the 30th Division Artillery operations officer, or S-3, Lieutenant Colonel F.C. Shepard commented that he "...did not realize until about the end of the 3d day that the Germans were making an all-out effort to break through to Avranches. If anybody around 30th Division Headquarters appreciated it, they did not say anything to him about it. VII Corps Headquarters apparently did not realize at the time how serious it was...." National Archives, Bureau of Records, College Park, Maryland.

2. Major Ralph A. Kerley, monograph prepared for Advanced Infantry Officers Course No. 1, 1949–1950, Fort Benning, Georgia, entitled *Operations of the 2d Battalion, 120th Infantry at Mortain, France, 6–12 August 1944*, p. 10.

Chapter 3
A Pleasant Little Town

1. Badsey, *Normandy 1944* (Osprey Publishing Ltd., 1990), p. 6.

2. After the battle, because of the destruction and lack of shelter, the population fell to 1,300. Gilles Buisson, *Mortain 44 Objectif Avranches* (Editions OGP, 1984), p. 122.

3. Field interviews with Colonel Hammond D. Birks and others on August 18–26, 1944. National Archives, Bureau of Records, College Park, Maryland.

4. Ibid.

5. Kerley, *Operations of the 2d Battalion*, pp. 9–10.

Chapter 5
We Dig In

1. See discussion of situation in Kerley, *Operations of the 2d Battalion*, pp. 9–10.

2. Ibid.

203

Chapter 6
"Want to Shoot Some Jerries?"

1. The official terminology for this vessel was Landing Craft, Infantry.

2. All fire missions are taken from the Message Log, 230th Field Artillery Battalion, 330-FA(230)-0.7, "Report-With supporting Docs and Journal," box 8883, entry 427, Record Group 407, National Archives, Washington, D.C. (located at Bureau of Records, College Park, Maryland). All messages and fire missions in the Message Log from "B3" were sent by the author. "B3" or "Baker 3" was the author's call sign.

3. The product of any exploding shell is sometimes erroneously referred to as shrapnel. Shrapnel, in fact, consists of round, usually steel, balls loaded in a shell which scatter upon explosion of the shell. Shrapnel was not used in World War II or in subsequent military actions.

4. Kerley, *Operations of the 2d Battalion*, p. 9.

5. Ibid. The efforts to dig in are described in the monograph.

6. Message Log, 230th Field Artillery Battalion.

7. Ibid.

8. Ibid. The log contains a telephone message sent at 9:30 p.m. from Division Artillery to this effect.

Chapter 7
Hitler's Counterstroke

1. Keegan, *Six Armies in Normandy* (The Viking Press, 1982), p. 224.

2. Ibid., p. 237.

3. The Hill has also been identified as Hill 317, a designation which occurs primarily in British literature describing the battle although some American authors, including Blumenson in his official history, *Breakout and Pursuit,* have adopted the Hill 317 terminology.

   Martin Blumenson wrote the author in a letter dated November 19, 1963 as follows: "On your question about the designation of the hill, the fact is that 314 and 317 are really the same height. Some maps have it one way, and some the other. It is called Hill 317 in BREAKOUT AND PURSUIT because the cartographer chose to follow the best (or most recent) maps rather than the maps that were available to the troops during the war. The text of the book was then made consistent to conform with the cartography."

   The map issued by the U.S. Army for use in the field and as a firing chart by artillery fire direction centers shows the elevation of the highest point of the Hill as 314 meters (Mortain, Sheet No. 34/10 N.E., First Edition, February 1944). This is the map we had on the Hill. Almost all contemporary reports referred to it as Hill 314, and this is how it was and is still known by the troops who fought there. Kerley, *Operations of the 2d Battalion*. The official histories of the 30th Infantry Division and its various units use that number to describe it. The order awarding Battle Honors, i.e., the Presidential Unit Citation, calls the location Hill 314. The French also refer to it as Cote 314. See, for example, Buisson, *Mortain 44 Objectif Avranches.* In any case, current topographic maps, such as the Institut Géographique National, Serie Bleue, 1:25000, now show the elevation as 322 meters.

4. Blumenson, *Breakout and Pursuit,* p. 466.

Chapter 9
"Enemy N, S, E, W"

1. Kerley wrote: "...Had it not been for the artillery there can be little doubt the battalion would have been destroyed or captured. The lions [sic] share must go to the artillery for the successful defense of this hill...," *Operations of the 2d Battalion*, p. 20.

2. Kerley, *Operations of the 2d Battalion*, p. 11.

3. Near the end of the war a proximity fuse which was designed to function automatically replaced the time fuse.

4. Post-battle interview with General Hobbs, dated August 21, 1944. Bureau of Records, College Park, Maryland.

5. Post-battle interview with Colonel Hammond D. Birks, commanding officer of the 120th Infantry Regiment, dated August 18, 1944. Bureau of Records, College Park, Maryland.

Chapter 10
Hand-Me-Down

1. "40 or 8" stood for "40 men or 8 horses."

Chapter 11
Hell Fire

1. Kerley, *Operations of the 2d Battalion*, p. 10.

2. *History of the 120th Infantry Regiment* (Infantry Journal Press, 1947), p. 52.

3. According to the statement of Major J. J. Parrish, Adjutant, 30th Division Artillery, given on August 25, 1944. Bureau of Records, College Park, Maryland. The Message Log of the 230th Field Artillery Battalion records the last radio message from Lieutenant Bartz at 0658 hours on August 8, 1944.

4. There was radio communication from K Company, commanded by Lieutenant Joseph C. Reaser, to a higher headquarters that resulted in some fire missions. The 230th Field Artillery was in direct support of the 120th Infantry. This meant that all artillery fire requested by any unit of the 120th Infantry, whether made directly by the infantry unit, by an artillery or cannon company forward observer attached to the unit, or by regimental headquarters would have been directed to the 230th Field Artillery for execution, and accordingly, should have been reflected in its Message Log. The Message Log for the period August 6–12, a contemporaneous record, contains only two entries, number seventeen on August 10 and number thirteen on August 11, that indicate a fire mission completed through infantry communication channels to the 230th Field Artillery. Although *History of the 120th Infantry Regiment*, which is dated three years after the event, at page 50 states that Lieutenant Kerley of E Company also had such radio capability, from personal knowledge, I can state that his radio was nonfunctional early in the engagement. The numerous messages that he had me relay to his regimental headquarters using the field artillery radio and communication network confirm this.

5. Kerley maintained that the Germans monitored our transmissions. See Kerley, *Operations of the 2d Battalion*, p. 14.

6. Although Blumenson states that 10 squadrons of Typhoons flew 294 sorties on August 7 in the Mortain area, these were the only ones I recall seeing over our front lines. See Blumenson, *Breakout and Pursuit*, p. 474.

Chapter 13
Notes for Company Commanders

1. 230th Field Artillery Battalion Log and after-action report, Headquarters, 230th Field Artillery Battalion, dated September 4, 1944. Bureau of Records, College Park, Maryland.

2. Kerley, *Operations of the 2d Battalion*, p. 14. This conforms with my own personal recollection. Kerley's view was that by the next day "morale was on a rapid decline." Ibid.

3. See, for example, the 30th Infantry Division Artillery Order of Defensive Fires for 8 August 1944, including attached list of 137 concentrations and overlay of plan of fires. Bureau of Records, College Park, Maryland. Not all of these concentrations, however, were fired in defense of the Hill. Division artillery had other missions in other sectors where the 30th Division was engaged in battle.

4. Headquarters 30th Infantry Division, G-2 Periodic Report from 08 0001 to 08 2400, dated 9 August 1944, Bureau of Records, College Park, Maryland.

Chapter 14

Meanwhile, Back at the Chateau...

1. Message Log, 230th Field Artillery Battalion.
2. Hewitt, *Work Horse of the Western Front, The Story of the 30th Infantry Division* (Infantry Journal Press, 1946), p. 74.

Chapter 15

"Surrender or Die"

1. These were code names: "Crow" for 230th Field Artillery Battalion, "Curtis" for 113th Field Artillery Battalion (155mm howitzers) and "Crunch" for 197th Field Artillery Battalion, which like "Crow" was light artillery equipped with 105mm howitzers.
2. It seems likely that these two messages were sent at Lieutenant Kerley's direction.
3. I made the first report of the incident in abbreviated form by radio at 6:50 p.m. on August 9, as shown by the Message Log of 230th Field Artillery Battalion. This would have been shortly after the incident occurred. The Message Log states: "Germans request B3 to surrender—have captured five officers, sixteen enlisted men. B3 answered—'HELL! NO.'" "B3" or "Baker 3" was my code designation. No doubt my message was that the Germans asked "us" to surrender, and the keeper of the Message Log interpreted "us" to mean the artillery forward observer, that is "B3," rather than the infantry unit to which I was attached.

   Subsequently, this incident has been reported in a number of publications, including at least two newspaper accounts published a week or more after the battle had concluded. Versions vary. Two are quoted here. One is from the 30th Infantry Division official history, written after the war was over. The second is a shorter and less dramatic version that forms a part of the report which I pecked out on a field typewriter the day after the battle ended, from memory and without notes when the events were fresh in mind. My report contains detail, particularly the reference to Lieutenant Pike, that is also in the official history and is consistent with it. From that and the record in the Message Log of the radio transmission of the event, quoted above, it follows that I must have been present.

   Yet I now have no personal recollection of the incident. Neither does Dan Garrott nor Armon Sasser, both of whom were there at the time. The reasonable explanation is that the incident was not significant when it occurred, that it was irritating, but also part of the condition of being surrounded, and that the episode took on dramatic proportions as the result of journalistic extravagance. As written by the newspaper reporters, it made a good story.

   The official historian wrote: "Then, at about 6:30 P.M., a German officer, accompanied by a soldier bearing a white flag, entered our lines in the edge of the Company E area. With great formality he told Lieutenant Rohmiller of Company E and Sergeant Wingate of Company G that he was an officer of the SS and prepared to give the Americans honorable conditions of surrender. The Germans knew they had the 2d Battalion of the 120th Infantry, 30th Infantry Division, surrounded, he said. They had captured a Lieutenant Pike (the battalion S-2) and a 'one-star' officer (evidently Colonel Hardway, whose silver leaves may have been confused with stars) among many other prisoners. The American position was hopeless. If they did not surrender by 8:00 P.M. they would be 'blown to bits.'

   "The lieutenant and the sergeant refused the offer out of hand, but sent the message back to Lieutenant Kerley, the E Company commander. According to one colorful story which later reached the newspapers, Lieutenant Kerley's reply, duly reported back to the surrender party, was that his men would not surrender as long as they had ammunition to kill Germans with or bayonets to stick in their bellies. More reliable sources indicate his reply was shorter and less printable, but equally to the point. Wounded Americans, lying near Lieutenant Kerley, cried 'No, no, don't surrender,' when they heard of the offer. The German officer returned to his lines...." Hewitt, *Work Horse of the Western Front*, p. 73.

Kerley was not given to Churchillian pronouncements, and his response would have been direct, showing more earth and less flower. That is indicated by my own report of the incident in the Message Log. No doubt what I wrote suffered from inaccuracy because of then current standards of what was acceptable language in print. More's the pity. Kerley himself stated that "Actually the reply wasn't quite so dramatic...." Kerley, *Operations of the 2d Battalion,* p. 14.

In my post-battle report I wrote: "...The troops to our rear asked us to surrender and reported the capture of 16 enlisted men and 5 officers, including Lieutenant Pyke [*sic*] of the 2d Battalion. Lieutenant Kerley told them 'HELL NO.' From this information, it looked as if the 2d Battalion staff had been captured. We believed the hill behind us to be occupied by approximately 35 men who were in a bad way and were bluffing (information from a prisoner). We didn't realize how many Germans were behind us...."

Kerley's answer, as I reported it in capital letters, was really shorthand for "expletive deleted," a phrase not then part of the jargon.

4. Kerley, *Operations of the 2d Battalion,* p. 14.
5. Ibid., p. 15.
6. Message Log, 230th Field Artillery Battalion.
7. Ibid.

Chapter 17
Sunshine and Other Military Technology

1. During the war the British bettered "daylight savings time" by adding an extra hour, giving two additional hours of daylight.
2. Hewitt, *Work Horse of the Western Front,* p. 67.
3. The entire process of preparing the "medical shells" and the way they were fired are described in two reports, one dated August 13, 1944, by Major Richard E. Evans, Jr., S-3 of the 230th Field Artillery Battalion, the officer who conceived the idea, and the other by the battalion surgeon, Captain Bruce D. Stern. Bureau of Records, College Park, Maryland.
4. I reported that the morphine syrettes were broken. Around 10:15 the 113th Field Artillery (code name "Curtis," 155mm howitzers) began firing medical shells. See reports of Evans and Stern, noted above, for results. "Custer," 120th Infantry Regimental Headquarters, apparently reported that only 50 percent were broken. But how could Custer have gotten such information except through our radio? Neither the radio of Bartz nor any of the infantry radios were functioning as far as we know at that late date in the battle, except possibly that of Lieutenant Joseph Reaser of K Company. See chapter 11, note 4. It seems likely, as is so often the case in truly desperate situations, that infantry headquarters and those in the artillery who had concocted the scheme of the medical shells were caught up in a whirl of wishful thinking. Anxiety for the well-being of the troops on the Hill and disbelief that we were beyond help may have created the images that they recounted.
5. See the reports of Evans and Stern cited in note 3 above.

Chapter 18
Last Chance

1. The 230th Field Artillery Message Log and G-2 Periodic Report, Headquarters 30th Infantry Division, for August 11, dated 12 August 1944.
2. In the first edition of his book, *Citizen Soldiers,* Stephen E. Ambrose has drawn on an early manuscript of this book for a description of the "Last Chance" mortar shot. At the outset of his description of the event, on page 97, he describes Lieutenant Kerley as "...discombobulated, on the edge of breaking...." This statement is the imaginative characterization of Stephen E. Ambrose and does not reflect Kerley's iron-tough character

or his incredibly cool behavior under fire. Kerley was never discombobulated or on the edge of breaking. No doubt there were many men who were. That they did not yield under pressure is in large part due to Kerley's strength and unyielding spirit from which they drew the will to fight on. He was a hero. Ambrose and the publisher agreed to delete this characterization of Kerley in subsequent printings of the book.

3. The 120th Infantry Regiment had been unable to obtain large-scale maps because of the suddenness of the order to move and take up positions near Mortain. Lieutenant Kerley and the other company commanders had obtained maps from the units of the 18th Infantry which they relieved on the Hill. "These had been in use for several days and were crumpled and badly marked." Kerley, *Operations of the 2d Battalion*, p. 8.

Chapter 19

"Without Reinforcements Can Hold Til Tomorrow"

1. Headquarters 30th Infantry Division, G-2 Periodic Report, dated 12 August 1944 for the period 11 August 1944. Bureau of Records, College Park, Maryland.

Chapter 20

Tattoo of Death

1. The report of Major Richard E. Evans, Jr., dated August 13, 1944, p. 2, cited in chapter 17, note 3, in connection with medical shells, confirms that the radio transmitted as long as we remained on the Hill even though we had no reception.

Chapter 21

Poison, My Dear Field Marshal?

1. Bradley, *A Soldier's Story*, p. 371.
2. Featherston, *Saving The Breakout* (Presidio Press, 1993), p. 84.
3. D'Este, *Decision in Normandy* (E. P. Dutton, Inc., 1983), p. 418. In General Collins' *Lightning Joe* (Louisiana State University Press, 1979, republished in paperback, Presidio Press, 1994) he states on p. 255 that "According to German reports they [the 2d Battalion] had been a 'thorn in the flesh' that helped paralyze enemy movements in the area."
4. Kerley, *Operations of the 2d Battalion*, p. 20. See chapter 9, note 1.
5. Reardon, *Victory at Mortain* (University Press of Kansas, 2002), pp. 293–94.

Chapter 22

Bunnies, Chickens and Ducks

1. All reports, including the Presidential Unit Citation awarded to the troops on the Hill, show 277 as the number of dead, wounded and missing. According to after-combat interviews in August 1944 with Colonel Hammond D. Birks, commanding officer of the 120th Regiment, and others, the number of infantrymen remaining on the Hill at the time the troops were relieved are listed below. Bureau of Records, College Park, Maryland.

Company	K	100 men
"	F	8
"	C	24
"	G	103
"	E	100
"	H	18
"	AT	4
Cannon Co.		5
823d TD		8

Afterword

1. *History Thirtieth Infantry Division Artillery*, typewritten, dated October 31, 1944. Bureau of Records, College Park, Maryland.

Glossary

Infantry Division. This was the basic unit around which U.S. field forces were organized. It was the smallest unit having all essential ground arms and services and capable of conducting by its own means operations of general importance. With normal attachments it had a strength of approximately 16,000, of which 9,000 were divided equally among three infantry regiments. Other units consisted of field artillery, antiaircraft guns, combat engineers, tank destroyers, reconnaissance troops, tanks, a signal or communications company, medical, quartermaster, ordnance, police and other services.

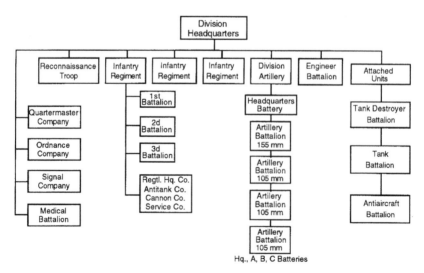

Typical Infantry Division Organization

Infantry Regiment. An infantry regiment consisted of approximately 3,000 men, divided into three rifle battalions, a cannon company, an antitank company and headquarters and service components. A colonel normally commanded a rifle regiment.

Rifle Battalion. A rifle battalion had a combat strength of approximately 800 men. It was the basic fighting unit. It was divided into three rifle companies, a heavy-weapons company and a headquarters company. Its commander was normally a lieutenant colonel.

Rifle Company. An infantry company had a normal strength of approximately 190 men, divided into three 40-man rifle platoons and a weapons platoon. In addition to rifles, a company was armed with antitank rocket launchers (bazookas), 60mm mortars, .30-caliber light machine guns and Browning automatic rifles. The commanding officer of a company would have been a captain, although frequently, because of battlefield casualties, an infantry company was commanded by a lieutenant.

Field Artillery. Field artillery, which normally formed an integral part of an infantry division, consisted of three battalions of light (105mm) howitzers and one battalion of medium (155mm) howitzers under control of Division Artillery and with headquarters and service units. Additional medium artillery and heavy (155mm) guns would normally be attached to a division and placed under Division Artillery control. At full strength, the four field artillery battalions under Division Artillery control had a total of slightly in excess of 2,000 officers and men. Division Artillery was commanded by a brigadier general. Higher units of command, such as a corps, also maintained artillery units, usually heavy artillery.

Light Artillery. The basic light artillery weapon was the 105mm howitzer. This field piece replaced the "French 75" of World War I fame. The 105mm howitzer fired a shell approximately four inches in diameter and weighing roughly 33 pounds, depending on the type of projectile. The 105mm howitzer weighed almost 5,000 pounds, had split trails for increased stability and accuracy in firing and was extremely mobile. Its maximum range was approximately 12,000 yards, or almost seven miles. The prime mover was the standard U.S. Army two-and-a-half-ton truck.

Field Artillery Battalion. This was the basic operational unit of light artillery and consisted of three 4-gun batteries, together with a headquarters and fire direction personnel, a service or supply battery and reconnaissance, communication and medical components. For more effective coordination, the infantry cannon company was usually placed under control of the field artillery battalion that supported the infantry regiment of which the cannon company was a part. A lieutenant colonel commanded a field artillery battalion.

Armored Division. The personnel of an armored division consisted of approximately 12,000 officers and men. As the name suggests, tanks formed its principal fighting units, supported by self-propelled artillery, some infantry and headquarters, service, communication and other groups.

Sources

Fifty years after the event, I have tried to be meticulous and accurate in reporting what happened. Fortunately, there are good sources to aid the telling.

First, there is the report which I pecked out on a field typewriter the day after the battle ended, when events were still vine-fresh in my mind. The report, published in a military history, has been a substantial resource. At the National Archives, Washington, D.C., 330-FA(230)-0.30, "Battle of Mortain," box 8881, entry 427, Records of the Adjutant General's Office, Record Group 407, National Archives—physically located at College Park, Maryland—I unearthed the original of that report, the sheets of paper now gray and fragile, but the typing errors, skips and overstrikes still fresh. Finding and holding it in my hands brought up unexpected excitement and emotion. It is reproduced in full in the appendix.

The report, as published elsewhere, contains several minor omissions, two of which are significant, and some differences in language from the original, probably resulting from copying or editorial error and oversight. In cases of discrepancy, I have relied on the original.

Of utmost significance at the National Archives was finding the handwritten Message Log of the 230th Field Artillery Battalion for the entire period of the battle. 330-FA(230)-0.7, box 8883, entry 427, RG 407, NA—also at College Park, Maryland. Reproduced in full in Appendix B. That battalion was the unit to which I and my forward observer party were regularly assigned. It was the unit to which all communications and fire missions from us were transmitted. As a log, it naturally inclines toward brevity, but the detail is significant showing who sent each message, the date and time, the mode of transmission, what it was about, and if it was a fire mission, the coordinates of the target or a concentration number, if one was designated, and often the adjustments in targeting that were made from the original target data transmitted. Some important messages are recorded verbatim. In addition, the National Archives has yielded unit journals, after-combat interviews at all levels of command, 30th Division intelligence summaries and other materials that have filled in many gaps in the story. For these, I am very grateful.

And finally there is memory. Some events after 50 years are forgotten or hazy in recollection. Others stick in the mind as if it were yesterday. Fortunately, I have been able to plumb the memories of Armon Sasser and Dan Garrott, who were there with me. Sasser was then a Tech 4 and in charge of the radio that became our lifeline. Garrott was at the time a corporal and member of the survey section, later staff sergeant and awarded the Silver Star for his heroism on the Hill. This is not to say that Corn and Sasser did not also play heroic roles. They did. Unfortunately, not all heroism is accorded formal recognition. The recollections of Sasser and Garrott have filled in many blank spaces. Although often together or in close proximity on the Hill, we were engaged in different tasks or were sometimes at different places, and our focus was not always the same. As John Hersey notes in the forward to a recent edition of his wonderful book *Into The Valley*, an account of a skirmish of the Marines on Guadalcanal, there are nearly as many versions of the truth about a battle as there were participants in it. In those few instances where our recollections differ, it is with respect to minor matters that are essentially meaningless in the context of the story—was Sergeant Corn on the right and I on the left, or vice versa?

Some small part of the dialogue has necessarily been reconstituted to aid in the telling of the story. Not all of it could be remembered verbatim from the past. For example, the exact language used for every fire mission that is described is not available from either a contemporaneous written record or from memory. Our observer party shot 193 targets during the time we were on the Hill, approximately one every 45 minutes for six days. That would have been a lot to record or remember, word for word. I have tried to recount events as they would have occurred, and I have conformed the language to procedures then used. The same is true of the scenes in the Fire Direction Center of the 230th Field Artillery Battalion. Every fire mission that is described is factual, each recorded in the Message Log which shows the time, type of target or enemy activity and location by map coordinates.

Some of the incidents involving Lieutenant Ralph Kerley are from memory with most of the dialogue taken from that etched inside Armon Sasser's skull and mine. A few words and details have been used to flesh out those that are intact in memory and to give proper dimension to the scenes without either enlarging or degrading them. These incidents have not to my knowledge been related elsewhere before, except in my own writings and in accounts of the battle that rely on what I have written. The men who observed them were generally not journalists or writers. Kerley, a man inclined to keep his own counsel, would have treated them as commonplace, all part of the job.

Those readers who are interested in other accounts of events of the "Lost Battalion" or the Battle of Mortain may find the following to be helpful:

Bradley, General Omar N. *A Soldier's Story* (Henry Holt and Company, 1951).

Blumenson, Martin. *Breakout and Pursuit* (Office of the Chief of Military History, Department of the Army, 1961).

Buisson, Dr. Gilles. *Mortain 44 Objectif Avranches* (Editions OGP, 1984).

Collins, General J. Lawton "Lightning Joe." *Lightning Joe* (Louisiana State University, 1979, republished in paperback Presidio Press, 1994).

D'Este, Carlo. *Decision in Normandy* (E. P. Dutton, Inc., 1983).

Fay, Norman F., and Charles M. Kincaid. *History of Thirtieth Division Artillery* (Mimeograph).

Featherston, Alwyn. *Saving The Breakout* (Presidio Press, 1993).

Hewitt, Robert L. *Work Horse of the Western Front, The Story of the 30th Infantry Division* (Infantry Journal Press, 1946).

Jacobs, John W. *"On The Way" a historical narrative of the Two-Thirtieth Field Artillery Battalion* (1945).

Keegan, Sir John. *Six Armies in Normandy* (The Viking Press, 1982).

Kerley, Lieutenant Colonel Ralph A. *Operations of the 2d Battalion, 120th Infantry at Mortain, France, 6–12 August 1944.* Monograph, Donovan Technical Library, Infantry School, Fort Benning, Georgia.

Officers of the Regiment, *History of the 120th Infantry Regiment* (Infantry Journal Press, 1947).

Reardon, Lieutenant Colonel Mark J. *Victory at Mortain* (University Press of Kansas, 2002).

American Military Cemetery at Normandy

Courtesy of David C. Grimwood

— The Author —

ROBERT WEISS founded and was senior partner in Weiss, Jensen, Ellis & Howard (now Holland & Knight LLP), where for many years he practiced business and tax law. He has served as special counsel to the governments of Jamaica and The Bahamas and to an agency of the People's Republic of China. An avid writer, Weiss has also published poetry, articles and a book of stories. His articles about World War II have been published in "Prologue: Quarterly of the National Archives," "MHQ: The Quarterly Journal of Military History," "FA Journal" and "World War II Magazine." He has appeared on the History Channel in its program "Dangerous Missions: Forward Observers," on CSpan-2 where he was interviewed about the Battle of Mortain and in 2005 on Oliver North's television program "War stories," also in connection with the Battle of Mortain. More recently, his participation in that Battle was reviewed in "Patton 360" on the History Channel. Father of two grown children, he lives in Portland, Oregon.

— Of Related Interest —

CONDEMNED TO LIVE!
A Panzer Artilleryman's Five Front War
Franz A. P. Frisch and Wilbur D. Jones, Jr.

Breakthrough to the subject of understanding the German common soldier. A gripping World War II memoir portraying the life, culture, and travails of Franz Frisch. The narrative includes extensive remembrances of a private soldier's small and volatile world, conforming to the level of authority and responsibility, viewpoint, and informality of the man who took the images. His American counterpart was immortalized as "G.I. Joe."

ISBN 978-1-57249-320-9 • Paperback

IRON KNIGHTS
The United States 66th Armored Regiment
Gordon A. Blaker

Tells the history of the 66th Armored Regiment from its creation in Wolrd War I through its triumphant entry into Berlin in July 1945. Placing the development of twentieth-century tank warfare under a microscope, Blaker combines the official history of the 66th Armored with oral history and archival research to tell its story.

ISBN 978-1-57249-122-9 • Hardcover

— COVER ILLUSTRATION —
Courtesy of Tom Bennett

WHITE MANE PUBLISHING CO., INC.

To Request a Catalog Please Write to:
WHITE MANE PUBLISHING COMPANY, INC.
P.O. Box 708 • Shippensburg, PA 17257
e-mail: marketing@whitemane.com
Our Catalog is also available online
www.whitemane.com

CPSIA information can be obtained
at www.ICGtesting.com
Printed in the USA
BVHW040943140821
613985BV00009BA/670